When in the Course
of Human Events

When in the Course
of Human Events

Arguing the Case for Southern Secession

CHARLES ADAMS

ROWMAN & LITTLEFIELD PUBLISHERS, INC.
Lanham • Boulder • New York • Oxford

ROWMAN & LITTLEFIELD PUBLISHERS, INC.

Published in the United States of America
by Rowman & Littlefield Publishers, Inc.
4720 Boston Way, Lanham, Maryland 20706
http://www.rowmanlittlefield.com

12 Hid's Copse Road
Cumnor Hill, Oxford OX2 9JJ, England

British Library Cataloguing in Publication Information Available

Library of Congress Cataloging-in-Publication Data

Adams, Charles, 1930–
    When in the course of human events : arguing the case for southern
secession / Charles Adams.
        p.   cm.
    Includes bibliographical references and index.
    ISBN 0-8476-9722-3 (alk. paper)
    1. United States—History—Civil War, 1861–1865—Causes.
    2. United States—History—Civil War, 1861–1865—Economic aspects.
    3. United States—Politics and government—1861–1865. 4. Taxation—
    United States—History—19th century. 5. United States—History—
    Civil War, 1861–1865—Foreign public opinion, British. 6. Public
    opinion—Great Britain—History—19th century. I. Title.
    E468.9.A33 2000
    973.7'11—dc21   99-41975
                                                                          CIP

Printed in the United States of America

♾ ™ The paper used in this publication meets the minimum requirements of
American National Standard for Information Sciences—Permanence of Paper
for Printed Library Materials, ANSI/NISO Z39.48–1992.

To the memory of hundreds of thousands of teenage boys and young men whose lives were snuffed out in the Civil War, a war that was caused by societies enamored of war and unwilling to settle their fiscal conflicts by civilized means.

Union means so many millions a year lost to the South; secession means the loss of the same millions to the North. The love of money is the root of this as of many many other evils. . . . The quarrel between the North and South is, as it stands, solely a fiscal quarrel.

Charles Dickens, December 1861

Contents

List of Illustrations

Preface

Many Northern historians and writers who are considered leading authorities on the Civil War have failed, in my opinion, to report the truth as they should have done. It is not that they have deliberately set out to mislead us; rather, they seem to behave like men and women in love. Polybius pointed out the folly of this partisan zeal, and in their persistent devotion to the memory of Lincoln and the Grand Army of the Republic, Northern historians maintain that Lincoln and the North acted with wisdom, virtue, and lofty ideals in instituting and prosecuting the war to end slavery and preserve the Union; but if, as Charles Dickens maintained, the Northern onslaught upon slavery was no more than a piece of specious humbug designed to conceal its desire for economic control over the Southern states—then it just may be that any wisdom, virtue, and lofty ideals were with the South, not the North.

In most aspects of life, we should not rule out partiality, as we recently saw in President Clinton's impeachment travail. A good person, even a political person, ought to love friends, country, and party, and should share their loyalties and hatreds. But a person who takes up the role of historian must discard all considerations of this kind. The historian may have to speak well of his or her enemies and even award them the highest praise should their actions demand this. As Polybius wrote in *The Rise of the Roman Empire* (1.14), "For just as a living creature, if it is deprived of its eyesight, is rendered completely helpless, so if history is deprived of the truth, we are left with nothing but an idle, unprofitable tale."

Because of the partisanship that has prevailed for almost 150 years among American Civil War history writers, bringing the most critical events of that struggle into proper focus is no easy task, but that is, to a large extent, what this book tries to do.

Charles Adams
Sedona, Arizona
March 1999

Acknowledgments

Jed Lyons of the Rowman & Littlefield Publishing Group first suggested this book idea following unusual interest in a chapter in my book *For Good and Evil,* "Was It Taxes, Rather Than Slavery, That Caused the Civil War?" At his suggestion I looked further into the tax factors behind secession and Lincoln's invasion of the South, and to my delight a number of Civil War scholars came forth with materials for this study. I am especially indebted to John Denson of the Mises Institute at Auburn University, who for over five years has been providing me with unusual materials not easily found in most libraries. I am also indebted to John Sophicles at Auburn University, Don Livingston at Emory University, Clyde Wilson at the University of South Carolina, and Marshall L. DeRosa at Florida Atlantic University. I am especially appreciative of the materials Jeffrey Hummel provided me that highlighted his *Emancipating Slaves, Enslaving Free Men,* such as Lincoln's warrant to arrest the Chief Justice of the United States, and lectures of Kenneth Stampp not found in his published books.

I am appreciative of Charles Hammel, publisher of the *Southern Partisan,* for publishing three of the chapters from this book, which has given his readers a preview of what was to come, and I want to express my appreciation to John Chodes for sharing with me his unpublished manuscript "The Union League: Washington's Klan," which provided some new insights into the Ku Klux Klan era during Reconstruction.

I must express my appreciation for my faithful editor, Jean Donelson, who has labored with me for a decade with considerable restraint. And, finally, to my most faithful fan, my wife, Tamara, whose support for almost thirty years has made all my works possible.

Credits

British Museum: Figure 1.1.

Punch magazine: Figures 1.2, 7.1–7.11, and 9.4.

Harper's Weekly: Figures 2.1, 2.5, 2.6, 2.7, 4.2, and 4.4.

Scribner's: Figure 2.2.

Phunny Phellows: Figure 2.3.

Library of Congress: Figures 3.1, 3.4, 4.3, 5.1, 9.1, 9.3, 10.1, 10.2, 10.3, 11.1, 11.2, 12.3, 13.1, 13.2, 13.3, and 13.4.

Maryland Historical Society: Figure 3.2.

U.S. Supreme Court: Figure 3.3.

Frank Leslie's Illustrated Newspaper: Figures 4.1, 8.1, and 8.3.

Mary Evans: Figure 6.1.

Picture Library: Figure 6.2.

Lincoln Library and Museum: Figure 9.2.

Museum of Confederacy: Figures 12.1 and 12.5.

New York Court of Appeals: Figure 12.2.

Washington and Lee University: Figures 14.1 and 14.2.

Department of the Interior: Figure 15.1.

Introduction

Charles Dickens, considered by many the leading man of English letters for the past two centuries, said the American Civil War was "solely a fiscal quarrel." He added, for emphasis, that "the love of money is the root of this as of so many many other evils." That fiscal view has not interested most of our Civil War scholars. Yet Dickens was a man of genius and greatness who wrote while the war was raging, and his views deserve serious attention. His use of the terms "solely" and even "evil" would challenge so many of our cherished beliefs about the war—its causes and justification. Even at that early stage of the war, he was debunking myths about the war, myths that survive to our day.

Recently a reader wrote to one of our Civil War periodicals, the *Civil War Times,* expressing anger at a 1996 postage stamp series entitled "The Civil War: The War between the States." This enraged New Yorker wrote, "Didn't they [Robert E. Lee, Jefferson Davis, Stonewall Jackson, et al.] to one degree or another, give active countenance to the enslavement of almost four million Africans in America just 130 years ago?" The writer seems to be unaware that the entire nation, with the exception of a minuscule number of abolitionists, "gave active countenance to the enslavement," with our revered Constitution giving the most countenance of all. Letters like this one make it hard for the historian to combat the specious history that created good guys and bad guys in a war in which slavery was not an issue until after almost two years of unimaginable slaughter; only at that point did emancipation become a war measure, limited to areas under Confederate control and designed to create slave uprisings and unrest in the South and thus shorten the war. As one prominent Northern historian had to acknowledge, "The Emancipation Proclamation was not the glorious human rights document it was held up to be . . . so celebrated and misunderstood by later generations."[1]

Erroneous thinking and misunderstanding about the Civil War make it clear that Americans need a lot of education about that most tragic era— tragic not only for America but for those who believed in democracy and

1

hoped that America and its new form of government would bring forth a better world free from the tyrannies of the old, with peace, prosperity, and brotherhood among men. With the Civil War, America failed the world as well as itself.

Like all Northerners, I was force-fed Lincoln adoration from early school days on into university history courses. The objective of preserving the Union, so I was taught, carried with it the emancipation of slavery as one of Lincoln's hidden motives; hence the Civil War was a war to abolish slavery as well as prevent the breakup of the federal Union. That, unfortunately, is part fable but was necessary to make the cause of the North seem just. But is that so bad? Don't the winners of wars have the right to sanitize their conduct as well as possess the spoils of war? With time, history's final verdict will be rendered, and the sanitation brigade will have to face up to its falsehoods and errors, however laudable its motives of patriotism may have been.

Understanding the motives for war may be one thing, but passing judgment at this later date is another. This could be criticized by saying that our standards are different from those of 150 years ago. In a sense, that is true, but hardly for the better. According to British military historian B. H. Liddell Hart, our Civil War marked a change, a revolution, in the code of civilized warfare that survived into the twentieth century. "Modern nations have reverted to more primitive extremes—akin to the practices of warfare between barbaric hordes that were armed with spear and sword."[2] As painful as it is to admit, our Civil War started that barbaric revolution.

By the 1860s the abolition of slavery was moving forward in Western civilization with great energy and force; only America had not caught the emancipation fever. Slavery was doomed everywhere, including America, even though the vast majority of Americans, North and South, had failed to sense the signs of the times. It is unfortunate that the Emancipation Proclamation came as a war measure and not as a humanitarian measure. Worse still was the lack of a positive, well-supported game plan to lift the slaves from abject poverty and illiteracy into the main stream of Western society.

There is a new breed of historians and writers willing to desanitize the Civil War, bucking so many historians of the past century with their zeal to make heroes out of Northern leaders and generals—not unlike Soviet historians of the recent past who glorified Lenin and the heroes of the Communist revolution. If the Communist revolution was a disaster for Russia, so was the Civil War a disaster for America. But, you may argue, it did bring about the end of slavery. That subject, too, however, needs to be examined to see how it failed to live up to even minimal expectations and possibilities. Of all the emancipations of the nineteenth century, ours was the worst. We will look into that.

We northerners like to read about Lincoln the martyr and the dying god, but do we want to know about Lincoln the dictator who circumvented the Constitution to wage war on the South? His best generals would have a difficult time avoiding conviction by a war crimes tribunal according to the laws of war at that time for their plunder of Southern civilization. Would such a treatise find favor with the dyed-in-the-wool northern apologists who don't want to see any tarnish on the northern assault and conquest of the South? Is America ready for that kind of insight and history? I think so. I for one, as a northerner educated in sanitized Civil War history, find a more truthful account of that war as refreshing as our honest accounts of Vietnam.

Wars have seldom been justified, and as the years and the centuries pass, war looks increasingly foolish. The gung-ho attitude in the North to punish the traitors in the South for wanting to withdraw from the federal Union looks ridiculous today; and the Southerners' belief that the North was out to destroy their slave economy looks equally absurd. That one Southerner could lick ten Yankees was soon proven false, and Lincoln's concern that government "of the people" would perish from the earth if the North lost may have been the biggest absurdity of all. Yet for all the vociferous absurdities, the Civil War, like most wars, had a rational basis and was objectively grounded in the economic realities of the times. If the Gulf War in the 1990s was justified for economic reasons, so was the Civil War. Men will not willingly, and with zeal, die for an economic purpose, but they will die for some "cause" that has a noble purpose. Governments, when engaged in war, have to keep a patriotic "cause" alive and motivational, and cover up the economic realities that are the true reason for the conflict. As we shall see, in analyzing the Civil War, foreign war correspondents and writers from Europe saw the issues more clearly, and we shall focus at times on what these foreign observers had to say. Their objectivity and distance from the conflict in America will help us to see this awful conflict for what it was, and most of all, to "fess-up" to what the war was all about and heal the breach with the Southerners.

To me, the slave issue and secession constitute the great enigma of the Civil War. There is something strange, even irrational, about the thesis that the solid South seceded over slavery, even though many Southerners said so. Jeffrey Hummel's remarkable study, *Emancipating Slaves, Enslaving Free Men,* points to the slave issue as the cause of the secession of the solid South, while Charles Dickens wrote that the South seceded in spite of slavery, not because of it.

The thesis that the solid South seceded to protect slavery just does not make sense. The institution of slavery had never been more secure for the slave owners, with the Supreme Court in their back pocket; with the Constitution itself expressly protecting slavery and mandating the return of fugitive slaves everywhere—a mandate Lincoln said he would enforce; with Lincoln also declaring he had no right to interfere with slavery and no personal inclination to do so; with Lincoln personally supporting a new constitutional amendment protecting slavery forever—an amendment expressly made irrevocable. Added to all these guarantees for protecting slavery was the most crucial one of all—money. Wars require money; Peter the Great called money "the heart of war." The money power of the nation, the commercial interests, the Wall Street Boys, the bankers, traders, manufacturers, businessmen in all forms, did not want to interfere with slavery or agitate the South over slavery. There is nothing the South could have asked for the protection of slavery that wouldn't have been gladly provided, just as long as the South remained in the Union. And there would be no money for a war to abolish slavery, period! Why secede, especially considering that throughout history secession wars had almost always meant disaster for the seceders.

Why did Southern leaders proclaim that slavery was in danger when it was not? I try to answer that. The facts belie their claim and must have irritated the Northerners who were trying to save the Union and appease the South, when their fears were illusory. It didn't take many astute Northerners pondering over the irrational behavior of the South to look behind this facade and find real answers.

The *North American Review* (Boston, October 1862) saw through the South's highly emotional charge that slavery was the reason for secession: "Slavery is not the cause of the rebellion. . . . Slavery is the pretext on which the leaders of the rebellion rely, 'to fire the Southern heart,' and through which the greatest degree of unanimity can be produced. . . . Mr. Calhoun, after finding that the South could not be brought into sufficient unanimity by a clamor about the tariff, selected slavery as the better subject for agitation."[3]

In other words, it was a political ploy, commonly resorted to by politicians then and now. So Southerners' proclamation—from the housetops so to speak—that they seceded for slavery was political cant. It was also the South's biggest blunder of the war, since it prevented European intervention. Britain and France, leaders in the worldwide abolition movement, turned away from active support because they couldn't see themselves aiding the biggest slave society of the day.

Even the territorial issue was a nonissue. It was a part of the Republican platform in 1860, although Lincoln did not mention it in his inaugural address. The only territory that could have benefited the South was New Mexico. At that time it included today's Arizona, 200,000 square miles, four times as big as England. Yet, after ten years as a slave territory there were only twenty-one slaves in the territory, and of the twenty-one, only twelve were resident—hardly a bastion for slavers. And what would the planters in Virginia and in the slave heartland care about having slavery in lands a thousand miles away? As for the adjoining Utah territory, it was almost exclusively controlled by Mormons who had no use for slavery. California, the other huge parcel swiped from Mexico, had already become a state and had rejected slavery. There remains Oklahoma, then called "Indian Territory," the focal point of America's ethnic cleansing at the time. Over one-third (more than sixty tribes) of all Native Americans had been rounded up and herded into this not-too-desirable territory. No room for slaves here.

Slavery simply was not in jeopardy, despite what the Southern leaders proclaimed, and it is hard to swallow the claim that the South seceded because of slavery. On the other side of the hill, the North cannot pretend that it was fighting for the cause of humanity to remove the blot of slavery from the Union—the North cannot even suggest that its zeal for the interests of the slaves was the cause of the alienation of the South—since there was no such zeal, except for a tiny number of abolitionists, and most of them were on the lunatic fringe, as we shall see. The more one looks behind the slavery facade, on both sides, the more one sees hypocrisy and subterfuge, designed to cover up the fiscal reality of the conflict.

This being so, the question naturally arises, what *was* the cause of offense? How did the views of the South come to be so opposed to those of the North that the South determined at all hazards and at any cost to renounce its partnership with the North and declare its independence? If slavery was not in danger, what else did the South have to fear?

The North and South had evolved in different ways since 1787 and no longer constituted a single nation and people. Their commercial interests had come into conflict, in contrast to the time of the founding. The North had built up a large and extensive manufacturing economy, and to foster that enterprise it demanded a protective tariff, a prohibition tariff, the burden of which fell on the South in two ways. First, because Southerners were large consumers of manufactured goods from their robust economy and, second, as agriculture producers and exporters, it was essential for their commerce to be able to exchange their products (e.g., cotton and tobacco) for manufactured goods in Europe. Otherwise the merchant ships would have to return home empty, and the Southern exporters would have to be paid in hard cash for their commodities, which meant much lower profits for the Southerners. When these same exporters chose to import European goods, notwithstanding the high tariff, this meant a high tax, increasing the cost to the Southern consumer and enriching the coffers of the federal government at the expense of the South, to benefit mostly Northern interests.

The battle over this tariff struggle began in 1828, with the "tariff of abomination," meaning the highest evil. The prospect that this tariff would split the nation and foster secession was expressed decades before 1860 by a Southern congressman in the debates in the House of Representatives in 1828: "If the union of these states shall ever be severed, and their liberties subverted, historians who record these disasters will have to ascribe them to measures of this description. I do sincerely believe that neither this government, nor any free government, can exist for a quarter of a century under such a system of legislation."[4] This prophetic statement came to pass thirty-two years later in 1860.

Even more enigmatic was the pro-Union, antisecession views of the slave owners in border states such as Maryland. They wanted to stay in the Union, since Union protection returned runaway slaves. With secession, once a slave went North, he was lost forever; with union, the slave had to go all the way to Canada to be truly free and safe. In short, there had to be something else that caused Southerners to fire the first shot—to leave the Union by force of arms. Yet slavery keeps rearing its ugly head, acting as a great catalyst in the monumental events of the war, and it becomes even more significant in the aftermath of the war. We shall, as the events require, focus on slavery throughout this book. What began as a nonissue became an overriding force as the war came to a close and the "tragic era" began.

1

The Dangerous Road to Secession

Since earliest recorded history, states have tried to secede from leagues, federations, or nations. Recently we have witnessed what is probably the most massive secession in all of history—the Soviet Union coming apart and being replaced with a myriad of new successor nations. For a brief moment Mikhail Gorbachev indicated a willingness to use force to hold the Soviet Union together, citing our Civil War as justification, but his better judgment prevailed. Only a few years before, in 1968, Soviet tanks rolled into Czechoslovakia in accordance with the doctrine of "limited sovereignty" that applied to all states in the Warsaw Pact (a league of states from which no people could secede without Moscow's consent)—a doctrine not unlike the one that justified using force against Southern states to prevent them from leaving the United States. Their sovereignty was also "limited," claimed Northern apologists for the aggression against the South.

Using force to hold a political union or even a nation together has been the rule throughout most of history, and most if not all attempts to withdraw have had disastrous consequences for the seceding states. The American Civil War is just one tragic example. An earlier example occurred in ancient Greece when the city-states Melos and Mytilene tried to secede from the Athenian League. The Athenians had exacted heavy taxes from the city-states, which caused the secession. The Athenians decided to use brute force against the seceders, killing the men and selling the women and children into slavery, as an example to the other city-states to not even think about seceding. None did.

The Romans too had a number of provinces that tried to secede, again over taxes. Not long after the Romans completed their conquest of Britain, the queen of East Anglia, Boadicea, led a revolt for English independence, exhorting her forces, "How much better it would be to have been sold to masters once and for all than possessing empty titles of freedom, to have to ransom ourselves every year? How much better to have been slain than to go about with a tax on our heads?"[1]

There were other attempted secessions from the Roman Empire, for example, in Gaul (France) and in Israel. The Jewish rebellion in A.D. 66 brought about the destruction of the temple in Jerusalem as well as the entire Jewish state. Taxes were at the core of this rebellion, which was followed by two other rebellions, both of which were also crushed. Secessions from a larger, more powerful state have more often than not failed, which is why we call them rebellions. The American Civil War was called the "War of the Rebellion" by the U.S. government. If it had succeeded, it would have been called the Second American Revolution. The term "Civil War" was used long before the war began—by Lincoln in his inaugural address and by numerous editorial writers in both North and South.

In the modern era, secession wars were common. The Dutch revolted against the Spanish and eventually the Spanish Netherlands seceded from the Spanish empire, following over sixty years of warfare. The Portuguese revolted successfully, but the Basque and Catalonians were not successful, and to this day the Basque are still clamoring for independence. The Netherlands, in turn, broke up with the secession of Belgium and Luxembourg. These nineteenth-century events involved some bloodshed, but nothing like the carnage of our Civil War. The war for Southern independence was the last great secession war; since then most secession struggles have been peaceful.

Until the twentieth century, the American Revolution represented the only successful attempt at secession from the British empire. The Irish battle for secession has lasted almost four hundred years and remains incomplete. This extended conflict explains the hatred for the "Brits" that has been passed from generation to generation among the Irish descendants of those who fought for independence—for secession first from English overlords and then from the British empire. Understand this and you can understand the apparent hopelessness of the struggle in Northern Ireland today.

The Scots' struggle for secession from the English and British empire cast remarkable shadows on events in America in the 1860s. Their struggle raged for five hundred years before they finally lost and became part of the Union known as Great Britain. The Act of Union in 1707 finally brought a legal end to Scotland's sovereignty. Then followed a period of "reconstruction" that sought to destroy Scottish civilization. The Disarming Act of 1756 took away the Scots' right to bear arms. The Second Amendment to the U.S. Constitution giving Americans the right to bear arms was a reaction to what happened in Scotland fifty years earlier. Americans, so many of Scottish descent, did not want that to happen in America. The Disarming Act responded to the British concern expressed in the following government proclamation: "Many persons within the shires [Highland Scots] continue possessed of great quantities of arms and war-like weapons."[2]

As part of the British "reconstruction" of Scotland, bagpipes were banned and their possession declared illegal, as was the traditional dress of the Highlanders. These laws further ordered the children of Scottish leaders to be educated by pro-British teachers "to prevent the rising generation being educated in disaffected or rebellious principles," that is, in secessionist ideas. A century later, in America's so-called North, secessionist ideas were treasonable ideas—dangerous criminal thought, which, as we shall see, often ended in imprisonment without any right of habeas corpus, ending free speech in America. When twentieth-century dictators locked people up for expressing ideas that opposed their regimes, they were emulating Northern Republicans.

The Scottish struggle can be traced back to 1297–1320 and the secessionist declaration of independence called the Declaration of Arbroath:

> So long as there shall be but one hundred of us to remain alive we will never give consent to subject ourselves to the dominion of the English. For it is not glory, it is not riches, neither is it honor, but it is freedom alone that we fight and contend for, which no honest man will lose but with his life.[3]

But the Scots failed, then and for the next four hundred years. The last dying attempt was made by Bonnie Prince Charlie as shown in the following illustration, as he triumphantly enters Edinburgh in his failed attempt to lead the rebellious Scots. But Bonnie Prince Charlie turned out to be more of a liability than an asset for the Scots. He claimed to be the legitimate king not only of Scotland but of Britain as well. Not satisfied with his successes in Scotland, he directed his armies south into England. When his military forces were less than a hundred miles from London, the British reacted, organized superior armies, and eventually defeated the forces of Charlie—in Scotland.

The struggle for Scottish independence died with Bonnie Prince Charlie after five hundred years of abortive rebellions. The British were just too powerful. One British commander, reminiscent of William Tecumseh Sherman, laid waste to the Scottish Highlands. Known as "Butcher Cumberland," he did to Scotland what Sherman did to the South. The planter class in the Confederacy was dispossessed of their lands after the Civil War, and the Highlanders suffered a similar fate after their final defeat at Colloden in 1746.

Figure 1.1. Bonnie Prince Charlie triumphantly entering Edinburgh after defeating the British. In time, the more powerful British invaded Scotland and defeated the secession struggle of the Scots. The prince fled (as Northerners said of Jefferson Davis) disguised as a woman. But unlike Davis, he succeeded in avoiding capture.

Many American Southerners were from Scotland. If they had reflected on the Scots' struggle for secession from the British empire, they might have been more cautious in bombarding Fort Sumter and taking on a vastly superior Northern opponent, just as the Scots had taken on a vastly superior British opponent. Was their failure foredoomed by the past—by the lessons of history they ignored?

Around the time of the Civil War there was another secession struggle that also had lessons for Americans—for the North as well as the South. The Poles had been fighting for independence since the time of the American Revolution, when Russia, Austria, and Prussia decided to carve up the Polish state for their empires, with the Russians taking the biggest piece.

In 1776, a Polish patriot, Thaddeus Kosciuszko, fled to America and joined the American Revolution. He became a war hero, and Congress granted him American citizenship, a pension, and a plot of land. Yet he returned to Poland to fight for his homeland's independence. Like the South, he won his initial battles but was finally defeated and imprisoned by the Russians for two years, not unlike Jefferson Davis. Thereafter he tried to persuade the tsar to grant some limited independence to Poland. He failed and died shortly thereafter, but his quest for Polish independence lived on for over a century.

Being defeated in the 1790s did not end the Poles' battle for independence. Each generation of Poles in the next eighty years rose up in revolt: in 1830, 1846, 1848, and finally in 1863, at the same time the South was battling for its independence. The British magazine *Punch* picked up on this and the similarities with the Civil War in America. Here Lincoln and

PUNCH, OR THE LONDON CHARIVARL—October 24, 1863.

EXTREMES MEET.

Figure 1.2. Abe: "Imperial son of Nicholas the Great, We air in the same fix, I calculate, You with the Poles, with Southern rebels I, Who spurn my rule and my revenge defy."
Alex: "Vengeance is mine, old man; see where it falls, Behold yon hearths laid waste, and ruined walls, Yon gibbets, where the struggling patriot hangs, While my brave myrmidons enjoy his pangs."

the autocratic tsar of Russia, Alexander I, are shown greeting each other as rulers battling secession movements from their respective empires.

The fact that the Poles rose up again and again must have been a lesson and warning to the North, for in 1867 they imposed on the South a harsh military occupation to make sure the Confederacy did not renew its struggle for independence as the Poles had done repeatedly over the immediate past. The North had good reason for fear because the Southerners often proclaimed, "The South will rise again!"

Thus it is hardly surprising that in 1861 the U.S. government would not allow a bloc of states to withdraw from the federal union. The right of self-determination, what Lincoln called "government of the people," is empty chatter when a larger power wants to hold on to its territories. The North went to war to preserve the Union, and that was the reason for the war. It was what Lincoln was fighting for. As with all secession wars throughout history, it was a fight for land and resources. Moral issues are not really motivating factors. William Shakespeare wrote three hundred years ago about the right of the victors in war to sanitize history. The Civil War has been more sanitized than any other American war, ad nauseam. With the passing of time, all wars seem pointless. The American Civil War certainly looks that way at this time in history. Heroes begin to look like fools. The glorious dead, the young soldiers who suffered and died, need to be pitied, and the leaders who led them to early graves need to be lynched. In that war, as in so many wars, the wrong people died. In 1862, the editors of the British periodical *Chambers's Journal* pointed out the immorality of the American war: "A calm European may surely question, not merely if it [preserving the Union] be worthwhile, but if it be allowable, in the eyes of God and man, for such an end to inflict so much evil."[4] The editor of the *Chambers's Journal* concluded with this further condemnation: "That wrongs so vast in their sweep and depth cannot pass without being followed by penalties as tremendous," that is, retributive justice. Could the racial consequences of America's Civil War, which have lingered to this day, be the fulfillment of that prediction? The South's objective brought no scorn or condemnation from this British writer: "Between being dragged at the chariot wheels of the North, and having its destinies in its own hands, the South has no room for hesitation. It would obviously be far happier in a separate state; and no wonder it fights for that objective."[5]

Shortly after Northern armies started invading the South and Northern navies started blockading Southern ports, the cause of the South took an even higher ground. In November 1862, Charles Dickens reported a dialogue between French correspondents and Confederate soldiers, from the generals to the privates:

They took high ground, which appeared to them above all discussion or controversy. They have vowed to the North a mortal hatred, they will wage against it an implacable war, because the North has made an armed invasion of their territories, their native land; because they are driven to defend against it their homes, their honour, and their liberty. From the general-in-chief to the lowest soldier, everybody held the same language with wonderful unanimity.[6]

The British were especially puzzled at the North's outrage over the South's wanting to withdraw from the Union. The Lincoln administration maintained that a person was a traitor to even talk about such a criminal act. It seemed self-evident to the British that America was founded on the right of secession—the right of a people by popular consent to secede from a larger nation or confederation when the people believed it no longer served their needs and interests, or that they, a minority, were oppressed by a larger power. Article after article and editorial after editorial commented on this enigma, for example, "It does seem the most monstrous of anomalies that a government founded on the 'sacred right of insurrection' should pretend to treat as traitors and rebels six or seven million people who withdrew from the Union, and merely asked to be let alone."[7]

British scholars haven't changed their position in a hundred years. J. K. C. Wheare, writing in 1961, stated the following:

It is startling to realize that Lincoln did not believe in the principle of the self-determination of peoples. . . . Lincoln fought against them [the South] with more determination than any British Prime Minister fought against Ireland. . . . Perhaps Gladstone's sympathy for the South is more understandable if this aspect of the case is considered. He saw them as a nation struggling to be free. . . . To those who associate the principle of self-determination with the United States it comes as something of a shock to find that Abraham Lincoln, associated in one's mind with liberty and democracy, should argue so firmly against it. Yet the fact is unavoidable.[8]

It was Massachusetts, not South Carolina, that asserted the right of states to secede and threatened to do so four times. First, in the early days, on the adjustment of state debts; second, on the Louisiana Purchase by Jefferson; third, during the War of 1812; and, fourth, on the annexation of Texas. One chamber of the Massachusetts legislature actually passed a resolution of secession. Thomas Jefferson clearly acknowledged the right of secession when there was talk of the newly formed territories following the Louisiana Purchase to withdraw from the Union. He actually wished them luck if they did so and hoped that they would get along with the original federation as brothers and friends.[9] Somehow, in the North in 1861, all this was ignored by those who opposed secessionist ideas. To believe in the right of secession was heresy; to express such views amounted to treason; and if two or more people got together and expressed such views, they were conspirators.

HOW CAN SECESSION BE TREASON?

If there is anything of which nineteenth-century Americans approved, it was rebellions. They delighted in the plight of rebels—provided, of course, the rebels were not opposing them. A rebel or revolutionary from any part of the world visiting America always received an enthusiastic reception. Pole, Hungarian, Italian, Ukrainian, Irishman—it mattered not, as long as he was a rebel, seeking secession from one of Europe's imperial orders. It seems clear that in 1860 the supreme right of rebellion and revolution was an article of political right for every American, unless the rebel happened to be a homegrown variety.

There was the Indian Sepoy Mutiny of 1857–1858 led by Nana Sahib; had he visited America, no doubt he would have received a tumultuous welcome. Louis Kossuth, the Hungarian rebel, did come. The eloquent Magyar entered New York like a great hero. He was, like Jefferson Davis, a defeated rebel. And in America, after his abortive revolution in the 1840–1850s, there was a great military procession and popular ovation, followed by a great public dinner at the Astor House, with a round of wonderful speeches for the rebel's cause. He then made a triumphal tour of the States. In Boston, Senator Daniel Webster delivered a moving oration on Kossuth's failed secession struggle, proclaiming that Russia violated civilized law in crushing this rebellion.[10] The Irish, especially, have long had their enthusiastic supporters throughout America, many of whom now support the Irish Republican Army.

Thus for Americans, the right of self-determination was self-evident. How did it happen that in America, of all places, secession was called treason? The Declaration of Independence, while setting forth specific acts of misconduct by the British, also set forth general principles for secession—the consent of the people. Contrary to the position taken by the Lincoln administration, the states were sovereign; even William Seward recognized that people were "citizens" of their states, for example, of Ohio or New York. It was the states that came first, that put together the federal constitution with its limitations.

With many states, Northern and Southern, asserting the right of secession, Lincoln's adamant stance against it makes no sense. He never in the slightest gave any credence to the right of secession, as if the idea was too absurd to justify any comment. In Lincoln's own words, from which he never wavered, as a matter of law no right to secede from the federal union ever existed. There was even no legal basis for discussion. How could Lincoln have been unaware of American history and the writings of the Framers and Founders? Three states—Rhode Island, New York, and, notably the most powerful at the time, Virginia—retained the right of secession in their act approving the Constitution on June 26, 1788:

> *Act of the State of Virginia adopting the Federal Constitution, passed the 26th day of June, 1788.*
> We, the delegates of the people of Virginia, duly elected in pursuance of a recommendation from the General Assembly, and now met in Convention, having fully and freely investigated and discussed the proceedings of the Federal Convention, and being prepared as well as the most mature deliberation hath enabled us, to decide thereon, DO, in their name and in behalf of the people of Virginia, declare and make known, *that the powers granted under the Constitution, being derived from the people of the United States, may be resumed by them, whenever the same shall be perverted to their injury or oppression;* and that every power not granted thereby remains with them, and at their will. That therefore no right of any denomination can be cancelled, abridged, restrained or modified by the congress, by the Senate or House of Representatives, acting in any capacity by the President or any department or officer of the United States, except in those instances in which power is given by the Constitution for those purposes; and that among other essential rights, the liberty of conscience and of the press cannot be cancelled, abridged, restrained or modified by any authority of the United States [emphasis added].

The Hartford Convention in 1814, attended by delegates from Massachusetts, Connecticut, Rhode Island, and parts of Vermont and New Hampshire, opposed the War of 1812 as well as many of the policies of Jefferson and his successors. One of their solutions was secession from the Union. They wanted to radically change the Constitution to improve states' rights. But the war ended shortly thereafter and the movement died. There were secessionist cries from some Northern states over the enforcement of the Fugitive Slave Act, the whiskey tax, the War of 1812, the admission of Texas, and the Mexican War. The Abolitionist party proposed that the Northern, nonslave states secede from the Union with the Southern states. The best way to get rid of the abominable institution of slavery, said the abolitionists, was to withdraw from any political union with the slave states. The right of secession was so deeply rooted in the early history of the nation that hardly any region did not at one time assert or recognize that right. Thus Lincoln's assertion that secession had no basis in law makes no sense. It is possible that Lincoln simply convinced himself that no right to secede existed or could possibly be discussed. His law partner, William Henry Herndon, as well as a local judge, David Davis, spoke of Lincoln's stubbornness: "He was the most secretive—reticent—shut-mouthed man that ever lived. He was so stubborn that nothing could penetrate his mind once he had made a decision."[11]

Yet he had been active in law, politics, and debates throughout his life. I submit that it was more than just stubbornness that determined his anti-secessionism. He knew that secession had solid credentials and that once he permitted discussion and debate, he would lose. Logic, history, constitutional law, and even his beloved Declaration of Independence were all against him. He had to close his mind.

What made the South blind to the dangers of secession? Southerners undoubtedly thought they had the Declaration of Independence on their side—government deriving its just powers from the consent of the governed. And then there was the Constitution, which the Founders declared to be a compact among sovereign states. Yet neither of these great documents could produce the battalions of troops and the weapons necessary to win a war of secession should the North not agree with the South's constitutional arguments. Southerners believed in the will and fighting ability of the Confederate armies to defeat the vastly superior numbers of men and arms that the North could muster. There was also the belief that European nations would come to the aid of the South because of King Cotton and their industries' need for this essential commodity. Even the industries of the North would need cotton and would not risk a disruptive war. But in the end, history once again repeated itself, and the South's bid for secession and independence went the way of most other secession wars over the past centuries.

Unlike other rebels such as the Poles, however, most Southerners, because of the devastation and slaughter, lost their stomach for continuing the war after only four years of carnage and civil devastation; it was a lost cause, however laudable. One Southern leader, Jabez Curry, expressed the view of many in the defeated South. At the dedication of a war memorial in Richmond, Virginia, in 1871, he told his audience:

> Crushed, subjected, impoverished as we were by the war, insulted, tyrannized over, outraged by the Reconstruction Acts, but to what avail is it to keep alive passion, and cherish hatred? Of the abstract right of a state in 1800, to secede, under our then form of government, I have not the shadow of a doubt, but no conquered people ever wrote the accepted history of the conquest. To go about shaking our fists and grinding our teeth at the conquerors, dragging as a heavy weight the dead corpse of the Confederacy, is stupid and daily suicidal. Let us live in the present, leaving the dead past to take care of itself, drawing only profitable lessons from that and all history.[12]

2

A Useless Fort?

The eyes of the whole nation were turned on Fort Sumter. One day a fleet of United States vessels appeared off the bar of Charleston, and the first gun was fired on the fortress. In one day, the whole North declared for war. The peace men were overborne; and, henceforth there was nothing heard of but vengeance, subjugation, and, if need be, extermination and annihilation, for the rebels who had dared fire upon the American flag.

Chambers's Journal, 5 December 1863

THE ROAD TO FORT SUMTER

Fort Sumter was the "last straw." Secessionist states had captured a long list of federal properties, including the largest force of Northern troops and supplies in Texas, seized by General Twiggs on 16 February 1861. President James Buchanan, serving as a lame duck from the November 1860 election to Lincoln's inauguration on 4 March 1861, did not block these takeovers:

December 27, 1860—South Carolina troops captured Fort Moultrie and Castle Pickney. The revenue cutter *Aiken* is surrendered by naval officer Coste.

January 3, 1861: Savannah troops capture Fort Palaski.

January 9: Steamship *Star of the West* is fired upon when entering Charleston harbor to reinforce Fort Sumter.

January 10: Louisiana troops take over forts Jackson, St. Phillips, and Pike, near New Orleans.

January 14: The Pensacola navy yard is taken over in Florida, along with Fort Barrancas and Fort McRae. The siege of Fort Pickens begins.

January: New Orleans customs house is seized, reputedly with $500,000 cash.

February 4: Arkansas troops seize the Little Rock arsenal.

February 16: General Twiggs transfers his military unit to Texas state authorities. Colonel Waite transfers San Antonio to the Texas Rangers.

March 2: The revenue cutter *Dodge* is seized by Texas Confederate naval units.

Figure 2.1. The residents of Charleston flocked to the rooftops as the bombardment of Fort Sumter took place. It was a great display of cannon and fireworks; amazingly, no one was hurt. But it aroused the anger of the North and the patriotism of the South, and the war was on.

It seemed obvious that Fort Sumter was next. It would be taken over peacefully or not, and its seizure would mark the beginning of the end for the remaining federal properties and forts in the South. Southerners had every reason to believe that this takeover would be like the dozen or more that had occurred in the past four months. But they figured wrong.

The following map (fig. 2.2), which shows Fort Sumter lying in the entrance to Charleston harbor entirely surrounded by water, gives us a clue to what was at stake. Charleston was the leading Southern port on the Atlantic Ocean. Federal troops were not in Fort Sumter when South Carolina seceded from the Union. The small garrison of less then one hundred men was stationed at Fort Moultrie, which was on the mainland and could not be defended from a land assault, as its batteries were directed toward the harbor. Realizing his vulnerable position, on Christmas night, 1860, Major Anderson moved his small garrison from Fort Moultrie to Fort Sumter.

President Buchanan had made an attempt to reinforce Fort Sumter before Lincoln's inauguration. In January 1861 he had sent a merchant ship carrying troops hidden below the deck to Sumter. Word leaked out, and the Confederates fired a cannon volley across the bow of the merchant ship, the *Star of the West*. With no response from the fort, the captain turned and fled.

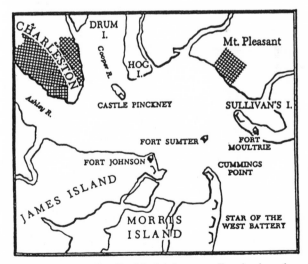

Figure 2.2. Charleston Harbor. Note that Fort Moultrie is on a small peninsula on the mainland; troops could easily storm the fort from the rear. Fort Sumter is in the middle of the entrance to the harbor, entirely surrounded by water. No ship could come or go without being in easy range of Sumter's batteries. Hardly a useless fort.

SUMTER AND THE REVENUE

Lincoln anguished over what to do about Fort Sumter. He had been in office only a couple of weeks and looked to his cabinet for advice. In his first meeting with the cabinet over Sumter, the secretaries of war, navy, interior, and state, as well as the attorney general, opposed provisioning Sumter. Caleb B. Smith, secretary of the interior, said that an attempt to send in provisions would "induce an attack," lead to the loss of the fort, and end in the "calamity" of civil war, which ought to be avoided at almost any cost. But the Treasury secretary, Salmon Chase, was cautiously for not abandoning the fort, as tax revenues were at stake, and it was his responsibility to protect the revenue. It was Montgomery Blair, the postmaster, who was alone in wanting aggressive action. The commanding general of the armies, Winfield Scott, never wavered in his opposition to sending provisions. The fort should be abandoned because it had no military value.

Taxes were foremost in Lincoln's mind, as he said in his inaugural address. He would collect the taxes. Sumter may have had no military value, but for protecting and collecting revenue it had value beyond measure—if it could be maintained. If not, then offshore collection would be the game plan.

The novel idea of having floating customs houses, with naval support, stop and collect taxes on incoming goods and thereby avoid provoking a war was supported by Unionists in the border states, which were still in the Union. They believed that responding with an armed force at Sumter would cause vacillating border states to join with the Confederates. Lincoln asked his attorney general if it would be legal to collect duties "on ship-board, off shore." It would be lawful, was the attorney general's opinion. Lincoln then asked the secretary of the navy to place its ships at the "disposal of the Revenue Service," and the meeting adjourned.[1]

Prior to seizing Sumter (April 12, 1861), Southerners had been taking federal property for months, including customs houses and military and naval installations, and had offered to pay for them. Sumter, however, was different because it was not taken by peaceful means. It was a great military display, not unlike a Fourth of July celebration. Amazingly, no one was killed. When Major Anderson ran out of ammunition, he surrendered the fort and he and his troops were sent home. Is this what opened the wallets of the Northern commercial interests who came to the aid of the president? There must have been something more than hurt pride and indignation to have the Northern money interests expend so much on the war, and to have Northern men sacrifice their lives. What then was behind the Fort Sumter episode—the decision to not let the fort go and the decision to go to total war? What was really at stake?

AN ANXIOUS MAMMA AND A FRACTIOUS CHILD
THE INFANT SOUTHERN REPUBLIC: "Boo hoo-hoo! I want Fort Sumter."
MRS. BUCHANAN: "Now, Baby, you can't have it. You've got two or three forts and a number of ships and arsenals already; and you won't be allowed to keep even them, for here comes Honest Old Abe to take them all away from you!"

Figure 2.3. This cartoon in a New York periodical pictures lame duck President Buchanan with her spoiled brat Southern Republic. The brat already has an arm full of Northern properties, naval ships, and forts. Sumter was one of the last federal holdouts not taken over by the Confederacy.

Fort Sumter wasn't a starving garrison that needed foodstuffs. The men at Fort Sumter may have needed provisions but not victuals. This yarn made for good propaganda, which continued after the war in the accounts by Lincoln's secretary, John Nicolay, as a noble reason for sending in "provisions only." It was said to be a great humanitarian effort. This falsehood got started within weeks after Sumter. On May 6, 1861, the *Cincinnati Daily Commercial* painted this account of the men at Sumter:

> The roar of the remorseless cannon which sought the destruction of Major Anderson and his brave little garrison, who were starving under the folds of the Stars and Stripes . . . the wanton inauguration of war by this unholy league of usurpers tore the film from the eyes of the most confiding advocates of peace and conciliation. It aroused us all to an appreciation of the fact that we have an armed aggression— not a peaceful secession to deal with.[2]

This starving garrison yarn is difficult to kill. But the federal garrison had been permitted to buy food and groceries and meats at the markets in Charleston, and it wasn't until after word of Lincoln's naval force reaching Charleston that the markets were cut off a few days before the bombardment. Major Anderson may have been running out of provisions, but it wasn't meat and potatoes.[3]

LINCOLN'S INAUGURAL: TAXES AND THE FORTS

Lincoln's inaugural address on 4 March 1861, certainly set the stage for war, and most of the South saw it that way. It sounded conciliatory, or at least peaceful, with his admission that federal services would not be forced upon the South and that there would be no invasion and no bloodshed, unless forced upon the federal government. He would, however, use federal power to hold federal property (the forts) and "to collect the duties and impost; but beyond what may be necessary for these objects, there will be no invasion, no using of force against or among the people anywhere." Southerners immediately saw the meaning behind Lincoln's words.

A few weeks later, on 30 March 1861, a Mobile, Alabama, newspaper published a speech by one of Alabama's most vocal antisecessionists (up to that time), who turned for secession after Lincoln's inaugural address:

> It is impossible to doubt that it was Mr. Lincoln's policy, under the name of reinforcing the laws, to retake the forts, to collect the revenue of the United States in our Ports and to reduce the seceded States to obedience to the behests of his party. His purpose therefore was war upon and subjugation of our people.[4]

In Lincoln's words, there were two instances in which war would be waged, which he seemed to indicate were unrelated. But they were not unrelated, and Lincoln knew it. The forts were intimately tied up with the collection of taxes. Control and fortify the forts in the great harbors in the South and you could cripple trade unless the South paid its duties. Sumter was such a fort.

As early as 15 January 1861, the *Philadelphia Press* spelled out the relationship between the forts and taxes, and this view seems to be the basis of Lincoln's inaugural address. If South Carolina were to take the forts by force, said the *Press,* this would be "levying war against the United States, and that is high treason by the Constitution." Lincoln undoubtedly took note. Continued the editors:

In the enforcement of the revenue laws, the forts are of primary importance. *Their guns cover just so much ground as is necessary to enable the United States to enforce their laws. . . .* Those forts the United States must maintain. It is not a question of coercing South Carolina, but of *enforcing* the revenue laws. . . . The practical point, either way, is—whether the revenue laws of the United States shall or shall not be enforced at those three ports, Charleston, Beaufort, and Georgetown, or whether they shall or shall not be made free ports, open to the commerce of the world, with no other restriction upon it than South Carolina shall see proper to impose. . . . Forts are to be held to *enforce the revenue laws,* not to conquer a state.[5]

The forts, then, would be the prize, not a useless piece of property. Without the forts, it would be necessary to station revenue ships outside these harbors, whose purpose would be to collect revenue from all incoming commerce. Not an easy task, as ships might slip by and make a run for the harbor. Not so with a fortified fort, capable of destroying any vessel refusing to submit to taxes.

The *Chicago Daily Times,* on 10 December 1860, saw the pending disaster Southern free ports would bring to Northern commerce:

In one single blow our foreign commerce must be reduced to less than one-half what it now is. Our coastwise trade would pass into other hands. One-half of our shipping would lie idle at our wharves. We should lose our trade with the South, with all of its immense profits. Our manufactories would be in utter ruins. Let the South adopt the free-trade system, or that of a tariff for revenue, and these results would likely follow.[6]

This editorial is remarkable. As yet there had been no secession, no new confederation, no free trade or low tariff zone. That happened three months later, when the North adopted the highest tariff in history (the Morrill Tariff)—not a revenue tariff but a prohibition tariff that kept a wide range of foreign goods out of U.S. markets. Foreign goods would almost have to go into the ports of the Confederacy, and the economic disaster these editorials predicted seemed most probable. Economics most of all would set the stage for war, and preserving the Union.

Many influential Northern newspapers initially did not see the secession of the Southern states as an economic threat. On 7 December 1860, the *New York Times* said, "We believe these apprehensions [economic losses] to be greatly exaggerated." The editorial then analyzed the commercial relations between the North and South and did not see any significant losses for the

North. Both the South and the North needed each other, and commerce would continue as before.[7]

In January, the editor in chief of the *Times* began to moderate his "no problem with a secession" theme. At that time there were no tariffs in place in the South, and a moderate tariff in the North. He predicted that dramatically different tariffs—if Southern tariffs were much lower than Northern—could spell disaster for Northern commerce.[8]

The most prominent newspaper in Pennsylvania, the *Philadelphia Press,* saw the tariff problem and a solution that would obviously mean war. On 21 December 1860, when South Carolina had just seceded, the editors proposed an idea that was later adopted by Lincoln:

> The government cannot well avoid collecting the federal revenues at all Southern ports, even after the passage of secession ordinances; and if this duty is discharged, any State which assumes a rebellious attitude will still be obliged to contribute revenue to support the Federal Government or have her foreign commerce entirely destroyed.[9]

Less than a month later, the *Press* emphasized the point: "*It is the enforcement of the revenue laws,* NOT *the coercion of the State,* that is the question of the hour. If those laws cannot be enforced, the Union is clearly gone; if they can, it is safe" (15 January 1861).[10]

The *New York Evening Post,* considered an extremely pro-Lincoln newspaper, picked up on the view expressed in the *Chicago Daily Times.* On 2 March 1861, the *Post* stated in an editorial, "What Shall Be Done for a Revenue":

> That either the revenue from duties must be collected in the ports of the rebel states, or the port must be closed to importations from abroad, is generally admitted. If neither of these things be done, our revenue laws are substantially repealed; the sources which supply our treasury will be dried up; we shall have no money to carry on the government; the nation will become bankrupt before the next crop of corn is ripe. There will be nothing to furnish means of subsistence to the army; nothing to keep our navy afloat; nothing to pay the salaries of public officers; the present order of things must come to a dead stop.[11]

The economic horror story goes on. All aspects of commerce will collapse, argues the editor: from iron and steel to woolens, clothing, and garment manufacturing; every shopkeeper will have to close his doors, as all kinds of goods from Britain and France will flood Northern markets. The whole country will be "given up to an immense system of smuggling," which cannot be stopped. And the solution?

What, then, is left for our government? Shall we let the seceding states repeal the revenue laws for the whole Union in this manner? Or will the government choose to consider all foreign commerce destined for those ports where we have no custom-houses and no collectors as contraband, and stop it, when offering to enter the collection districts from which our authorities have been expelled?

The editor concludes that the president should call a special session of Congress to "abolish all ports of entry in the seceding states."[12] (Within less than a week after Sumter, Lincoln ordered a blockade on his own, without any Congressional authorization. The dictatorship of the presidency had begun and the checks and balances in the Constitutional scheme of government would be ignored.)

It was reported in the Cleveland *Daily National Democrat* on 20 November 1860, that the English cabinet had entered into a secret trade agreement with the South for free trade in which cotton would be exchanged for British goods, duty free for both parties. This would, said the editors, "cripple" Northern commerce in these products and strike "a deadly blow" at the United States.[13] In short, a free and independent South would be an economic dagger ready to plunge into the heart of the nation.

Warmongers in the North raised their voices dramatically after the two opposing tariffs were adopted in early March. What a difference a few weeks can make when taxes are in the forefront! The newspapers and their hostile attitude no doubt caught the attention of the cabinet. In less than two weeks after Lincoln first asked the cabinet if it was "wise" to send in reinforcements, he once again met with the cabinet and confronted them with the desirability of reinforcing Sumter. This time the majority favored this aggressive action, although it was likely to start a war. Lincoln's cabinet read the newspapers and got the message. In the second cabinet meeting on Sumter the cabinet changed its tune and voted for war. Lincoln was with them.

The shift in the mood of the cabinet corresponded to the shift in the mood of the newspaper editors. After the first cabinet meeting over Sumter the major newspapers in Boston, New York, and Philadelphia came out demanding war, in the strongest language possible, after the tariff war became apparent. These cities were the three chief trading ports of entry into the nation. If trade were to shift to the Southern ports because of a free trade zone, or extremely low duties relative to the North, then these great cities would go into decline and suffer economic disaster. The image painted by these editorials is one of massive unemployment, the closing of factories and businesses, followed by unrest, riots, and possibly revolution. The inland cities would also go into decline, like Pittsburgh, where duty-free

British steel and iron products would cripple the American steel industry. The clothing industry would collapse if the South charged an export duty on cotton. And it could also charge duties on trade on the great inland rivers—the Ohio, the Missouri, and the Mississippi. Smuggling along a 2,000-mile border could not be checked by any means.

Fort Sumter must have been a fascinating problem for the president. As already noted, the fort held a strategic position. Yet the military insisted it would be difficult to maintain the fort with sufficient military supplies. To the last, General Scott opposed military action, indicating that a force of 20,000 men would be needed to maintain the fort. But by now war fever and a sense of its inevitability had infected the cabinet. If there had to be a war—if secession was to be checked—then why not at Sumter, here and now. Following this cabinet meeting on 29 March, Lincoln gave orders to prepare a naval force to provision Sumter.

Lincoln had given the South the option of taxes or war in his inaugural address. The mere suggestion that the South could secede unmolested as long as it paid taxes to the U.S. government was a demand for tribute, which was an outrage. Such a tax policy would never be tolerated. War was a certainty.

Throughout history most wars have included economic factors as well as armies and navies. Imperialism usually ends with colonies being exploited by the conquerors. There is an analogy between the Gulf War of 1991–1992 and the American Civil War with respect to the motive for invasion. Saddam Hussein had seized Kuwait under some claim of legitimacy, but this gave him control over much of the Middle Eastern oil, and his armies could easily keep going and take over the other oil-producing nations in the Arabian Peninsula. This, so the leaders of the West believed, could strangle the business and commerce of all Western oil-consuming nations. The horror story that the North used to justify its war against the South was also used to justify the Gulf War. Economic catastrophe was in the making. War was the solution in both instances, and war put an end to the threat, whether real or imaginary.

In the Gulf War the moral issue was decidedly in favor of the West with Iraq's military invasion of Kuwait, whereas in the Civil War, the North had to rely on some rather strained and myopic interpretation of the Constitution. The North couldn't find a good reason in history or constitutional law to justify its military onslaught on the South, so it resorted to a bad one. The war was fully justified for economic reasons—on both sides. The high tariff in the North compelled the Southern states to pay tribute to the North, either in taxes to fatten Republican coffers or in the inflated prices that had to be paid for Northern goods. Besides being unfair, this violated the uniformity command of the Constitution by having the South pay an undue proportion of the national revenue, which was expended more in the North than in the South: when some of the compromise tariffs of the 1830s and 1840s are analyzed, the total revenue was around $107.5 million, with the South paying about $90 million and the North $17.5 million. These are round numbers but they also coincide with export numbers. In 1860, total exports from the South totaled $214 million, and from the North around $47 million. In both instances the percentage for the South (taxes and exports) was approximately 87 percent, and 17 percent for the North. To add further salt to the wounds of the South on matters of revenue, fishing bounties for New Englanders were approximately $13 million, paid from the national Treasury, hence 83 percent from the South. And with a monopoly on shipping from Southern ports, the South paid Northern shipping—$36 million.[14] So the numbers show that the South's claim to be, in effect, paying tribute to the North has a factual basis.

It seems obvious that Lincoln's concern over secession, "What then will become of my tariff?"[15] was a serious matter. And a low Southern tariff, a free port, was a serious threat to Northern commerce on top of everything else. Business, commerce, investments, even people are drawn to low taxes. Taxes do motivate and can easily destroy a nation. In the second century B.C., a free port set up by the Romans on the island of Delos drew the commerce in the eastern Mediterranean from the commercial giant, Rhodes, which only charged a 2 percent tax. A free port destroyed this once commercial colossus. If a free port by the Romans could destroy Rhodes over a 2 percent tax, think what the Southern free or low tax ports could have done to Northern commerce and prosperity.

Thus the decision by Lincoln and his government to start the war over a fort made sense. Forts were capable of frustrating the South's free trade zone. They were capable of blocking low tax commerce. Lincoln's game plan was almost foolproof from a psychological sense. No matter what happened, the South would be the aggressor unless it permitted the provisioning. Lincoln notified the governor of South Carolina that he would send in provisions only, and that was enough to entice the Confederates to bombard and seize the fort. Lincoln's orders were to send in supplies peacefully but if attacked to respond with whatever force was necessary, thus compelling the Confederates to fire the first shot.

Not everyone in the leadership of the South wanted to take Fort Sumter by force. Secretary of State Robert Toombs, second in authority to President Davis, saw the madness of this action. At the cabinet meeting held on 9 April 1861, the Confederate leaders made the fateful decision to bombard the fort. Robert Toombs argued as strongly as he could to avoid resorting to force: "The firing on that fort," he warned, "will inaugurate a civil war greater than any the world has ever seen. Mr. President," he said, "it is suicide, it is murder, and will lose us every friend at the North. You will wantonly strike a hornet's nest which extends from mountains to ocean; and legions, now quiet, will swarm out and sting us to death." He then paused, and began, "It is unnecessary, it puts us in the wrong. It is fatal."[16]

But Toomb's pleading and arguments fell on deaf ears, especially those of the president, Jefferson Davis. A telegraph was written and handed to a youthful courier who rushed to the telegraph office across the street. It was a message to General Beauregard ordering the bombardment of Fort Sumter. The Civil War was to begin, as Lincoln had intended it, at the hands of the South.

The outrage resulting from the firing on the flag and the taking of Fort

Figure 2.4. This caricature of Robert Toombs in the *New York Illustrated News* shows him as an avid secessionist, which he was as a senior senator from Georgia. Nevertheless, he was the only member of Davis's cabinet with enough sense to condemn the bombardment of Fort Sumter. His predictions that this would arouse the North and become a rallying cry for military action against the South was a remarkable insight for the fanatical secessionist who dominated Southern politics.

Sumter by force of arms did just as Robert Toombs had predicted. It lost almost every friend that the South had in the North, and it stirred up a hornet's nest that turned the resources of the North into a great war machine that turned on the South. The South, on the other hand, had every reason to defend itself from foreign invaders. It was a tragedy unparalleled in American history that has had repercussions to this day.

Thus we had two fateful decisions. The first, by Lincoln, to reinforce the fort, by force if necessary; and the second, by the Confederate cabinet, to seize the fort before the relief squadron arrived at Charleston harbor.

Immediately after the bombardment, Northern newspapers took up the cause of the president, and his call for 75,000 volunteers to raise an army was quickly answered by most Northern states. The border states—Virginia, Tennessee, North Carolina, and Arkansas—had just voted to stay in the Union but refused to take up arms against the Southern states, which they believed was against the Constitution. As a result, they soon joined the Confederacy. Kentucky and Missouri did not join the Confederacy but refused to send troops for Lincoln's invasion of the South. Overnight the battle lines were drawn and the Confederacy had doubled in size, manpower, and resources, and all because of what many called the conflict over a useless fort.

On 4 March 1861, the day of Lincoln's inauguration, an Arkansas lawyer, Albert Pike, published a pamphlet on the secession crisis entitled *State or Province? Bond or Free?* He thought the best way to achieve peace was for Arkansas and the border states to join the Confederacy; with that show of force, civil war would be avoided. In the pamphlet Pike explained his ideas about what was going on in the nation and why the secession problem existed in the first place: "There was no necessity for any irrepressible conflict between the sections. There was no necessity for hatred, jealousies, and wrong-doing. We have been unnecessarily set against each other, by fanatical folly and unprincipled ambition in the North, and passion and rashness in the South. The harm is done."[17]

Historical studies on Fort Sumter usually argue over whether or not Lincoln provoked the South into firing on the flag and the fort, and thus providing him with the excuse he needed to wage war and to force the seceding states back into the Union. The firing on the flag outraged the North and ended its indifference to the secessionist crisis that had been smoldering for many months. Now the nation would rally around the flag and punish the traitors for waging war against the United States. There is little doubt that this was the most foolish thing the South did, even though Southern cannon didn't hurt anyone. This was an age in which war and imperialism were greatly admired, and both the North and the South were ready to settle their differences by war.

Both sides cried foul—the South in being denied the right of self-determination—the right of the people through the democratic process to withdraw from the Union. They had a right to cry foul over Northern domination of the Congress and a tariff injurious to the South. Just plain unfair. The North also had the right to cry foul. Not in the tongue-in-cheek assertion that no state could withdraw from the Union, which was on shaky ground. But the free trade zone and its threat to Northern prosperity was a serious matter, justifying a strong response in one form or another. Northerners could also cry foul for the firing on the U.S. flag and on U.S. property at Fort Sumter. And that foul, though insignificant compared to the bigger economic issues, caused the people of the North to rally around the flag and preserve the Union, however irrational that battle cry may appear today. Preserving the Union was so important economically and for the destiny of the American nation that the country as a whole didn't seem to mind if Lincoln pushed the Constitution aside, ignored its checks and balances, and assumed the role and power of a Roman consul, a dictator in fact, for the duration of his life. Lincoln's dictatorship survived and flour-

Figure 2.5. The *Star of the West* attempted to enter Charleston harbor under cover of darkness on 10 January 1861, supposedly to carry food and clothing to the garrison. But secretly there were troops and military supplies below deck. The South Carolinians were aware of the subterfuge and were on guard, watching for the ship. Once the cannons opened fire across the bow of the ship, it turned and fled. It was not a navy vessel but a private contractor used to help disguise its military purpose.

ished because the people wanted it, and their voices and demands, along with Lincoln's strong-arm tactics, silenced the few dissenters who spoke out against the tyranny of the Republican administration.

War fever was even more intense in the South. History was in the making—a new nation was being born—and the excitement over this remarkable event blinded the populace to the horrors of war. This patriotic fervor for the new nation gave rise to ceremonies all over the South—raising the new flag of the Confederacy. This was the official flag, the Stars and Bars, used in the early days of the war. But at a distance it had been mistaken for the Stars and Stripes, and that led to the well-known battle flag that has caused such controversy today, the crossed bars of blue and white stars on a red field.

Historians have focused on Fort Sumter's bombardment and its overriding

Figure 2.6. Following the bombardment of Fort Sumter, Lincoln called for 75,000 recruits to the state militias. The quota was quickly oversupplied by thousands of angry Northerners who demanded war against the traitors in the South who had fired on the flag. Here, less than a week after Sumter, New York volunteers parade down Broadway amid cheering crowds and waving flags with guns in arms and ready for war, answering Lincoln's call for troops.

importance at the time as the immediate cause of the Civil War. But on 12 January 1861, Fort Barrancas, the federal fort at Pensacola Bay, was seized by troops from the state of Florida under the governor's direction. President James Buchanan deplored the assault and seizure but assumed a policy of wait and see and hope for a peaceful settlement of the crisis. By Lincoln's time, the battle lines were being drawn, with the war of the tariffs emerging in March 1861 and the war of violence commencing in April at Fort Sumter.

Blood was first spilled in Baltimore a week after the firing on Fort Sumter.

Here on 19 April, troops from Massachusetts, sent by the governor to protect Washington, D.C., fully armed and marching in military ranks, fired on civilians, killing twelve of them. The civilians fired back and killed four soldiers. The problem came about because there was no train directly to Washington. Troops from Pennsylvania had arrived before those from Massachusetts, but they walked one by one through the streets of Baltimore from the East Side depot to the Camden Street station, where they then boarded another train to Washington. The Massachusetts regiment, however, marched

Figure 2.7. First Blood. A Massachusetts regiment, marching through Baltimore on 19 April 1861, fired on civilians and killed twelve of them. The Baltimoreans fired back and killed four soldiers.

into Baltimore like an invading army. The mayor of Baltimore, George Brown, wrote to the governor of Massachusetts and explained the incident: "Our people viewed the passage of armed troops to another state through the streets as an invasion of our soil, and could not be restrained." Massachusetts governor John Andrew replied, "I am overwhelmed with surprise that a peaceful march of American citizens over the highway to the defence of our common capital should be deemed aggressive to Baltimoreans."[18] The complaint that armies from the North were invading states in the South soon became the main battle cry for the defense of the Confederacy.

An English visitor to the South in the early summer of 1861 gives an account of the celebrations raising the new flag of the Confederacy throughout the South: "The raising of the Secession flags has been one of the most popular amusements in all the Southern States during the past spring. The war is the people's, and the excitement of preparation for it has been so much romance — that as yet it has seemed more like the fitting out for a summer trip, or preparing for an archery party, than any really serious and solemn undertaking."[19] It was all so much fun. The citizenry would meet at the local church, and the new flag would be displayed by a number of teenage girls, dressed in their spring outfits, and then a similar number of teenage boys would hoist the flag above the church to the salute of rifles and pistols and the cheering of the crowd. Speeches would follow speeches, and more salutes. The local minister would have the final say and pray for the new nation and for victory over the "Yankees." One pastor, taking the lead, pronounced himself "ready, not only to preach the cause of liberty, but to go himself and join the ranks if need be, as many of his brethren had done."

The English observer, perhaps because of the well-publicized account of the horrors of the recent Crimean War only five years before, pondered: "When these light-hearted girls began to lose their lovers and brothers, when lists of killed and wounded are passed around, and we read of the thousands slain, then the reality of war and all its terrors will crowd around them." How unreal, how dreamlike and incredible, "did all this farce appear as we rode through the woods and lanes, glorious with floral beauty . . . of Virginia's loveliest season."

The war had not begun except for Fort Sumter, but armies were forming, and sons were leaving home to fill the ranks. This was an exciting time, for the glories of war and the new nation. But, noted our observer, this was to become "a land of war and terror; that the very next mail may bring us tidings that the terrible warfare has begun . . . that the inevitable result must be the sacrifice of precious lives, of human beings, living souls, sent recklessly into the presence of their Maker, *to answer for the sins of their leaders*" [emphasis added].

3

Lincoln Crosses the Rubicon

Liberty lies in the hearts of men and women: when it dies there, no constitution, no law, no court can save it.

Learned Hand (1944)

When civil war developed in the Roman Republic, Julius Caesar defied the civil authority and crossed the River Rubicon in 49 B.C. This was a violation of the Roman constitution, for no army was to cross the Rubicon and enter Rome, under arms. Within a few months Caesar was master of Rome and Italy. He was elected by the senate as consul and appointed dictator for "life," something unknown in the Roman Republic when such appointments were for six months only. No one in the Republic had received so much authority, but with the military power of Caesar breathing down every senator's neck, what choice did they have? In time the civil war ended with the triumph of Caesar's adopted son Octavian. He became emperor, Caesar Augustus, and the Roman Republic was no more.

Cicero, the great Roman lawyer, lived during these troubled times. Upon Caesar's ascension to dictatorship after he crossed the Rubicon illegally and defied the civil authority, Cicero lamented, "Our beloved Republic is gone forever."[1] How right he was, for strong men would rule Rome for another five hundred years, and they would rule civilization for another fifteen hundred years. Republican government would not return as a major force in civilization until the Netherlands' successful revolt against the Spanish empire in the sixteenth century.

Caesar may be remembered for introducing many worthwhile laws to improve Roman society. The one I like was his plan to reduce the number of Romans on perpetual welfare by having them removed and resettled in the provinces where they could work for a living rather than survive on government handouts. Maybe that is the only way to cut down on the welfare state. But for all his benevolent acts as dictator, Caesar rode roughshod over the Roman constitution, and that resulted in his assassination; the

35

killing of a tyrant was a patriotic act, a belief held by both the Romans and the Greeks. John Booth felt that way about Lincoln.

There are other similarities between Caesar's story and that of Lincoln. Both held command of the military. Both suspended civilian authority. Both had indeed ridden roughshod over their respective constitutions. Both set up military rule and dictatorship. Both intimidated the civil authorities and tossed the constitution out the window in the interest of public safety. Both were assassinated as tyrants. The final outcome was different, however. As Cicero lamented in Rome, the Republic was gone forever.

It is not necessary to go back into ancient history to see a common pattern unfold: A time of national crisis, a strong leader assumes extraordinary powers, constitutional rights are suspended; rule by executive order with the legislature following and sustaining whatever the executive deems necessary for the public safety. We saw this happen in Germany in the early 1930s, which ended the Weimar Republic and put the National Socialist party in control after suspending the constitution and civil liberties.

Fidel Castro is an even more vivid example, close to home. As a student revolutionist, he opposed the ruling dictatorship. Eventually, after a long struggle to overthrow the Batista regime, he rode to power with the support of many groups: the peasants, the middle class, the army, and the moderates. In the summer of 1958 Castro gained support from the many antigovernment factions with what was called the "Caracas Pact." He agreed to reinstate democracy through the restoration of the 1940 constitution and to hold free elections. But once in power, Castro assumed and kept dictatorial powers. This is the normal historical pattern when constitutions and civil liberties are suspended during times of national crisis. America was lucky. This dictatorial pattern did not remain in place following the Civil War. But it could have, and for a time the Constitution hung by a thread.

LINCOLN VERSUS THE CONSTITUTION

After the attack on Fort Sumter, Lincoln assumed dictatorial powers. He circumvented his constitutional duty to call Congress in times of emergency by delaying the meeting for almost three months. In the meantime, he made the decisions, which, according to the Constitution, the Congress should have made. The first thing he did was to call out the militia from the states to put down what he said was an insurrection in the South. Even assuming this to be true, it is the duty of Congress to make such a decision according to Article 1, section 8 of the U.S. Constitution: "The Congress shall have the power . . . To provide for calling forth the Militia to execute the Laws of the Union, suppressing Insurrections and repel Invasions." Here are the exact words of Lincoln's demand upon the states:

By the President,
William H. Seward, Secretary of State,
    The following call on the respective state governors for troops was simultaneously issued through the War Department:
    Sir, Under the act of Congress for calling out the militia to execute the laws of the Union, to suppress insurrection, to repel invasion, etc., approved February 28, 1795, I have the honor to request your excellency to cause to be immediately detailed from the militia of your state the quota designated in the table below, to serve as infantry or riflemen for a period of three months, unless sooner discharged. Your excellency will please communicate to me the time at about which your quota will be expected at its rendezvous, as it will be met as soon as practicable by an officer or officers to muster it into service and pay of the United States. At the same time the oath of fidelity to the United States will be administered to every officer and man. The mustering officers will be instructed to receive no man under the rank of commissioned officer who is in years apparently over 45 or under 18, or who is not in physical strength and vigor. The quota for regiments from each state is as follows:

Maine	1
New Hampshire	1
Vermont	1
Massachusetts	2
Rhode Island	1
Connecticut	1
New York	17
New Jersey	4
Pennsylvania	16
Delaware	1
Tennessee	2
Maryland	4
Virginia	8
North Carolina	2
Kentucky	4
Arkansas	1
Missouri	4
Ohio	13
Indiana	6
Illinois	6

Michigan	1
Iowa	1
Minnesota	1
Wisconsin	1

It is ordered that each regiment shall consist, on an aggregate of officers and men, of 780. The total thus to be called out is 73,391. The remainder to constitute the 75,000 men under the President's proclamation will be composed of troops in the District of Columbia.

Lincoln, through his secretary of state, called out the militia of twenty-four states, using as authority a 1795 act of Congress that gave the president authority to do so, providing that the authority would cease thirty days after the beginning of the next session of Congress. In other words, it was a temporary measure in the case of an emergency, to be ruled on by Congress as the Constitution requires. With the craft of an attorney, Lincoln delayed calling Congress for almost three months, in effect giving him four months to operate his military forces without any determination by the Congress. By then, he had the war in full operation, and the Congress could do little else than sanction his caesarian acts. Six of the governors saw through this subterfuge, refused his call for troops, and rebuked his constitutional gamesmanship with these words:

I have only to say, that the militia of Virginia will not be furnished to the powers at Washington for any such use or purpose as they have in view. Your object is to subjugate the Southern states, and a requisition made upon me for such an object—an object, in my judgment, not within the purview of the Constitution or the act of 1795—will not be complied with. You have chosen to inaugurate civil war, and having done so, we will meet it in a spirit as determined as the administration has exhibited toward the south. (Governor Letcher, Virginia)

Your dispatch is received; and, if genuine, which its extraordinary character leads me to doubt, I have to say in reply, that I regard the levy of troops made by the administration for the purpose of subjugating the states of the South as in violation of the Constitution, and a usurpation of power. I can be no party to this wicked violation of the laws of the country, and to this war upon the liberties of a free people. You can get no troops from North Carolina. (Governor Ellis, North Carolina)

Your dispatch is received. I say emphatically that Kentucky will furnish no troops for the wicked purpose of subduing her sister Southern states. (Governor Magoffin, Kentucky)

Tennessee will not furnish a single man for coercion, but fifty thousand, if necessary, for the defense of our rights, or those of our Southern brethren. (Governor Harris, Tennessee)

In answer to your requisition for troops from Arkansas, to subjugate the Southern states, I have to say that none will be furnished. The demand is only adding insult to injury. The people of this commonwealth are freemen, not slaves, and will defend to the last extremity their honor, lives, and property against Northern mendacity and usurpation. (Governor Rector, Arkansas)

There can be, I apprehend, no doubt that these men are intended to make war upon the seceded states. Your requisition, in my judgment, is illegal, unconstitutional, and revolutionary in its objects, inhuman and diabolical, and can not be complied with. Not one man will the State of Missouri furnish to carry on such an unholy crusade. (Governor Jackson, Missouri)[2]

If Lincoln had respected the provision in the Constitution that puts the power of calling out the militia with the Congress and not the president on his own, who knows what would have happened? The border states that joined the Confederacy after Lincoln's call for troops would have had a voice in the Congressional debate that would have followed. War may have been averted, for it seems clear that an abundance of the people in both the North and South did not want war but a peaceful solution to the crisis.

Under the Constitution, it is the duty of the president to call the Congress into session during "extraordinary occasions." Sumter, like Pearl Harbor, was such an occasion. Why didn't Lincoln follow the commands of the Constitution and call the Congress forthwith? Why did he, on 15 April 1861, call Congress to meet *almost three months later* in July? And then only after he had driven the nation headlong into war? Obviously, he did not want Congress to get involved—did not want the Constitution to get involved. Lincoln was assuming all the powers of a dictator.

After calling forth the militia, within less than a week after Sumter, Lincoln ordered the blockade of Southern ports. A blockade is an act of war, requiring Congressional resolution. On April 21, he ordered the navy to buy five warships, an appropriations act requiring Congressional approval. On April 27, he started suspending the privilege of habeas corpus, in effect just about nullifying every civil liberty of every citizen. Soon thereafter he started shutting down newspapers that were not supportive of the war on the South. On May 3, he called for more troops, this time for three years, again a prerogative of the Congress.

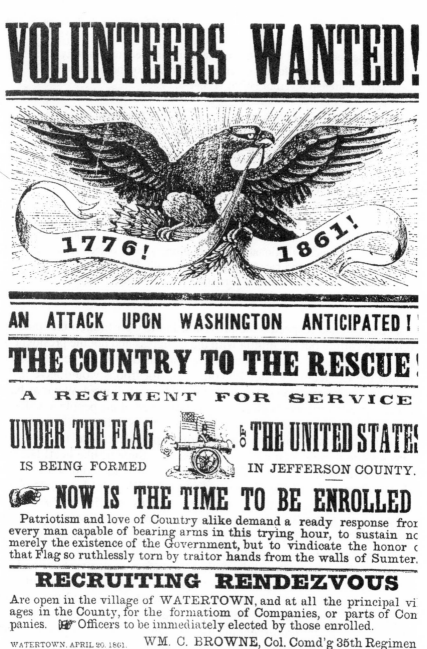

VOLUNTEERS WANTED!

1776!   **1861!**

AN ATTACK UPON WASHINGTON ANTICIPATED !

THE COUNTRY TO THE RESCUE!

A REGIMENT FOR SERVICE

UNDER THE FLAG ^{OF} THE UNITED STATES

IS BEING FORMED   IN JEFFERSON COUNTY.

☞ NOW IS THE TIME TO BE ENROLLED

Patriotism and love of Country alike demand a ready response from every man capable of bearing arms in this trying hour, to sustain no merely the existence of the Government, but to vindicate the honor of that Flag so ruthlessly torn by traitor hands from the walls of Sumter.

RECRUITING RENDEZVOUS

Are open in the village of WATERTOWN, and at all the principal vil ages in the County, for the formatiom of Companies, or parts of Con panies. ☞ Officers to be immediately elected by those enrolled.

WATERTOWN. APRIL 20. 1861.   WM. C. BROWNE, Col. Comd'g 35th Regimen

Ingalls, Brockway & Beebee. Printers, Reformer Office, Watertown.

Figure 3.1. A recruiting poster in response to Lincoln's call for 75,000 volunteers. Note the absurd appeal for volunteers on the basis that Washington would be attacked. By comparison, consider the acts of President Roosevelt when the Japanese attacked Pearl Harbor on 7 December 1941. He called Congress into session the next day and addressed them in these words: "I ask that the Congress declare."

He directed the Treasury Department, at this time, to pay $2,000,000 to a private firm in New York to start buying military equipment, also an appropriations act that required Congressional approval—before the fact.

When he finally got around to calling Congress to meet in July, he was already laying plans to invade Virginia to make a quick knockout blow and end the war. He went ahead with those plans, with the battle cry "On to Richmond."

When Congress convened in July, it went along with all Lincoln had done: the time for any debate had passed, and any expressions of doubt about all these extraconstitutional acts would have put one in danger of being arrested by a military officer, tried for treasonable speech, and then locked up for who knows how long. Unquestionably, the Congress was scared to death about what the Lincoln administration would do to them if they did not support his acts of war. The Constitution was hanging by a thread, if that.

Northern informers had identified members of the Maryland legislature who might support secession when the legislature met. Mind you, these were the people's elected officials. Secretary of War Simon Cameron issued an order to Major General Banks in Maryland that "all or any part of the Legislative members must be arrested" to prevent secession. By the darkness of night, on September 12–13, all suspected Southern sympathizers in the Maryland state legislature were arrested along with other influential citizens, and all were locked up in prison at Fort McHenry. In the end, fifty-one citizens were arrested, and the democratic government in Maryland ceased to exist. Here, with a state government, Lincoln had indeed crossed the Rubicon. But Lincoln was not alone, and not without support. Both the *Annapolis Gazette* and the *Baltimore American* applauded the act of the federal government.

But that was not the end of the destruction of the democratic process in Maryland. In November there was an election, and to make sure only Union people were elected, all members of the federal armed forces voted, even though they were not residents of the state. At the voting booths, other voters had to pass through platoons of Union soldiers who had bayonets affixed to their rifles. The elections were a fraud, and finally the democratic system of government in Maryland breathed its last breath. In London, commenting on what happened in Maryland, the *Saturday Review* noted, "It was as perfect an act of despotism as can be conceived. It was a *coup d'etat* in every essential feature."[3]

Even earlier, by the time Lincoln reluctantly called the Congress in July 1861, a reign of terror had enveloped the nation. Hundreds of newspapers were being shut down by Lincoln's order. But for what purpose? What motive? The *Chicago Times* had the courage to raise that question:

PROCLAMATION OF GENERAL LEE.

HEADQUARTERS ARMY N. VA. }
Near Fredericktown, Sept. 8, 1862. }

TO THE PEOPLE OF MARYLAND:

It is right that you should know the purpose that has brought the Army under my command within the limits of your State, so far as that purpose concerns yourselves.

The People of the Confederate States have long watched, with the deepest sympathy, the wrongs and outrages that have been inflicted upon the Citizens of a Commonwealth, allied to the States of the South by the strongest social, political and commercial ties. They have seen with profound indignation their sister States deprived of every right, and reduced to the condition of a conquered province.

Under the pretense of supporting the constitution, but in violation of its most valuable provisions, your Citizens have been arrested and imprisoned upon no charge, and contrary to all forms of law ; the faithful and manly protest against this outrage made by the venerable and illustrious Marylander to whom in better days no citizen appealed for right in vain, was treated with scorn and contempt ; the government of your chief city has been usurped by armed strangers ; your Legislature has been dissolved by the unlawful arrest of its members ; freedom of the press and of speech has been suppressed ; words have been declared offences by an arbitrary decree of the Federal Executive, and citizens ordered to be tried by a military commission for what they may dare to speak.

Believing that the people of Maryland possessed a spirit too lofty to submit to such a government, the people of the South have long wished to aid you in throwing off this foreign yoke to enable you again to enjoy the inalienable rights of freemen, and restore independence and sovereignty to your State. In obedience to this wish, our army has come among you, and is prepared to assist you with the power of its arms in regaining the rights of which you have been despoiled. This, Citizens of Maryland, is our mission, so far as you are concerned. No restraint upon your free will is intended, no intimidation will be allowed. Within the limits of this army, at least, Marylanders shall once more enjoy their ancient freedom of thought and speech. We know no enemies among you, and will protect all of every opinion. It is for you to decide your destiny, freely and without constraint.

This Army will respect your choice, whatever it may be : and while the Southern people will rejoice to welcome you to your natural position among them. they will only welcome you when you come of your own free will.

R. E. LEE, General Commanding.

Figure 3.2. Southern leaders were well aware of what had happened in Maryland with the arbitrary arrests that shut down the Maryland government by federal military forces. When Lee invaded Maryland in 1862, he issued this proclamation to the local citizenry listing the crimes against Marylanders by the federal government. Unfortunately his army was defeated in the battle of Antietam a short time later. His battle plans fell into Union hands, but he was still outnumbered three to one, and for almost any offensive operation, that means defeat. Gettysburg, in July 1863, had the same problem.

> It can not be possible that a Christian nation can desire to see thousands and tens of thousands of their people and tens of thousands of a kindred people butchered, and all the expenses and horrors of a civil war incurred without some adequate motive. To assume a different ground, would be to confess ourselves barbarians or demons. We then repeat the question as to what adequate motive we have for inaugurating a civil war?[4]

After examining the question in "the light of reason and uninfluenced by passion," the newspaper could find no sufficient moral reason to justify a civil war. The article was reprinted in the Indianapolis *Daily State Sentinel*. In a short time, a military officer arrived at the *Chicago Times* and shut down the newspaper and sealed its presses. Yet all they had asked for was a proper, moral basis for civil war, and they could find none. And, frankly, neither could anyone else. Thus the freedom of the press, as guaranteed by the First Amendment, was curtailed not from calls to support the South or to take up arms against the federal government, but just from asking for the right to question the right to invade the South and engage in civil war. Legitimate questions were denied a voice in the press and in the whole country, questions that demanded rational answers, not an iron fist.

Besides the *Chicago Daily Times,* the government ordered scores of newspapers shut down.[5] The *Journal of Commerce* (New York City), a large commercial paper, supported Southern rights and attacked the suspension of the right of habeas corpus. The publisher stood up against a mob attack, but he was forced to sell the paper after the government ordered the post office to refuse to mail the paper. A new owner was willing to follow the government's party line.

The *Morning News* (New York City), a Democratic daily, opposed the war and was shut down by order of Secretary Seward. *The Day-Book,* another daily, was similarly shut down for opposing the war, as was *The New York World.* The *Freeman's Journal* (New York City), a Roman Catholic weekly, was not only shut down, but its editor was imprisoned without a trial and was held in the government's prison in New York Harbor.

Other newspapers that were shut down include the *Philadelphia Evening Journal,* the *Christian Observer,* the *Republican Watchman* (Pa.); the *Journal,* the *Missourian,* the *Herald* (Mo.); the *Democrat* (Concord, N.H.); the *Farmer* (Bangor, Me.); and the *Sentinel* (Bridgeport, Conn.).

The *New York Herald,* at that time the largest newspaper in New York City, maintained the right of secession and opposed a war of coercion against seceding states. But a mob compelled the publisher to change his tune, and editorials stopped expressing hostility to Lincoln's war.

One of the foreign newspapers in New York, the French *Courier des*

États Unis, was ordered to print the news of the day only, no commentaries, and its editor, M. E. Masseras, was ordered to resign. He resigned, as ordered, and wrote to Paris: "The belief on the part of the Washington Government that such extreme measures are necessary, proves conclusively that there must be a strong feeling of disapprobation on the part of the people against the war."

As the attack on the press continued, which Lincoln supported throughout the war, the game plan changed somewhat. Instead of shutting down the presses, which upset the citizenry, Seward and his henchmen would simply throw the editor in prison. His successor would naturally get the message and comply, and the readers would not see the heavy hand of government.

Lincoln was not interested in having Congress take up the issues raised about secession and the Fort Sumter affair. By the time Congress convened, he had the army fully mobilized and had plans to invade the South. Public discussion, free speech, and a free press were strangled by Lincoln. He became master of the lives of men captured from the Confederacy, and he was fully prepared to hang them, especially those seized on Confederate ships—they were pirates under the law as he saw it. Lincoln was thus an imperial magistrate, with full despotic powers, and his rightful master, the Congress, was not allowed to say anything or decide the issues.

In fact, there was no Congress to speak of, and when they met there was nothing to do but vote the money Lincoln wanted and ratify all his acts. By that time, "the mob spirit had America in its grips." And how would any member of Congress dare to challenge what was being done? Thinking men were filled with fear, and justifiably so. There was nothing, and no one, in the history of the nation who could support what Lincoln and his government had done. Even extreme Unionists, like Daniel Webster, would not support what had been done.

Thirty years earlier, when it was rumored that President Jackson would blockade Charleston and invade South Carolina over the nullification crisis, Daniel Webster, as strong a Unionist as any who ever existed, responded, "The President has no authority to blockade Charleston; the President has no authority to employ military force, till he shall be required to do so by civil authorities. His duty is to cause the laws to be executed. His duty is to support the civil authority."[6]

Lincoln said that constitutional legislative powers applied to the commander in chief in difficult times. He did, as caesars and dictators have done throughout history, assume the powers of the legislature in time of crisis. Lincoln told Congress that he had the right to suspend the Constitution in order to save it—constitutional gospel according to Lincoln. He also felt he had as much right to interpret the Constitution as did the Court or the Congress, an idea erroneously attributed to Andrew Jackson.

Jackson said he had the right to make constitutional determinations when he was acting in the legislative process—vetoing or approving congressional acts. Henry Clay initiated the rumor that Jackson had said to a Georgia congressman, regarding the Georgia—Cherokee Indian dispute, "John Marshall has made his decision, now let him enforce it." Clay was after Jackson's job as president, and this bit of slander served his ambitions.

A national debate ensued over this rumor. Newspapers came out with editorials demanding that Jackson be impeached if he should ever refuse to enforce or abide by a Supreme Court ruling. One editorial ended by saying that if Jackson ever rebuked the Court without being impeached, then "the Constitution was at an end."

Scholars now believe there was no truth in the "rumor" and no evidence to suggest that Jackson would have flouted a Supreme Court order. Henry Clay hated Jackson. For decades Clay sought the office of president and was narrowly defeated time and time again. Jackson was the least educated president the country ever had. To the leaders of the nation in the East he was an ignorant bumpkin and a soldier of fortune—a man Lincoln could identify with. And the mere rumor that Jackson had expressed words implying that the Court could be ignored was all the authority Lincoln had.

THE THREAD: SUSPENDING THE PRIVILEGE OF HABEAS CORPUS

Within a month after the bombardment of Fort Sumter, Lincoln and his cabinet and military started suspending the right of habeas corpus. First in Florida, and soon thereafter, "from Washington D.C. to Bangor, Maine." A British publication saw Mr. Lincoln's deeds as those of a dictator:

> There is no Parliamentary [congressional] authority whatever for what has been done. It has been done simply on Mr. Lincoln's fiat. At his simple bidding, acting by no authority but his own pleasure, in plain defiance of the provisions of the Constitution, the Habeas Corpus Act has been suspended, the press muzzled, and judges prevented by armed men from enforcing on the citizens' behalf the laws to which they and the President alike have sworn.[7]

The Republican administration began making arrests based on unfounded rumors. Some officers and officials with a tinge of paranoia came to see traitors behind every bush. Arbitrary arrests and trials before military commissions were not uncommon.

The Supreme Court made a valiant effort to check this reign of tyranny. In the case of *Ex Parte Merryman* (1861), a citizen of Maryland, John Merryman, was arrested at night in his home and imprisoned at Fort McHenry under the orders of General George Cadwallader, commander of the fort. From his military prison, Merryman petitioned for a writ of habeas corpus to Chief Justice Roger B. Taney, whose circuit included Maryland. Taney granted the writ and set a date for a hearing, but neither the general nor Merryman showed up. Instead, the general sent a letter to the Chief Justice explaining his actions and citing the decree of President Lincoln suspending the writ, which meant that Merryman could languish in prison forever, if the general so decided, with no right to a trial or an inquiry into whatever charges the general decided to make.

The writ of habeas corpus is probably the most important provision of the Bill of Rights. It can be traced to the Magna Carta, and even today, in many countries without this protection—this most fundamental principle of English liberty—people are arrested and confined in prison indefinitely, with no trial and no means of ever being freed or even tried if the government should so decide. If Lincoln and his generals could get away with this kind of imprisonment, the liberties of all Americans would be at the whim of the generals.

In response to the general's letter, Chief Justice Taney ordered federal marshal Washington Bonifant to bring the general before the court on the next day along with the prisoner. Bonifant went to Fort McHenry, but the soldiers refused to admit him. The marshal had legal authority to summon a posse to arrest General Cadwallader and bring him into court, but this would have produced an armed conflict and bloodshed. Taney had no other recourse but to write his opinion and send a copy to President Lincoln who ignored the writ; Merryman remained in prison.

Lincoln had taken the position that he had the right to suspend the writ without Congressional approval, and that he also had the final say on the Constitutional question, not the court, and his power to make such a determination was a higher power than the Supreme Court. Lincoln thus put himself above the Congress, above the Supreme Court, and above the Constitution. He was an absolute ruler, like the tyrants of Greece and the Caesars of Rome.

Taney wrote a blistering opinion, today a great classic in constitutional law, holding that the arrest was unlawful and violated the Constitution and that only Congress can suspend the writ of habeas corpus. If Lincoln's actions were allowed to stand, said the Chief Justice, then "the people of the

Figure 3.3. Roger Brooke Taney, recognized by legal scholars as one of our greatest chief justices. He reluctantly wrote the *Dred Scott* decision that tarnished his image, especially since he had freed his own slaves and wrote against "the evils of slavery" throughout his life. His most courageous opinion was *Ex parte Merryman,* which rebuked President Lincoln for taking away the people's right to habeas corpus. Lincoln ignored the Supreme Court's ruling and in his wrath signed an order to arrest the chief justice. Lincoln was saved the condemnation of history by a reluctant federal marshal, Lamon, who wisely refrained from arresting the chief justice.

United States are no longer living under a Government of laws, but every citizen holds life, liberty and property at the will and pleasure of the army officer in whose military district he may happen to be found."

Lincoln not only ignored the Supreme Court's ruling, he then wrote out a standing order for the arrest of the Chief Justice, who was then in his eighties. The arrest was never made. But one wonders how Lincoln, who justified the war on the South because of his duty to enforce the law, could in good conscience turn around and flout the Supreme Court and its court orders and rulings on the Constitution, which he was bound to obey. Chief Justice Taney reminded Lincoln of this in his opinion. Some Lincolnite scholars argue that the Constitution is not clear on the question of who suspends the right of habeas corpus, so Lincoln was within his rights to ignore the Supreme Court. It is the Supreme Court that decides such issues, not the president, and once decided the issue is settled.

Taney's opinion irritated Lincoln, especially when the Chief Justice had a copy served on the president. The situation in Maryland was in a critical phase, and Merryman was a known agitator. It was necessary to keep Maryland in the Union, and the only threat was a real threat—the Maryland legislators who could meet and then decide that issue. By arresting the people's representatives, there would be no problem with secession, as they could not meet and could not vote and decide the issue.

To Lincoln, the Supreme Court was as much a threat as the Maryland legislators. According to the federal marshal, Ward Hill Lamon, after "due consideration the administration was determined to arrest the Chief Justice." They had already arrested members of the Maryland legislature who had been less than supportive of the Republican administration and its zeal for war on the Confederacy, so why not the justices of the Supreme Court? Lincoln issued an arrest warrant for Taney, but " 'then arose the question of making service.' Who should make the arrest, and where should the Chief Justice be imprisoned?"[8] Tough questions.

Lamon recalled, "It was finally determined to place the order of arrest in the hands of the United States Marshal for the District of Columbia."[9] Lincoln personally gave the warrant to Marshal Lamon, instructing the marshal to "use his own discretion about making the arrest unless he should receive further orders." Lamon wisely decided to not serve the warrant unless specifically ordered to do so. These orders never came. But Taney must have received some information that his arrest was in the making, for, after reading the text of his opinion in open court, he remarked that before nightfall he might also be imprisoned in the fort.

The account of the plan to arrest the Chief Justice and the execution of the order for his arrest is confirmed by two trustworthy independent sources of information—Lamon himself, in his personal papers in the Huntington Library's rare book and manuscript collection, and Professor Francis Lieber, author of the famous Lieber Code, which Lincoln endorsed (the code is discussed at length in chapter 8). Both Lamon and Lieber were, throughout their lives, ardent Unionists. Lieber's private papers are also at the Huntington Library. Lieber noted that Lincoln gave Marshal Lamon the arrest warrant for Taney along with permission to make the arrest. This confirms Lamon's account in detail.[10]

Fortunately, the marshal saved the president from what would have been his worst crime against the Constitutional scheme of government. Arresting and imprisoning state legislators was bad enough, but arresting and imprisoning the Chief Justice of the United States for rendering an opinion the president disliked—an opinion required by his high office and under the Constitutional scheme of government—would have cut the thin thread upon which the Constitution hung at that time.

Lincoln's order to arrest the Chief Justice of the United States was another Rubicon, and fortunately for the survival of republican government, it was never crossed. If Lincoln had established the precedent that a president could not only flout the orders of the Supreme Court but also arrest the Supreme Court justices if he disagreed with their opinions, then the United States, like the Roman Republic, would have evolved into a military despotism under the will of the commander in chief, as happened in Rome two thousand years ago.

Fortunately, Lincoln did not cross his Rubicon, and republican government did survive. It was shaky throughout the nation during the war, and was suspended in the South during Reconstruction when military generals held life, liberty, and property in their hands, at the whim of their military tribunals and officers. But the thread did not break, and in time it strengthened. The Constitution survived, but not as originally intended and not as conceived of during pre–Civil War years. A new nation was brought forth with an all-powerful federal government, obliterating the sovereignty of the states, as Lincoln conceived it. Lincoln's war to preserve the Union turned out to be a war that destroyed it.

Chief Justice Taney's decision and subsequent opinion ordering the president to respect the Constitution and the orders of the Supreme Court—the final arbiter of constitutional issues that no president had the right to evade or ignore—is probably the most courageous decision ever handed down by the High Court. At a time when there were wholesale arrests of innocent people whose only offense was to disagree with the Republican administration, Taney stood up to a president who thought that because of the rebellion in South Carolina and the secession, he justifiably held all the reins of government: legislative, executive, and judicial.

Taney, in his decision, cited William Blackstone's *Commentaries on the Laws of England* (1765), one of the great discourses on common law, a treatise that was cited more times by the Framers than any other book except Baron de Montesquieu's *The Spirit of Laws*. Blackstone, in his work, cited the great Justice Lord Coke on the matter of habeas corpus:

> Of great importance to the public is the preservation of this personal liberty . . . confinement of the person, by secretly hurrying him to gaol, where his sufferings are unknown or forgotten; is a less public, a less striking, and therefore a more dangerous engine of arbitrary government; and yet sometimes, when the state is in real danger, even this may be a necessary measure. But the happiness of our constitution is, that it is not left to the executive power to determine when the danger of state is so great, as to render this measure expedient. For the parliament only, or legislative power, whenever it sees proper, can authorize the crown, by suspending the habeas corpus act for a short and limited time.[11]

Blackstone's *Commentaries* were unquestionably the leading treatise on common law throughout the English-speaking world, cited with great frequency in court cases and legal treatises. Taney, as well as anyone with any legal education, was aware of this work, and citing Blackstone was great authority. How Lincoln could evade this great giant of the law, as well as the opinion of the Chief Justice, is beyond comprehension. When Lincoln finally decided to explain his position, that the executive also had the power to suspend habeas corpus, he did so in his written treatise to the Congress when they assembled on July 4. Lincoln showed that he had no significant understanding of the law, and he zigged and zagged trying to excuse himself. He cited no authority because there wasn't any, only the Constitution according to Lincoln.

Blackstone wasn't the only authority against what the president had done. One of the leading scholars in the United States was Justice Joseph Story, the Dane Professor of Law at Harvard University. Besides being on the Supreme Court, and a strong supporter of a powerful federal government, he wrote a series of treatises on important legal subjects, and one of them was *Commentaries on the Constitution*. He wrote that "hitherto no suspension of the writ has ever been authorized by Congress since the establishment of the Constitution. It would seem as the power is given to Congress to suspend the writ of habeas corpus in cases of rebellion or invasion, that the right to judge whether the exigency had arisen must exclusively belong to that body [Congress]."[12]

In addition to Justice Story's commentary, we have Thomas Jefferson, who even disliked the power given to Congress to suspend the privilege of habeas corpus. To Jefferson, there should never be any suspension of this ancient right; he was in favor of "the eternal and unremitting force of the *habeas corpus* laws."[13] On another occasion he wrote, "If the public safety requires that the government should have a man imprisoned on less probable testimony in those and other emergencies, let him be taken and tried."[14] During the Aaron Burr conspiracy, when Jefferson was president, the Senate introduced a bill to suspend the right of habeas corpus; it passed the Senate but was overwhelmingly defeated in the house by a vote of 113 for rejection and only 19 in favor.

And if Story, Blackstone, and Jefferson weren't enough, there was Chief Justice John Marshall himself who wrote in the case of *Ex Parte Bollman and Swartwout:* "If at any time the public safety should require the suspension of the powers vested by this act in the Courts of the United States, it is for the legislature to say so. That question [suspension of the writ] depends upon political considerations, on which the legislature is to decide."[15]

Justice Taney cited John Marshall's decision in his opinion that rebuked President Lincoln. Lincoln must have been enraged to have the Chief Justice sending him personally a copy of his opinion, together with the overpowering authorities on habeas corpus law, but it did not move him. His own legal education was minimal, and his comprehension of the law was often impaired by this limitation. He was more a politician or a trial lawyer who could sway the masses but not the courts of law or experienced, learned judges. So he simply ignored their opinions, ordered more arrests, and snubbed the Supreme Court. After all, he held the power of the military, and all that the courts had to stand up to him were words, history, the law, and that piece of parchment called the Constitution, plus the English constitution and common law. The history of liberty and of tyranny was also against him, but so what? Caesar didn't have to win the argument with the senate for his extraconstitutional powers, and neither did Lincoln. They both had the army on their side.

As noted, Lincoln said that the commander in chief had just as much right to interpret the Constitution as did the Court, but even he had some doubts about this crackpot interpretation of the Constitution. Lincoln should have been brought to trial before the Congress for impeachment. Instead, in July a compliant Congress simply granted the president powers to suspend the writ of habeas corpus. The Congress during Lincoln's reign of terror could well be called "the rubber stamp Congress," not unlike the Roman senate after Caesar assumed the powers of government.

A few months later, a Philadelphia lawyer tried to come to the aid of Mr. Lincoln and justify his power to suspend the writ. The argument was that the president was a better judge of when to suspend the writ, and because he was ultimately responsible to the people every four years, that distinction made the English rule inapplicable. That opinion set off vicious responses by the bench and bar everywhere. One legal scholar made a long roll of "eminent judges, lawyers, and statesmen on the subject," and found without exception that from the "birth of the Constitution to the present day," not one respectable lawyer supported the position of the president and his attorney general.[16] Lincoln didn't fool anyone, nor did he persuade anyone that he was in the right. So while the debate seemed hopeless on the side of the president, the suspension of the writ continued under the approval of the Congress. As time passed, the suspension of the writ put over ten thousand men into prison. Men who had done nothing other than express their opinions about the despotic course of events—words opposing Lincoln's rule. They were not secessionist sympathizers, but Lincoln opponents—against the wholesale destruction of the Constitution. By comparison, Mussolini is reported to have jailed around two thousand men.

This wild state of wartime hysteria, heated up by the president, his fanatics in the cabinet, and the military, had no restraint—no checks and balances once the Court was snubbed. There was the cry of treason throughout the land for any that opposed the president, yet the crime of treason was of serious concern by the Framers of the Constitution, since it had been used rather loosely throughout Western civilization as a device to oppress society and silence any political dissent. Yet even that provision in the Constitution was given no more respect than the other provisions Lincoln ignored.

The reign of terror, and excuse of "public safety" to justify what was done, was a term used in the French Revolution. The only thing missing was the guillotine. The Congress and the Courts were without either the will or the ability to check the president's dictatorial rule. Caesar was given dictatorial powers, not for six months as the Roman constitution provided, but for life. Were Lincoln's powers any less? Lincoln had no more respect for the American Constitution than did Caesar for the Roman constitution.

When Chief Justice Taney rebuked Lincoln for asserting his power as commander of the military to suspend the right of habeas corpus, Taney said:

> And if the President of the United States may suspend the writ, then the Constitution of the United States has conferred upon him more regal and absolute power over the liberty of the citizen than the people of England have thought it safe to entrust to the crown—a power

which the Queen of England cannot exercise to this day, and which could not have been lawfully exercised by the sovereign even in the reign of Charles the First.[17]

Military dictatorship weakened in 1866 after the war ended. Another court challenge was made to the military trials of civilians that had raged in the country for the past five years. In the case of *Ex Parte Milligan,* the Supreme Court had another chance to deal with military judicial despotism. Milligan's supposedly treasonable conduct was presented to a Grand Jury in Indiana, where the jury found insufficient evidence to indict Milligan. But a military court then took over, convicted Milligan and gave him the death penalty. President Andrew Johnson had restored the right of habeas corpus, so the matter could be brought before the High Court for review. The Supreme Court released Milligan and then condemned the past five years of arbitrary, even phoney, military tribunals.

The government made the established Lincoln argument that the commander of American armies could, in times of war, within his military district, suspend all civil rights, and subject the citizens as well as the soldiers, to the rule of his will, and this could take place if "in his opinion the exigencies of the country demand it, and of which he is to judge," and even if the district is no war zone, and civilian courts are open. In reply, the Supreme Court said in the Milligan case:

> If true, republican government is a failure, and there is an end of liberty regulated by law. Martial law, established on such a basis, destroys every guaranty of the Constitution and effectively renders the military independent of and superior to the civil powers. . . . Civil liberty and this kind of martial law cannot endure together; the antagonism is irreconcilable and, in the conflict, one or the other must perish. . . . Martial rule can never exist where the Courts are open, and in the proper and unobstructed exercise of their jurisdiction.[18]

Hence, the military commissions of the Civil War era were held to be illegal. The military courts of President Lincoln were illegal. The opinion was delivered by Justice Davis, a personal friend of Lincoln. "No graver question was ever considered by the Court, nor one which more nearly concerns the rights of every American citizen charged with a crime."

The decision was a two-edged sword. Not only did it make Lincoln's military tribunals illegal, it even made illegal all those military arrests and trials by Lincoln after he received congressional approval—after Congress suspended the privilege of habeas corpus. In short, the *Milligan* case held that not even Congress can suspend the writ in those areas where civilian courts are open.

THE RADICALS: ON THE ROAD TO A LASTING SOLUTION

Republicans who hated the South were called "radicals." They condemned the *Milligan* decision as an outrage to the purposes of the war. The decision, they said, was designed to aid and abet the rebels and the Confederacy. One editorial said, "It virtually declares that Lincoln's assassins suffered a juridico-military murder."[19] In other words, the military court that put to death those accused of conspiring to assassinate Lincoln was illegal. One of the lawyers in that military trial, who defended Mary Surratt, acknowledged afterward that the military tribunal was organized to convict, whatever the evidence, and was illegal. The *Milligan* decision confirmed that, but there is no appeal once one is hanged until dead.

That same editorial called the decision "the most dangerous opinion ever pronounced by that tribunal." Said another, "This two-faced opinion of Mr. Justice Davis is utterly inconsistent with the deciding facts of the war, and therefore utterly preposterous. These antediluvian Judges seem to forget that the war was an appeal from the Constitution to the sword." Worse still, said another editor, "The hearts of traitors will be glad by the announcement that treason, vanquished upon the battlefield and hunted from every other retreat, has at last found secure shelter in the bosom of the Supreme Court."

The leading Republican newspaper in the capital, the *Washington Chronicle,* that always stood by the Lincoln administration during the war, said, "We have not yet met a Republican who does not speak with contempt of the language of Justice Davis. . . . The people have said, if it is not lawful to whip traitors, we will make it so."[20]

With this furor over the *Milligan* case in 1866, it naturally followed that the Senate, the *Chronicle,* the Bureau of Military Justice, and others, called for the impeachment of the Justices of the Supreme Court, even to reconstruct the Court, FDR style. The attack on the Court indicates the hate that was pervasive among the radicals—hate that all wars too often engender. The Civil War was no exception, and, as the reader will discover, most shocking of all was the call for the extermination of the Southern people—man, woman, and child!

The radicals, who included the Christian clergy, the press, leaders of the Republican party, and a host of minor politicians and leaders, spewed forth venom in their writings and demands on the government. They wanted to slaughter every Southern white in sight and then repeople the Southern territory (discussed in chap. 9).[21] Was not this to be ethnic cleansing at its best?

In the Congress, there was a significant group of South haters, with murderous demands. The chairman of the Ways and Means Committee of the House of Representatives, Thaddeus Stevens, was willing that the South "be laid waste, and made a desert, in order to save this Union from destruction." Before a Republican state convention in September 1862, he urged the government to "slay every traitor—burn every Rebel Mansion. . . . unless we do this, we cannot conquer them."[22] The *New York Times* wrote in March 1861 that the North should "destroy its commerce, and bring utter ruin on the Confederate states," and this was before the bombardment at Fort Sumter.

Congressman Zachariah Chandler expressed the spirit of so many in the Congress: "A rebel has sacrificed all his rights. He has no right to life, liberty, property, or the pursuit of happiness. Everything you give him, even life itself, is a boon which he has forfeited."[23] Such sentiments found their way to the European observers of the war, who found them hard to believe from a civilized people. A correspondent for the pro-Northern *Macmillan Magazine,* in December 1863, wrote, "How can you subjugate such a people as this? And even supposing that their extermination were a feasible plan, as some Northerners suggested, I never can believe that in the nineteenth century the civilized world will be condemned to witness the destruction of such a gallant race."[24]

On 5 May 1861, this genocidal passion against the South found analysis in the *New York Herald.* It quoted the views of the abolitionists: "When the rebellious traitors are overwhelmed in the field, and scattered like leaves before an angry wind, it must not be to return to peaceful and contented homes. They must find poverty at their firesides, and see privation in the anxious eyes of mothers, and the rags of children."

Another radical editor noted that the *New York Herald* called "for the punishment of all individuals in the South by hanging, and the confiscation of everybody's property in the seceding States." "Richmond," said another, "must be laid in ashes," and as for Baltimore, "it must become a heap of cinders and ashes, and its inhabitants ought either to be slaughtered, or scattered to the winds." Virginia and Maryland deserve to be "laid waste and made desolate" and 500,000 troops should "pour down from the North, leaving a desert track behind them." The editor responded, "Submission on the part of the South would not satisfy these bloody journalists of the Republican party. Far from it. They cry out: 'We mean not merely to conquer, but to subjugate.' " The editor then adds, "The people of the North are prepared for no such extremities as the brutal, bloodthirsty journals of the abolitionist school suggest."[25]

On 24 May 1861, the *Daily Herald* in Newburyport, Massachusetts, said that "if it were necessary, we could clear off the thousand millions of square miles so that not a city or cultivated field would remain; we could exterminate nine millions of white people and re-settle—re-people the lands. There is no want of ability; and if such a work is demanded, there would be no want of a will."[26]

It is no wonder that the Civil War generated hatred for the North and the Republican party among Southerners for well over a hundred years. The bloodthirsty rhetoric of the radicals in the North in time found expression in the devastation of civilians and civilian property by Sherman, Sheridan, Grant, and the commander in chief—Lincoln. It didn't end with the war, for it was then carried on in a less violent form in the Reconstruction laws for the South by the radicals. The object was to exterminate the culture of the Southerners, and to subjugate then destroy the political force of the Southern establishment, and not just the planter–slave owner class. There was to be a new order in the South, excluding the established Southerners of all classes. The radicals succeeded for a while and then moved on, leaving a wasteland in which secret societies and lawlessness prevailed. Thus, in a sense, the Northerners did exterminate a society in every way except genocide. By contrast, no such genocidal threats were made by Southerners against the North.

There is no doubt that during the Civil War era the U.S. Constitution held by a thread. People today have no idea of the real dangers to American society that were on the line, and few realize just how fortunate succeeding generations are that the military despotism that plagued the land for over five years did not last forever. The radicals eventually were toppled from power and disappeared. Only their literature survives to our day. Their hatred of the South has also disappeared. In time, the Constitution and the ideals of civil liberty and limited government came back as the Bureau of Military Justice disappeared from civilian life. The evil these men did is there for us to see and to make us realize how vulnerable civil liberties are in times of crisis. Perhaps it was the deep-rooted love of liberty the Founders passed on to us that reasserted itself in the men who followed the Civil War and directed the affairs of the American people. In other times and places, like Rome, military dictators assumed power, and civil government and liberties died forever.

Finally, many Northern historians continue to ignore the depth and tragic significance of the military arrests, trials, and even hangings by Lincoln's administration during the war years. Lincoln's refusal to respect the Supreme Court's decision—that he had no power to suspend the privilege of habeas corpus—is cited as a differing of opinion on the Constitution. The issue was not one of differing opinions but of the duty to respect the decisions of the Supreme Court as the final arbiter of Constitutional issues.

Regardless of what Lincoln's personal views were on the Constitution, it was his absolute and unconditional duty to obey the Court. It is well-known that President Eisenhower did not like the antisegregation ruling of the Court under Chief Justice Warren, but he did his duty and enforced desegregation of the Little Rock public schools. He did his constitutional duty; Lincoln did not. But Eisenhower never again invited Chief Justice Earl Warren to the White House for dinner.

These same historians ignore the awful consequences of imprisonment in federal prisons, for months and even years. The death toll was outrageous. How many innocent people, languishing in a federal military prison, died as a result? Here are the numbers: On 19 July 1866, Secretary of War Stanton published a report on the prisoners in federal prisons during the Civil War, and this included Confederate POWs. There were approximately 220,000 prisoners, of which 26,576 died in custody. The death toll in Confederate prisons, even Andersonville, was not any worse.[27] The POWs could have been exchanged for Northern POWs, but it was Lincoln who refused to exchange prisoners, and that makes the horrors of Andersonville partly his responsibility, especially since he refused to permit medical supplies to be exported to the South. He wanted the Southern people to suffer, and as a consequence thousands of Northern POWs died in the process. It is no wonder that Lincoln finally blamed the Civil War on God, as otherwise he had an enormous amount of blood on his hands.

In summary, Lincoln seemed to believe that there were no limits to his powers as president if they were exercised to prevent secession. He summoned the militia when that was a power the Constitution gave to Congress (Article 1, section 8) as well as the authority to "suppress Insurrection." He spent millions of dollars for war materials, when that was also a congressional power. He authorized recruiting, decreed a naval blockade (an act of war), defied the Supreme Court, and even signed an order to arrest the Chief Justice of the United States for writing an opinion telling him that the president alone had no right to suspend the privilege of habeas corpus. It was an easy opinion to write, since legal authorities including Blackstone and Justice Joseph Story, as well as the plain language of the Constitution, gave that dangerous power to the Congress. Blackstone had said this power to suspend habeas corpus could only be used for a short, limited time, and then only by the legislature. Lincoln usurped this congressional power, and then with Congress's blessing created an American gulag for an estimated 20,000 political opponents who disagreed with him. He personally pledged the nation's credit, when that was also for Congress to do. He arrested members of state legislatures, preventing them from debating the secession issue. He closed more than three hundred newspapers that disagreed with him. When his reelection was on the line, he corrupted the voting process.

In one of his strangest acts of contempt of the Constitution he created the state of West Virginia, in contravention of Article 4, section 3, which required the approval of Virginia. No such approval was obtained. Lincoln excused this because it was "expedient."

The worst of his malfeasance was as commander in chief, when he authorized and promoted a policy to decimate civilian property and life, violating the laws of war at that time. All of these acts, so common for an autocrat like a Russian tsar, were done with the enthusiastic support from the moneymen of the North. When Lincoln was willing to toss the Constitution out the window, he had the blessing and the approval of those who financed the war and thus made it possible. It was more their war than it was Lincoln's war. They bear the ultimate responsibility for the war. The Wall Street boys and the men of commerce and business were determined to preserve the Union for their economic gain. They were anxious to appease the South over the slave issue, but when secession came, they were then for preserving the Union by war. In the final analysis, it was the nation's business leaders who beat the war drum for preserving the Union, which really meant preserving their prosperity and bank accounts.

When Chief Justice Taney wrote his opinion, telling the president that he could not lock people up at his will and throw away the key, it was the leading New York newspapers that blasted the Chief Justice: He was a traitor, using "the powers of his office to serve the cause of traitors" (*New York Times*). The *New York Evening Post* wrote that Taney was serving "treason . . . those who are armed against the Union." The *New York Tribune* attacked Taney's age: "When treason stalks . . . let decrepit Judges give place to men capable of detecting and crushing it. . . . No judge whose heart was loyal to the Constitution would have given such aid and comfort to public enemies [using words in the Constitution that define treason]."[28] However, many other newspapers outside of New York—in Boston, Cincinnati, Baltimore, even Washington D.C.—defended the Court. Today, Taney's opinion is studied in law school as one of the great decisions on constitutional law, with no dissenters. The Chief Justice was courageous, and when he sent his opinion to the White House, he commented that he expected to be arrested and imprisoned within the hour. He almost was.

Lincoln came as close to crossing our Rubicon as any other president. He did not go as far as Julius Caesar—he was not appointed dictator for life—but he did in fact serve as such for a few years. Why did dictatorship emerge in Rome and rule for centuries, whereas Lincoln's dictatorship lasted only for the war years? It was only a year or two after the Civil War

Figure 3.4. Lincoln's policy of letting generals try, convict, and punish civilians, even when civilian courts were open to guarantee compliance with the Bill of Rights, eventually ended with judicial murder. Here on the left is Mary Surratt, hanging by her neck until dead, ostensibly for being a conspirator to assassinate Lincoln. She just happened to operate a boarding house where John Wilkes Booth occasionally visited. It was guilt by very remote association. Mary Surratt's lawyer, John Bingham, who later became a man of considerable stature in American law, commented that the generals would have convicted her no matter what the evidence. These are the kinds of tribunals associated with totalitarian states, which America was at that time.[29]

The army wanted to try Jefferson Davis along with the others and had some trumped-up evidence that would have been enough for this tribunal but decided that a great state trial for treason would provide worldwide publicity. As we shall see, this great trial of the century never took place.

that the Constitution was resurrected, that the Supreme Court's decisions were respected by the other branches of government, and that the separation of powers was once again restored. Was it the inherent vitality of the Constitution and its wisdom in the format of government that prevailed? Or was it the strength of the American people and their belief in limited government? Whatever the reason, although big government had its origin in Lincoln's war government, dictatorship died with the war and Reconstruction, and even the imperial presidencies of our era have been puny by comparison.

But the tyranny of the Civil War era should be a sobering lesson, not to be lost or brushed aside. For unless we focus on what happened, and make sure it does not happen again, another national crisis may produce a strong executive who overpowers the other branches of government, even the Constitution itself, and we may end up as Benjamin Franklin is reported to have predicted about the new Constitution in 1787: "That it might last for ages, involve one quarter of the globe, and probably terminate in despotism."[30]

At the end of the war, British writers predicted that the despotism had indeed arrived, and America as a free society had ended.[31] Throughout the war, the British press focused on the despotism that had taken over America, arguing that the American government "has disgracefully and ignominiously failed."[32] Even the London *Times* saw it that way, and blamed the American system of government: "This Republic has been so often proposed to us as a model for imitation that we should be unpardonable not to mark how it works now. . . . We believe that if the English system of Parliamentary action had existed in America, the war could not have occurred, but we are quite sure that such Ministers [Republican leaders] would have long since been changed."[33]

Why didn't the people in the North see what Lincoln was doing? What had happened to constitutional government? Was it not the passion of war, which even blinded them to the destruction of their civil liberties? If so, the American Civil War proved the adage that the first casualty of war is truth. So where do we look for objectivity at that time? Surely not at home. But there was objectivity abroad from the writers, editors, and correspondents in Europe. Those foreign observers saw the war for what it was.

4

Whose War Was It, Anyway?

Money, and not morality, is the principle of commercial nations.
Thomas Jefferson, letter to John Landon, 1810

The Civil War has also been called "Lincoln's war." Modern historians have been compelled to acknowledge that it was a war Lincoln could have avoided or ended at his will.[1] It was Lincoln who made the call to arms and who, on his own, proceeded to gear up the nation for war—depriving the Congress of its constitutional responsibilities to make that fateful decision. But was it really Lincoln's war? If not, then whose war was it?

The war has also been labeled the "rich man's war," an accurate but not entirely popular label. Without the strong support from the Wall Street class and the merchants and men of commerce, especially in New York City, Lincoln could not have gone to war against the South. Indeed, his first inaugural address could have been written by Northern businessmen. However, a few weeks before Sumter, businessmen had almost universally favored peace and had fostered attempts to save the Union by compromise and by appeasing the slave owners. There were rich and continuing profits for them with the Union as it was, and they had no interest in joining the abolitionists or the secessionists. For the sake of their commercial interests, they would sympathize with the slave owners and could see no virtue in disrupting the slave economy of the South, which, by the way, benefited them. They had too much to lose to disrupt the Union in any way. Money makes the world go around; money was the moving force behind the Gulf War in 1992, and it was the moving force behind the Civil War in 1861.

Lincoln was right when he later said that he did not cause the events of his time, but he was moved by them—by forces greater than he was. That is true, but it was not the force for abolition that moved him, nor was it God, even though that seems to be a noble interpretation of his thinking. It seems to this historian that financial prosperity was the powerful force that moved the nation into war. All other events and motives were secondary. Here is the story.

THE FIRST SUBSCRIPTION.

Figure 4.1. An early etching showing the support of New York's moneymen subscribing to loans to the federal government shortly after the bombardment of Fort Sumter. Without the support of these moneymen—the Wall Street boys and New York's leaders of commerce and trade—no war could have been waged for long.

THE FATEFUL MONTH

The fateful decisions that caused the war are often traced to the Fort Sumter event. It was fateful for Lincoln to have made up his mind to reinforce the fort. It was fateful when the Confederate cabinet sent a cable to General Beauregard to take the fort by force of arms. And it was perhaps most fateful of all when Lincoln made his call for 75,000 troops to go to war against the South and to order a blockade of Southern ports. These were all fateful decisions, the more immediate causes of the war. But it was in March 1861 that the fateful event occurred that made these later fateful decisions possible. If, during March, both the Confederate and Federal congresses had not created a "war of the tariffs," the war over Sumter may never have occurred.

Before the "war of the tariffs" in March 1861, the merchants, bankers, brokers, and investors in the North were all in favor of appeasing the South and allowing it to keep its "peculiar institution." Let the South have its way over slavery, if that is necessary to preserve the Union. But once it became clear, by mid-March, that a low tariff was in place at Southern ports to challenge Northern commerce and even undermine Northern business and trade, the policy of "preserving the Union" then shifted from appeasing the slave owners to going to war. A low or free trade zone in the South meant disaster for Northern commerce. An independent Southern nation could easily hold Northern commerce as its prey and exact a tribute if it so desired. The Yankees would squirm now! The North needed the South for its prosperity and commerce; the South did not need the North—it could buy the goods it needed from Europe and could strangle Northern business at its pleasure. It could require tolls for goods bound for the northwest, traveling up the Mississippi River onto the Ohio and Missouri Rivers. Its low trade zone would foster smuggling along the 2,000-mile border from the Atlantic Ocean to New Mexico. None of these fears were irrational, or even exaggerated, and war would be far more tolerable than a Southern Confederacy hell-bent on punishing the North over the tariff issue, which had been a bitter pill for the South to swallow for over thirty years. The Civil War got started as a "rich man's war" and not as a war over slavery. The leading abolitionist newspaper editor and writer, Horace Greeley, was delighted with secession. What a great way to rid the nation of the evil of slavery—to purge the evil that affects the whole. Good riddance was his theme, on learning of secession.

"Peaceful separation had died in the war of the tariffs," wrote Professor Philip Foner in 1941, in his remarkable book *The New York Merchants and the Irrepressible Conflict*. There was only one path for the government to follow, wrote Foner: "Collect the revenue at the seceded states, impose duties on goods entering the ports of these cities, and in general enforce the laws and compel obedience to the government. This might bring war, but even that would hardly mean 'a change for the worse.' "[2]

Lincoln got the message in many ways—from leading newspapers, as we shall see, but perhaps even more from public letters sent to the president from America's leading moneymen, demanding that the federal government act firmly to protect Northern commerce. When John A. Dix retired as secretary of the Treasury in March 1861, more than one hundred leading merchants, both Democrats and Republicans, sent him a public letter demanding action and praising the secretary for his stand against secession. One such prominent and wealthy merchant tried to send a ship to reinforce Fort Sumter, on his own, in late February. But Buchanan was still president and an informal truce was in place to maintain the status quo while the government of Lincoln was preparing to take over the reins of power and make the decisions. Most of the merchants were not for provoking war, and many admitted that the government had no right to coerce a state to remain in the Union. Either the Union should be preserved peacefully or the Southern states should be permitted to go in peace. War has most often been the archenemy of commerce, and these merchants wanted prosperity. War was to be avoided at all costs, or so they believed up until early March 1861.

By the end of March, the whole Northern world had changed, with the businessmen and newspapers leading the way. Whenever the historian reads Northern newspapers and articles that favor secession, or just tolerate it as a constitutional right, it is important to look at the date on the article. For by late March the business circles saw clearly that slavery was a nonissue for them—the tariff was *the* issue. There was already a cold war, a war of the tariffs. This was the real issue of the American crisis, as European writers saw the conflict. Now Lincoln had become a hero. He had said in his inaugural address that "physically speaking we cannot separate. We cannot remove the respective sections from each other, nor build an impassable wall between them." The business community in the North suddenly realized that it was not an issue of slavery, as many in the South had so vociferously maintained. Rather it was "now a question of national existence and commercial prosperity," wrote August Belmont, a leading banker in New York connected to the European Rothschild banking establishment. Originally a champion of peaceful secession, Belmont was all for a hot war once the tariff war began.

Figure 4.2. Lincoln on his way to his inauguration, 4 March 1861. He gave the South the option of "taxes or war."

THE NEWSPAPERS SPEAK

In early March, even before Lincoln took the oath of office, Congress passed the Morrill Tariff, the highest tariff in American history, with duty on iron products of well over 50 percent. On the average, rates were about 47 percent. It was not a revenue tariff but a prohibition tariff, according to the British and foreign newspapers. On March 11, the Confederate Constitution was adopted, and a low tariff was instituted immediately, essentially creating a free trade zone in the South. Within less than two weeks Northern newspapers grasped the significance of these two tariffs—the high Morrill tariff in the North and the low tariff in the South—and, as one historian called it, the "war of the tariffs" began. This soon led to the hot war of the armies. Prior to the two tariffs, most Northern newspapers had called for peace through conciliation, but many now called for war.

On 18 March 1861, the *Philadelphia Press* demanded war: "Blockade Southern Ports," said the *Press*. If not, "a series of customs houses will be required on the vast inland border from the Atlantic to West Texas. Worse still, with no protective tariff, European goods will under-price Northern goods in Southern markets. Cotton for Northern mills will be charged an export tax. This will cripple the clothing industries and make British mills prosper. Finally, the great inland waterways, the Mississippi, the Missouri, and the Ohio Rivers, will be subject to Southern tolls."

Previously, on 18 January 1861, the *Press* had opposed military action, arguing that the secession crisis should be settled peacefully and not by conquest, subjugation, coercion, or war.

The economic editor of the *New York Times* changed his tune in late March. For months he had written that secession would not injure Northern commerce and prosperity. The economies of the two sections were tied together and would stay together. But on 22–23 March 1861, he reversed himself with a vengeance: "At once shut down every Southern port, destroy its commerce and bring utter ruin on the Confederate States."

Perhaps the best example is an editorial that ran in the *Boston Transcript* on 18 March 1861. After pointing out that the Southern states had claimed to separate on the slavery issue, now "the mask has been thrown off and it is apparent that the people of the principal seceding states are now for commercial independence. They *dream* that the centres of traffic can be changed from Northern to Southern ports. The merchants of New Orleans, Charleston, and Savannah are possessed of the idea that New York, Boston, and Philadelphia may be shorn, in the future, of their mercantile greatness, by a revenue system verging on free trade. . . . The government would be false to its obligations if this state of things were not provided against."[3]

Following these and a host of other editorials and demands from the merchant classes, Lincoln called his cabinet together twice for advice on sending reinforcements to Sumter. At the first meeting cabinet members were against doing so, as it would mean war. It was the secretary of the Treasury, Salmon Chase, who was in favor of military action, as might be expected. In the next cabinet meeting, the call for war was given support, and the Sumter expedition was ordered the next day. The cabinet also read the mail and the newspapers.

There were a few who saw the coming war of the tariffs and its significance months before either tariff was proposed or adopted. In a speech to New York merchants, Henry J. Raymond, who founded the *New York Times* and was a prominent journalist, said that "there is no class of men in this country who have so large a stake in sustaining the government, whose prosperity depends so completely upon its being upheld . . . who have so much to lose . . . as the merchants of this city."[4] That was in January 1861, but by the end of March, the merchants grasped the significance of Raymond's remarks and were prepared to support strong action against the South and its tariff. Lincoln's request for a loan from these bankers, which was swiftly taken up, reveals their awareness of the commercial prosperity that was in danger with the war of the tariffs.

Perhaps the most intriguing development occurred in late March when the two tariffs stood side by side. Over a hundred leading commercial importers in New York, as well as a similar group in Boston, informed the collector of customs they would not pay duties on imported goods unless those same duties were also collected at Southern ports. This threat forced the Lincoln administration, and certainly Lincoln himself, to abandon his initial plan to turn over Fort Sumter to the Confederates. Only a month before, these merchants had favored giving up the forts, especially Sumter, but by early April they were all for reinforcing both Fort Sumter and Fort Pickens (which was in Florida at the entrance to Pensacola's harbor).

At the very end of March, at the very time Lincoln told his cabinet he was going to reinforce Fort Sumter, a committee of these New York merchants visited Lincoln. We have no record of what was said, but a Washington newspaperman learned that at the meeting the merchants had placed great emphasis on the tariff issue and that it was destroying trade and legitimate business. He then wrote that "it is a singular fact that merchants who, two months ago were fiercely shouting 'no coercion' now are for anything rather than inaction."[5]

The mood in the banking and business circles in New York and throughout the nation had changed dramatically. When it was reported that Lincoln was going to evacuate Fort Sumter on 12 March 1861, the stock market was buoyant, since this move indicated that Republicans were taking a much desired step toward peace, which excited investors in a positive way. Less than a month later, on April 7, after the war of the tariffs emerged, news of Lincoln's decision to send a relief naval task force to Sumter hit Wall Street, and investors were overjoyed at the reversal. There was great excitement again, and stock prices jumped. Why the change? In the interim, the significance of the two opposing tariffs became apparent. The newspapers had painted a gloomy, almost disastrous, picture for Northern commerce. Sumter could easily cripple Southern commerce and shut down a free trade port. Lincoln was going to protect Northern commerce—that was the message of the Sumter expedition for Northern businessmen.

Support for war poured into Washington, and the swift change in the attitude of New York's commercial interests had to have a powerful influence on the Lincoln administration. One merchant wrote to the secretary of the navy, Gideon Welles, that the business community was now in full support of the administration, especially if the administration would "per-

Figure 4.3. Early secessionist caricature showing the nation as a mother hen with seven ducks having left the flock. An anarchy hawk circles over the ducks while the hen complains of her empty treasury resulting from the ducks having left. As Lincoln said soon after he became president, "What about my revenue?"

severe and crush this thing out." A Wall Street man said that if the government embarked on an armed policy (war) "a hundred million dollars can be raised on Wall Street to sustain the government." Undoubtedly music to the president's ear.

> If each member of the cabinet could see the elation upon the countenance of the influential classes of the community within the two or three days past he would need no other witness to the approval of the efforts now making the rescue of our country from destruction.[6]

There were a few newspapers that had failed to sense the mood of the businessmen. The *New York Daily News* was convinced that there would be peace within a week after Sumter for the simple and compelling reason that the New York moneymen and merchants would refuse to support the war, and without their support and money there could be no war. That was compelling logic, for "money is the heart of war," as Peter the Great once said. The editor went on: "The wealthy will not supply the means to depreciate the rest of their property by prolonging this unnatural war." Even the *New York Herald*, on April 14, played the same tune: the merchants were against war and "in favor of peace and against civil war and coercion." But in a few days, these dailies had to eat their own words as the merchants and businessmen of all classes came out fighting mad against the South, secession, and the breakup of the Union. Business wisdom made policy. Nothing else mattered.

Southern newspapers were just as blind. The Richmond *Examiner,* immediately after Sumter, editorialized: "Will the City of New York 'kiss the rod that smites her,' and at the bidding of her Black Republican tyrants war upon her Southern friends and customers? Will she sacrifice her commerce, her wealth, her population, her character in order to strengthen the arms of her oppressors?"[7]

Of course she would, for the Southern friends were not friends at all but rivals in trade who had set a course to destroy the prosperity of the North and especially New York. Like the New York *Herald* and *Daily News,* the Southerners had got it all wrong—they had their heads in the sand.

NEW YORK PANICS

When the merchants of New York (and Boston) threatened to stop paying import duties as long as the Southern ports were not paying the same tax, they cited the constitutional provision that taxes had to be uniform—the same rate for all. This threat sent shock waves through the administration in Washington, but it was mild compared to the next threat from New York to withdraw from the Union and establish a free trade zone. In effect, New York would be a free port, a free city. In other words, it too would secede from the Union, over taxes.

This was only a partial solution. Granted that goods would flow into New York harbor from abroad, the importer paying no taxes. But how would the goods find their way to the markets in the North and the Northwest? The importer might pay no taxes, but the merchant sending the goods on to Northern markets would pay the same taxes that would have been paid if New York City had not seceded. But the main purpose was to receive goods tax free for shipment on to the Southern markets, and thus secession would not hurt them.

A plan not to pay any import taxes was just as foolish. The commissioner of customs would deny entry into the country; an importer who tried to force the issue would have to contend with the police and would face criminal charges for evasion of taxes. Although it was a crazy idea, it got the

THE STATE OF AFFAIRS AT WASHINGTON

Figure 4.4. This Civil War cartoon, published shortly before Lincoln's inauguration, shows an empty treasury as Southerners run off with the loot. President Buchanan is shown as an old woman, wringing her hands and doing nothing to stop the pillage while the Southerners leave Washington with the government's wealth.

attention of the president and made it clear that taxes were the issue of the day, not slavery. Many in the North suddenly realized that secession under the pretext of protecting slavery was a monstrous deception. And this explained why all the attempts to appease the South had come to naught. Now the Southerners were "demagogues of the South," and the slavery issue had been employed for years as a "pretext for the destruction of the Union."

The merchants of New York and the North, whether Democrat or Republican, now saw that there was only one course for them. They had prospered under the Union as one nation, and they now believed that prosperity would continue only if the United States was maintained as one nation. They had no choice but to support Lincoln and his policy of preserving the Union. Better to pay for armed conflict now than suffer prolonged economic disaster in a losing trade war. The president was given the message: "Wall Street . . . is ready to sustain the government heartily and liberally." The war was welcomed as the only solution for Northern commerce that would protect the nation's prosperity, which depended on one nation—and one tariff. John Bigelow, editor of the *New York Evening Post,* immediately after Fort Sumter (18, 20 April 1861), wrote that the majority of New York businessmen were supporting the president—a great majority—for they believed that "efforts and money expended *now* will reestablish the Union and give them a firm government."[8]

New York's chamber of commerce met on April 20, a week after Sumter, and attendance at the meeting was the largest ever. The president of the chamber of commerce wrote in the *New York Tribune:* "Nearly all the heaviest firms were represented. . . . We are either for the country, or for its enemies." Whether they had been Democrats or Republicans, regardless of their past political beliefs and "regardless of [their] differences earlier in the secession movement as how best to end the crisis, [they] were determined to maintain the government in its efforts to defend the country and preserve the Union."[9]

Although the abolitionists were ready to support secession to sever the ties of the North from slavery, the moneymen, the merchants, the traders, the manufacturers—businessmen everywhere—were in favor of war in order to prevent secession and maintain one nation. No constitutional rhetoric or discussion, just hard-nosed economic reality—money. And that, as we shall see, is how the British saw the war.

5

The British Press Views the War

The struggle of today is on the one side for empire and on the other for independence.

Wigan Examiner (UK), May 1861

The Southerners are admired for everything but their slavery and that their independence may be speedily acknowledged by France and England is, we are convinced, the strong desire of the vast majority, not only in England but throughout Europe.

Liverpool Daily Post, 11 March 1862

When the American Civil War, or War of the Rebellion, as it was officially called, erupted in 1861, an editorial in the British periodical *Quarterly Review* said that it could not comment on the war because "the catastrophe is too fresh, too sudden, and too terrible in its consequences."[1] Even the British House of Commons refused to allow any discussion at that time. What was so shocking was "the calamity of a people who are our kinsmen by blood, who speak the same tongue and inherit the glories of a common literature." Worse still, here was the greatest democracy of all time, "a great experiment, ostentatiously set up in the face of all the world, designed to teach the nations wisdom, and to confute the prejudices of old times." It was a new form of government "never tried before . . . For a time the experiment succeeded."[2]

The editor then lists the advantages and benefits of the American system: "The Government was cheap and free from debt, the taxes were light, emigrants poured in from Europe, and the increase and prosperity of the new country under its new form of government were beyond anything that the history of the world could parallel." This was the sum total of the great benefits and achievements of American society, achievements, we must note, that ceased to exist once America decided to emulate European ways and get involved in its wars and problems. Gone is the government that is "cheap and free from debt," nor are the "taxes . . . light." But to this editor, those were the keys to America's greatness, and the attraction to immigrants wanting to get out from under governments in Europe where debts and taxes were horrendous.

Democracy in America was on the line, and it failed with the Civil War—proving that democracy requires leaders who believe in it and honor the will of the people. As the London *Times* wrote about the American crisis: "Democracy broke down, not when the Union ceased to be agreeable to all its constituent States, but when it was upheld, like any other Empire, by force of arms."[3] The government in Washington, wrote the *Times,* was no different than the government in St. Petersburg—an autocracy, preserving its empire. How could a nation, argued so many British observers, which professed such a strong belief in government by the people, turn on its own citizens and deny them what it supposedly stood for. The *Cornhill Magazine* (London) chided the North: "With what pretence of fairness, it is said, can you Americans object to the secession of the Southern States when your nation was founded on secession from the British Empire?"[4]

Northern apologists to this day have been unable to justify the war on the grounds that the North had the right to force the South to remain in a political union that they abhorred. As one British editor expressed it: "Twenty millions [the North] say to the other ten millions [the South], 'You shall continue to live under a government you detest, you shall submit to laws you wish to change, you shall obey rulers you repudiate and abjure . . . their inherent right to secede if they chose, can, it seems to us, be denied by no one but a *nisi prius* lawyer [i.e., a trial lawyer pleading his client's case]."[5]

Within less than a year, British periodicals started to shift from legalism and constitutional arguments to the horrors and ugliness of the war. They saw the war to be much worse than any European conflict as it degenerated into cruelty unknown in Western history:

> The barbarous character of the warfare is a subject too painful to be needlessly dwelt upon . . . There are "traitors" in all the departments of a public service which has suddenly changed hands at the most critical moment of the republic. What was patriotism a year ago has become treason. The friendships a year ago have become snares; the commercial partnerships of the two sections have become embarrassments; the family ties have generated hatreds; sectional grudges have grown into fierce revenges. The brigands of the whole country have come to the front; and the worthiest citizens retire into the darkness to grieve unseen. The sacking and burning of homesteads and undermining railway bridges; the infliction of torture and murder for sup-

posed opinions; the suspension of law and rights—these scandals and miseries are of a nature and extent never required or imagined in international wars.[6]

This editorial ran in late 1861. By 1865, these acts of barbarism would expand beyond anything imagined by a civilized society. The rage generated in the victims would last for generations, even to this day.

The Civil War was the first modern war with ironclad naval vessels, rifling for cannon and small arms, interchangeable parts, extensive amphibious operations, submarines and torpedoes, balloons, and so on. Another innovation was the foreign war correspondent. These foreigners were granted audiences with Lincoln, Davis, cabinet officers, and generals, as well as citizens in all walks of life. One British correspondent in the company of Prince Napoleon of France tells of his visits with Lincoln, Seward, General Scott, and a Union military camp. They were then escorted to neutral ground and were met by "a troop of Virginia Confederate cavalry, strong and hardy horsemen," who conducted them to the camp at Fairfax, Virginia, where they met with Confederate generals Johnston and Beauregard. Another special correspondent from *Macmillan's Magazine,* a British monthly, was sent by his editors to America to answer the question that puzzled so many English readers—"What on earth is the North fighting for?"[7]—indicating a sense of bewilderment, which was common throughout Europe.

To most Europeans, Lincoln had a serious morality problem when he rejected all offers and attempts at settlement and compromise. Even American newspapers focused on that idea as a solution to the conflict. The gist of the condemnation of Lincoln was that it was immoral and even illegal—against the law of nations—for a Christian nation to go to war except to defend itself. It was obvious that the South was defending itself, not the North, so, what was the North *really* fighting for? Some of the Northern ambassadors tried to make slavery the issue—the North was fighting to end slavery. But upon careful analysis that just didn't hold water. Neither did it hold water as an explanation for the secession by the South, despite the flood of verbiage from Southern leaders and writers that this was the cause of secession—that slavery was in danger if they remained in the Union. It wasn't.

Thus the slave issue shows up on both sides, and in both instances the arguments don't stand up after careful scrutiny. The inquiry by the special correspondent for *Macmillan's Magazine,* could be paraphrased as: Why on earth did the South withdraw from the Union? Slavery is a bad answer to both questions, and the more objective investigating reporters in Europe saw through the facade. Said one London editor: "It is not then surprising

Figure 5.1. Frank Vizetelly, artist-correspondent for the *Illustrated London News,* was pro-Southern, as were most of the British media. Despite their pro-Southern sentiments, the foreign correspondents were decidedly anti-slavery, and this was a major stumbling block for Britain giving support and recognition to the Confederacy. To get out from this dilemma, the media came forth with the idea that the Confederacy would most likely abolish slavery on its own, and do so sooner than if the slave states remained in the Union.

that the South is tempted to regard the clamour of the North against slavery as something very like hypocrisy, and to resent with bitterness a cry which it knows to be injurious and believes to be insincere." The writer goes on to point out that "we have seen that he [Lincoln] was prepared to give slavery more protection than it had ever before enjoyed."[8] Said another, "If slavery were alone, or principally, in issue, the conduct of the South would not only be unreasonable, but unintelligible."[9]

Charles Dickens, who wrote a great deal about the American Civil War, said that "the South, instead of seceding for the sake of slavery, seceded in spite of the fact that its separate maintenance will expose them . . . to risks and losses against which the Union would afford security."[10] Under the protection of the Constitution and the Supreme Court, the entire nation was one gigantic prison from which the fugitive slave could not escape, which explains why the so-called underground railroad ended up in Canada. Lincoln said in his inaugural address that he would enforce the fugitive slave laws, hardly the philosophy of an abolitionist. There were many slave owners who opposed secession, especially, we now know, in Maryland, which bordered on the North. To protect their slave property, staying in the Union was the wiser course to take.

Despite the vast amount of pompous rhetoric by so many Southerners on the slave issue, many scholars have accepted this grandiloquence as sincere and truthful and then have had to offer an explanation. After boiling off all the fat, the reasoning goes like this: True, slavery was not in any danger from the North, but it could be. The Republicans could gain control of Congress. They could then, with a two-thirds vote, put forth a constitutional amendment abolishing slavery, and then if a few more free states joined the Union, they would have the necessary three-quarters vote to approve the amendment. The scholars then have to explain how rational Southern men would go to war, create enormous economic and political problems, and disrupt the commerce and affairs of the people, all to prevent something hypothetical, some pyramid of "what ifs" from happening.

Some scholars have added that the grievance of prohibiting slavery in the territories was a major factor in secession. But even that had not happened, and it faced formidable difficulties with the Dred Scott case and Stephen Douglas's law of "popular sovereignty," still the law of the land. (The essence of the Dred Scott case was that a slave's status had to be respected even in free territory. Popular sovereignty meant that each state or territory would decide the slave issue, not the federal government.) Even this was a "what if," and with secession, the South would have been shut out of any new territories. Lincoln's inaugural didn't even mention prohibiting slavery in the new territories as a purpose of his administration. As the British editorial said, if slavery was *really* the motive for secession, then the South's conduct was not only unreasonable but unintelligible. Unless, of course, there was another grievance having a basis in reality. Giving some credence to the slavery complaint, this British editor explains the Southern position as well as possible:

The grievances which to the South seemed so intolerable that civil war itself was the lighter evil, were two—one was actual, the other, in the main, hypothetical. They were suffering, and had long suffered, from the effects of the various Northern Tariffs; and they believed from past experience that as soon as the North had the power in its hands, they should be exposed to some perilous dealing with their slaves. . . . it is clear that the first reason was the one on which the South mainly acted. The proof is simple. Secession was an absolute and immediate remedy for the free-trade grievance . . . founded on long experience . . . The protective system had been won as a triumph by the North. . . . The South felt the double sting of humiliation and of loss. They felt that they were wronged. And it did not seem likely that the evil would abate of itself in the course of time; the wants of the Treasury were growing, and as those wants grew, the tariff was likely to rise.[11]

This editor did give some credence to the abolition issue, but most Northerners, Lincoln included, saw emancipation as a difficult problem. Lincoln, like others, thought of relocating black people to some new land as a solution.

PRESERVING THE UNION

Our correspondent from *Macmillan's Magazine* did a thorough job of investigating the war while in America. He wrote that he talked with hundreds of people in the North, from all walks of life, and he was convinced that slavery had nothing to do with Northern motives or purposes. This was in 1861. He summarized the answers he had been given with these words: "We do not claim to be carrying on a war of emancipation. We are not fighting for the blacks, but for the whites. . . . The object of the war is to preserve the Union. . . . [It even had nothing to do with the Constitution.] It was for clear matter-of-fact interests."[12]

When the correspondent tried to pin down these so-called "matter-of-fact interests," the answers did not show a moral or legal justification for a war of aggression with the carnage that was taking place; a war waged, in the words of this correspondent, "with a ferocity which must have been learned not from Europeans, but from Red Indian precedents." High noble principles were not involved, as they rarely are in warfare. What was involved was usually commerce and trade, money, and empire building. He came to the conclusion, as did so many other foreign correspondents, that the preserving of the American empire was what was at stake, with all the economic ramifications that means. The British empire was a pride to all

Britons, and no doubt an American empire was equally a matter of pride to all Northerners, wrote this English correspondent.

The correspondent's notion of an empire motive was further strengthened when he visited with the aging commanding general of all Northern armies, General Winfield Scott, hero of the Mexican War (1846–1847). The general answered him with a question, "The British empire was worth fighting for, wasn't it?" The Englishman understood. In 1862, the *Quarterly Review* (London) analyzed "The American Crisis" in these words: "For the contest on the part of the North is now undisguisedly for empire. The question of Slavery is thrown to the winds. There is hardly any concession in its favor that the South could ask which the North would refuse, provided only that the seceding States would re-enter the Union. . . . Away with the pretence on the North to dignify its cause with the name of freedom to the slave!"[13]

The "pretense" that the North was really fighting to end slavery had made a few converts in Europe, but when General Fremont emancipated the slaves in his military district in Missouri, Lincoln promptly dismissed Fremont, rescinded his emancipation order, and sent the slaves back to their masters. This shocked the deceived Europeans. A French newspaper, in an article filled with disillusion over the Northern cause, wrote that "Fremont's dismissal [has] stopped the American conflict from becoming a cause of our civilization. . . . what should we hate if not slavery."[14]

Thus it became clear to the majority of British writers that preserving the Union really meant preserving the empire. In the strangest places this became the dominant interpretation of Lincoln's war motive. Horace Greeley, the radical editor of the *New York Tribune,* wrote a two-volume work on the war. In 1865, as the war ended, Greeley's first volume was reviewed by the *Athenaeum,* a highly respected British weekly. The reviewer was quite familiar with Greeley's abolitionist interpretation of the war but considered it more nonsense than truth:

> Many different motives urged her [the North] to begin the work on which she lavished blood and treasure. She fought . . . for all those delicious dreams of national predominance in future ages, which she must relinquish as soon as the union is severed. . . . They saw the necessity for an undivided nation: they knew that banded together they might achieve all their promises and predictions, but that their historical pre-eminence would be sacrificed as soon as they consented to a dissolution of partnership.[15]

To fully appreciate the North's zeal for empire—a view still held in high esteem by European historians—we need to examine the political psyche of the nineteenth-century American. There was an English proverb, War is the sport of kings. After the victory at Fredericksburg, Robert E. Lee said, "It is well that war is so terrible—we would grow too fond of it." Today, we abhor war, but this was not so in the mid-nineteenth century. In Kenneth Clark's marvelous book *Civilisation* (1969), he sums up the thinking of that age as "the insatiable urge to conquer and explore."[16] What was Manifest Destiny but a label for American imperialism? America was building an empire across North America, with Alaska, Canada, and Cuba on the list, and this is what the Europeans saw as a very understandable reason to preserve the Union.

Of course, today war and imperialism have fallen into disrepute. All of us are children of our time, and we have learned through the horrors of war in this century to hate both war and imperialism. But in 1860, civilized man felt otherwise.

The *Cornhill Magazine,* in late 1861, got wind of the Northern idea of aggression against Canada: "The proposal that the North and South should forge their differences in a joint piratical attack upon Canada and Cuba is worthy only of the infamous source from which it proceeds."[17] At the same time, the *Quarterly Review* noted that Canada had called out its militia and fortified her frontier. "We earnestly hope," said this editorial, "that immediate steps will be taken to place Canada in such a state of permanent defense as to relieve both her and ourselves from anxiety in case of a sudden attack from her restless neighbors."[18]

As the war progressed and the idea of the North and South joining forces against Canada faded, British writers were silent on any danger of attack. But in 1865, as the war came to a close with a Northern victory (and destruction of the South), the fear of a Northern attack on Canada reappeared, and this time from periodicals that had been pro-North. The April 1865 edition of *Macmillan's Magazine* pleaded with the Northern policy makers to abandon any thought of now turning its large armies and navy against Canada. Instead of a docile conquered people, the Canadians would be to America what Ireland had become to England. The reason for "annexing Canada would be the extension of their commercial frontier with a view to the increase of their import duties (which form their chief fiscal resource of a permanent kind). . . . Canada is a most dangerous point of contact; and from its openness to invasion, a temptation, and even a positive incentive, to war." And what would be the other motive for invasion? "Territorial aggrandizement,"[19] that is, imperialism, said the editorial.

The correspondents from Europe all returned home with some bewilderment at the cause of the North—of preserving the Union. The constitutional issue was always very thin and hardly very moral. It became unavoidable in an age of Western imperialism for the "empire" motive for the Civil War to override all others. The preservation of the empire is really what the preservation of the Union was all about.

On 13 December 1860, the *New York Times* published a letter from one of its readers, which went to the heart of the "matter-of-fact interests" that so many Northerners were talking about. If imperialism was a dominant motive in all European politics—and it was—then it was an even greater motive in America. Said the writer: "There is no nation in the world so ambitious of growth and power—so thoroughly pervaded with the spirit of conquest—so filled with dreams of enlarging dominions as ours. In New England these impulses have lost something. . . . But in the Centre and the West, this thirst for national power still rages unrestrained."

Along with the zeal for empire, which the British focused on, the French saw even more sinister forces. In a letter to his diocese, a French monsignor noted what seemed to be a view of Americans by many French. "We must fear the growing power of a people [the Americans] whose example and conquering bent menaces the world."[20] The British also condemned the aggressiveness of the American character and threat to European interests:

> The aggressive character of the people, the confidence they felt in their constantly increasing strength, and their contempt for many of the rules which regulate the intercourse of the old monarchies of Europe, held out prospects little favourable to peace. What they called their "manifest destiny" was territorial aggrandizement; and every fresh accession of territory seemed only to whet their appetite for more. It was impossible that this could go on without bringing them into collision with the nations of Europe, which have interests on the other side of the Atlantic too great to be sacrificed to the ambition of one overweening Power.[21]

A TARIFF WAR?

The war between the North and the South is a tariff war. The war is further, not for any principle, does not touch the question of slavery, and in fact turns on the Northern lust for sovereignty.

Karl Marx[22]

Karl Marx summarized what the major British newspapers were saying— the *Times,* the *Economist,* and the *Saturday Review* were all strong on the tariff interpretation of the conflict. In 1862, in the House of Commons, a member named William Forster said it was generally recognized that the war was caused over slavery. He was answered from the House with cries of "no, no!" and "the tariff!"[23] The commercial interests that dominated the House were more in tune with the economics of the war than were the intellectuals.

Fraser's Magazine, a popular British publication, contained a number of articles on the tariff, as not only a cause of war but also as a tragic event that made any reconciliation between the North and South impossible: "Congress was rapidly passing a new tariff of the most stringent protectionism to Northern manufacturers! . . . The untimeliness of the measure has filled all England with astonishment. It is a new affront and wrong to the slave states, and raises a wall against the return of the seceders."[24]

The wrong to the Southern states had a long history. John C. Calhoun had explained the problem ten years before in a reply to Daniel Webster's famous speech on the Union. Calhoun listed three main grievances that could lead to secession. The first was the exclusion of the South from most of the new territories, upsetting the balance of power. The second was the growth of federal power despite the limits set in the Constitution. He could see on the horizon the coming of an all-powerful national government obliterating state sovereignty. He had remarkable vision. His fears have come to pass, but in 1850 an all-powerful national government was a long way in the future. The third grievance, the one concrete complaint, involved taxation as a two-edged sword against the South. Said Calhoun: "The North had adopted a system of revenue and disbursements in which an undue proportion of the burden of taxation has been imposed upon the South, and an undue proportion of its proceeds appropriated to the North . . . the South, as the great exporting portion of the Union, has in reality paid vastly more than her due proportion of the revenue."[25]

Even Northern-oriented historians acknowledge that "indignation against the tariff as an unfair tax injurious to their economy was general throughout the South."[26] Before the ultra-high Morrill Tariff adopted in March 1861, Southern indignation found forceful expression in the House of Representatives by John H. Reagan of Texas on 15 January 1861:

> You are not content with the vast millions of tribute we pay you annually under the operation of our revenue laws, our navigation laws, your fishing bounties, and by making your people our manufacturers, our merchants, our shippers. You are not satisfied with the vast tribute we pay you to build up your great cities, your railroads, your canals. You are not satisfied with the millions of tribute we have been paying you on account of the balance of exchange which you hold against us. You are not satisfied that we of the South are almost reduced to the condition of overseers of northern capitalists. You are not

satisfied with all this; but you must wage a relentless crusade against our rights and institutions.[27]

Some history is helpful to understand the forces that brought forth the ultra-high Morrill Tariff in early 1861, immediately after the new Congress assembled in Washington. It was the highest tariff in history, with rates for iron products of over 50 percent; rates for clothing ran over 25 percent. It was a major plank in the Republican platform. When this matter came before the delegates to the Republican convention in the summer of 1860; there was "hoopla and howling" with canes and hats thrown into the air, "as if a herd of buffalo had stampeded through the convention hall."[28] When Southerners realized what they were up against with respect to a high tariff and a new Congress and Republican administration, only two courses of action seemed open to them—secession from the Union and a low tariff for the Confederate states. James Spencer, a British cotton trader and trade adviser writing in a Scottish journal, saw this as the inevitable consequence of Lincoln's high tariff obligations to Northern industrialists and manufacturers. The

> tariff question, again, enters largely—more largely than is commonly supposed—into the irritated and aggrieved feelings of the Southerners. And it cannot be denied that in this matter they have both a serious injury and an unconstitutional injustice to resent. . . . All Northern products are now protected; and the Morill [sic] Tariff is a very masterpiece of folly and injustice. . . . No wonder then that the citizens of the seceding States should feel for half a century they have sacrificed to enhance the powers and profits of the North; and should conclude, after much futile remonstrance, that only in secession could they hope to find redress.[29]

The weekly *Athenaeum* added this bit of insight into Southern feelings: "As a rule, the great mass of the public expenditures were made from the North, not in the South, so that Southerners found themselves doubly taxed—taxed first for the benefit of the Northern manufacturers, and then, in the disbursement of the public funds, denied an equal participation in the benefits accruing therefrom."[30]

The most stinging criticism of the North came from *The Quarterly Review* in 1862, taking apart just about every virtue and principle the North supposedly stood for:

> Fate has indeed taken a malignant pleasure in flouting the admirers of the United States. It is not merely that their hopes of its universal empire have been disappointed . . . the mortification has been much deeper than this. Every theory to which they paid a special homage . . .

has been successively repudiated by their favourite statesmen. They were Apostles of Free Trade: America has established a tariff, compared to which our heaviest protection-tariff has been flimsy. . . . she has become a land of passports, of conscriptions, of press censorship and post-office espionage, of bastilles and *lettres de cachet* [a letter bearing an official seal, authorizing the imprisonment without a trial of a named person]. . . . there was little difference between the Government of Mr. Lincoln and the Government of Napoleon III. There was the form of a legislative assembly, where scarcely any dared to oppose, for fear of a charge of treason.[31]

It seems clear that British war correspondents and writers saw the war between the states as caused by the forces that have caused wars throughout history—economic and imperialistic forces behind a rather flimsy facade of freeing the slaves. It was not until this century that American historians of Northern persuasion began to abandon the noble but phony virtues for Lincoln's aggression against the South. Charles and Mary Beard wrote the first scholarly in-depth economic study of the war and came to this conclusion: "Since, therefore, the abolition of slavery never appeared in the platform of any great political party, since the only appeal ever made to the electorate on that issue was scornfully repulsed, since the spokesman of the Republicans emphatically declared that his party never intended to interfere with slavery in any shape or form, it seems reasonable to assume that the institution of slavery was not a fundamental issue during the epoch preceding the bombardment of Fort Sumter."[32]

Finally, the war correspondents saw two main causes behind the war. On the Northern side there was the obvious and unquestionable desire for an American empire—taking in all of North America, Mexico, Cuba, and much of the Caribbean. Ample evidence existed to support this conclusion as a force behind the "preserve the Union" facade. In the South, they saw economic forces behind secession, which is why the war has been called "the rich man's war and the poor man's fight," a term which, most of the time, applies to most wars.

These writers and correspondents were not fools and had little difficulty condemning the North and supporting the South, even to the point of urging the British government to join in the conflict for Southern independence. As *Blackwoods Magazine* (London) urged early in the war, "A war between England and the North will, at least, have the good effects of shortening the sufferings and hastening the independence of a people who are proving themselves very capable of self-government, who will at once assume a creditable position among nations, and who will act as a permanent check on Northern turbulence. And it is to be hoped that, if war is to be, we may put our whole strength and will into it, and conduct it so as to leave the orators and writers of the North, with all their skill and practice in the falsification of history."[33]

Suppose England had joined in the fight and provided the naval and military strength the South needed to win her struggle for independence — what would North America be like today? And what role in world affairs would the two nations have played in this century? "For of all sad word of tongue or pen," wrote John Greenleaf Whittier, "the saddest are these: 'It might have been!' " The South is still haunted by what "might have been."

As the world's great empires have broken up in the latter half of this century, with the Soviet Union being the latest casualty, only America remains as the last of the great empires. The European writers saw the inevitability of secession in that the Union did not have the right ingredients for permanence except with military force. James Spence (whose book, *The American Union,* was popular throughout Britain at the time), writing for the Scottish periodical, *North British Review,* made this intriguing observation in February 1862:

> In truth, the Union itself was artificial in its origin; and its artificial character has long been increasingly apparent, and increasingly felt. Spontaneous and self-supporting political combination, compact and enduring nations, are the result of many convergent influences. There must be some degree at least of homogeneousness; there must be harmony, if not identity, of interests; there must be mutual liking, if not mutual respect. Or, in default of these binding links, there must be power . . . to enforce union and compel submission. Which of these necessary elements existed in the United States? Scarcely one.[34]

Of course, the British writer was wrong. The North did have the last element — the power to enforce union and compel submission. What the British had been doing to Ireland and Scotland for centuries.

We have considered the writings of British journalists, but what did English scholars have to say? It was one of the world's most noted men of letters, John Stuart Mill, who shocked the British intelligentsia by concocting the idea that slavery was the one cause of the Civil War, thus repudiating the main stream of British and European thinking, which focused on the economic and tax issues. He gave Northerners a much needed moral basis for their onslaught on the South, a fable to be sure, but a cause Europeans could look upon as justification for the war against the Confederacy. In time, Northerners, even Lincoln, would latch on to Mill's thesis and put emancipation into the forefront. Eventually Lincoln's morally dubious objective of preserving the Union would be complemented with a more morally appealing justification — freeing the slaves.

6

British Scholars Speak

Charles Dickens and John Stuart Mill were both in their fifties and at the height of their literary careers and fame when the Civil War was under way. Both took great interest in what was going on in America. Since they were living in Britain, they did not have to worry about going to jail for expressing themselves. In America, at this time, criticizing one's government was a dangerous undertaking.

Dickens and Mill had been carrying on a verbal war for over a decade. First, when Mill wrote his famous *Political Economy* (1848), Dickens responded with two novels—*Bleak House* (1853) and then *Hard Times* (1854). The latter novel, according to historians, "manhandled" Mill's treatise. After reading *Bleak House,* an enraged Mill wrote that "that creature Dickens," was filled with "vulgar impudence," and that the book was written in the "vulgarist way." Mill said Dickens's writings were "extremely repugnant to me." Besides this clash, and the clash over the American war, they also battled over a rebellion in Jamaica in which the British governor took harsh reprisals against the leaders of this uprising. Mill organized a committee to bring criminal charges against the governor. But he failed, primarily because Dickens took up the cause of the governor and defeated Mill's efforts. This long-running feud between Dickens and Mill found expression in their views on the American conflict between the North and South.

CHARLES DICKENS SPEAKS: "THE LAST GREAT MAN"

Charles Dickens is as alive today as he was over a hundred years ago. As long as there is Christmas, there will be Ebenezer Scrooge. Most bookstores have a full shelf of Dickens's books, and libraries often have close to five hundred different volumes about him. One biography calls Dickens "the last great man." He had a feel for life and society unsurpassed by anyone before and probably since.

Dickens's great intellect and genius were nurtured in the soil of his early life—the slums and squalor of London. He was only twelve years old when he had to abandon any formal education. Growing up in these terrible conditions colored his view of life and found expression in his novels. He saw the plight of the slum children, and his novels made their suffering real because they were not a figment of an imagination run loose; they were real people from his real world.

Dickens's interest in the political and social problems of his day stemmed from his early effort to break away from this poverty in London. He traveled to America, saw the South and slavery, and even visited a slave auction in Richmond. When comparing the plight of the children of American slaves to that of the children of London's poor, there was no doubt in his mind that the poor of London, though free, were free to starve, free to be homeless and to live in rags. He even fostered a small pamphlet comparing the West Indies slave children to those of London's slums.

Although he was a strong advocate for emancipation everywhere, he thought it was a great error to focus on slavery as the great social evil of the age when there were evils at home that deserved equal if not higher rank among the social cruelties of his time. A baby born into slavery had the right to be taken care of from cradle to grave. The child of the slums had a much more miserable life—one of hunger, cold, homelessness, disease, illiteracy, and little chance of rising above this deplorable condition.

In the recently published biography of Mary Boykin Chestnut, a Southern woman whose diaries caught the attention of historians soon after the Civil War, she writes of the terrible financial losses her family suffered and of the horrendous debts they incurred. Yet, in spite of this financial ordeal for a once wealthy plantation family, one of the family obligations Mary Chestnut lists was to seventeen ex-slaves who had to be cared for in their old age, even though they had been emancipated with the Thirteenth Amendment and were no longer a legal obligation. But they were a moral obligation, and however financially distressed the family was, these elderly ex-slaves would be taken care of. No such moral obligation existed for the workers in London or elsewhere. No slave was human rubbish like the disabled or elderly workers in the free societies of that day.

As an advocate for helping the poor and for reform, Dickens was able to enlist some of London's wealthy. He engaged in welfare work, slum clearance, schools for poor children, and even a home for the rehabilitation of unfortunate women. In addition to Charles Dickens's extraordinary talents as a novelist, his interest in contemporary affairs led him to found his own

THE CONDITION

OF

THE WEST INDIA SLAVE

CONTRASTED WITH THAT OF

THE INFANT SLAVE

𝔍n our 𝔈nglish 𝔉actories.

———

WITH FIFTEEN ILLUSTRATIONS FROM THE GRAVER OF

ROBERT CRUIKSHANK.

———

" Truth is strange,—stranger than Fiction."

NEGRO SLAVERY. | ENGLISH LIBERTY

LONDON:

W. KIDD, 14, CHANDOS STREET, WEST-STRAND;

AND

SIMPKIN AND MARSHALL, STATIONERS'-HALL-COURT.

West Indian slave-owners were shocked at what they saw in English mills '

Figure 6.1. A Dickens pamphlet comparing West Indian slave children to those in England's factories. When West Indies planters visited London, they were shocked at the deprived children they saw in London's factories. Dickens condemned those whose attention was focused abroad on the misfortunes of people in faraway places whose miseries did not match those of the English at home.

periodicals, first *Household Words* in 1850, and then his biggest love, *All the Year Round,* in 1859. This periodical continued weekly for almost two decades after his death. He was its primary contributor.

When the American Civil War broke out, Dickens was absorbed in understanding the forces behind the conflict, and he wrote two articles for his London readers on the "American Disunion." The first article, appearing in *All the Year Round* on 21 December 1861 was to show "what the cause of the disruption is not. We shall show next week what the cause of the disruption *is*." His London readers must have looked forward with great interest to his views, for by this time he was the leading man of letters in Britain—no other writer had his fame or admiration. Here was the great sage of the Victorian era about to tell the British people what the hottest news event of the day was all about.

WHAT THE CAUSE OF THE DISRUPTION
IS NOT: SLAVERY? AH HUMBUG!

In the article of 21 December 1861, Dickens traces the history of the United States. The initial constitution was framed by slave-holding states. There were thirteen states, twelve of which permitted slavery in 1781. But by 1860, slavery had proven useless in the Northern states, setting the North apart from the South. Dickens had done considerable research and had given a lot of thought to the American disunion. He quotes Jefferson and Washington, who both predicted that the Union would not last. Even in the early 1800s, it was too big and too unwieldy. Travelers to America, like Alexis de Tocqueville and a Russian visitor, Ivan Golovin, had both predicted that the Union could not last because of its changing character. Dickens summed up the current strain between the North and South in these words: "The struggle between North and South has been of long duration. The South having the lead in the federation had fought some hard political battles to retain it . . . But in the last presidential election, which was a trial of strength between South and North, the South considering itself subject to the North within the federation, carried out its frequent threat and desire of secession."[1]

Dickens cites a quote that Jefferson made after the Louisiana Purchase, when there was talk of dividing the Union into an Atlantic federation and a Mississippi federation: "Let them part by all means if it is for their happiness to do so. It is but the elder and the younger son differing. God bless them both, and keep them in Union if it be for their good, but separate them if better."[2] No statesman today in the North, said Dickens, would dare repeat what Jefferson had said.

Another factor that supports secession, said Dickens, was a defect in the American political system, especially in the selection of president. The U.S. presidency was a flawed concept. It produced corruption and mediocrity that was impossible to root out during a four-year tenure. The most talented men in America were "very rarely" placed at the head of state, yet to make the system work, the presidency required an "extraordinarily great man." Once the Founders had passed away, the system no longer produced any great men as president. A mediocre man as president, with corrupt ministers, would "plunder the public treasury."[3] Watergate and the innumerable scandals of corruption that seem to routinely infect the executive branch today would confirm the insight of Dickens, and we haven't yet found a way to correct the problem. Under the British system a corrupt prime minister can be removed instantaneously, without the great national crisis a Watergate would create.

Prior to 1860, both political parties—the Democrats and the Whigs— represented people in both the North and the South. But Lincoln was a Northern leader from an exclusively Northern political party. The election of a Republican administration, being for the first time a sectional party with absolutely no affinity for the Southern states, made secession justifiable. The South was fully aware of what a sectional pro-North, anti-South presidency would do, and they would be stuck with this outrage—this "foreign ruler"—for four years. The time to get out of the federation was now.

Focusing on the slave question, Dickens contended that the "Constitution was framed by slave owners, and gave the whole might of the Union for suppressing slave insurrections" and enforcing the rights of slave owners. There was no lawful place a fugitive slave, seeking freedom, could go. With secession, slave owners exposed themselves to losses of their slave property and would lose the protection of the federal Constitution. Dickens cites Lincoln's inaugural address, which expressed a firm determination to enforce the fugitive slave law and to support a new Constitutional amendment to protect slavery in any state, denying Congress the right to interfere with slavery. This amendment was quickly approved by three states in a matter of weeks before the bombardment of Fort Sumter.

Dickens concluded that slavery was not a reason for the Civil War, and this view was recently highlighted by a Dickens biographer, Peter Ackroyd: "The Northern onslaught upon slavery was no more than a piece of specious humbug designed to conceal its desire for economic control of the Southern states."[4] Dickens condemned slavery as an evil for the slave, an evil for the slave owner, and an evil for the white working class in the South. He predicted, as other British writers had predicted, that a secession from the Union by the South "would, in fact, bring us very many years nearer to the end of slavery than a continuation of the old system under the great Union pledge to support as a whole the evil that afflicts a half."[5]

WHAT THE CAUSE OF THE DISRUPTION *IS:* MONEY!

Dickens began his next article, "If it be not slavery, where lies the partition of the interests that has led at last to actual separation of the Southern from the Northern States?" In the original constitution of the Union, wrote Dickens, "it was provided that all taxes 'shall be uniform throughout the United States.' "[6]

When the new nation began, there had been few manufacturers. Import duties fell evenly among the states. But manufacturing got started after the War of 1812, and a modest protective tariff seemed to be in everyone's interest for the infant industries. But by 1828 the protective tariff had become a prohibitive tariff, and it provided fat profits to manufacturing interests in the North that really didn't need to be protected anymore. The tariffs turned into "a system that compelled it [the South] to pay a heavy fine into the pockets of Northern manufacturers." Southern ships that carried cotton and tobacco to Europe were paid by an "exchange of commodities," that is, European manufactured goods that now had a high tariff charge, thus draining money from the pockets of the people in the South into the federal Treasury, which the people of the North were not paying—a tax lacking in uniformity or equality in the nation, an unconstitutional tax for certain. James Spence, a British trade minister, said he was astonished that such a law could be passed at the present time, in the modern world. It wasn't a protective tariff, it was a prohibition tariff, said Britain's leading periodicals.[7]

The South had hated the tariff for almost forty years. No matter how low it was (20 percent in 1857), it was not low enough for most of them. It caused their cotton and tobacco prices to decline. Since they could not receive British or French goods in exchange with a high tariff, they would have to demand hard cash, which in turn would require a lower price for their commodities. Dickens explained the South's predicament: "Every year, for some years back, this or that Southern state had declared that it would submit to this extortion only while it had not the strength for resistance. With the election of Lincoln and an exclusive Northern party taking over the federal government, the time for withdrawal had arrived."

Secession, reasoned Dickens, was not like an English county departing from the Crown. "The conflict is between semi-independent communities," he said, in which "every feeling and interest on the one side [the South] calls for political partition, and every pocket interest [the North] calls on the other side for union."[8] "So the case stands, and under all the passion of the parties and the cries of battle lie the two chief moving causes of the struggle. Union means so many millions a year lost to the South; se-

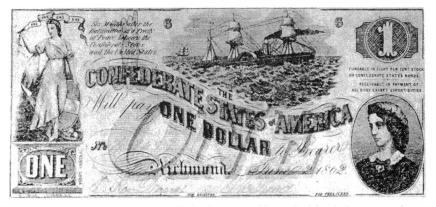

Figure 6.2. The Confederate one-dollar bill showing a steamship, emphasizing the importance of commerce and trade to the new nation. Shipping from Southern ports had been an exclusive monopoly for Northern shipping interests, much to the dissatisfaction of Southern commercial traders. Now shipping would take place in Southern vessels, or so it was hoped. But an effective blockade soon ended those dreams of commercial greatness.

Charles Dickens saw commerce and money as the real reason for the South's scession; concern for the perpetuation of slavery was just a facade.

cession means the loss of the same millions to the North. The love of money is the root of this as of many many other evils." He ends with these words: "the quarrel between North and South is, as it stands, solely a fiscal quarrel."[9]

SLAVERY: THE ONE CAUSE OF THE CIVIL WAR, ACCORDING TO JOHN STUART MILL

Most Britons and the major periodicals accepted the tax-and-tariff interpretation of the American disunion. But one highly respected man of letters, John Stuart Mill, proclaimed in an article published in *Fraser's* magazine, shortly after Dickens's articles, that slavery was the one cause of the Civil War. And while the economic forces were obvious to most European observers, Mill had a formidable case if you take the Southerners' ranting and rhetoric seriously. After all, the Southern leaders had said that they "separated on slavery, and proclaimed slavery as the one cause of the separation."[10]

There were, as Mill wrote, many Southern politicians who said that slavery was the reason for secession. And if there had been formidable opposition to slavery in the North and proposals to end slavery through some means other than the John Brown approach, then Mill may have been right.

The vice president of the Confederacy, Alexander Stephens, had said the issue was slavery, as had a host of others. Yet it didn't make sense, when the Northern leadership and the vast majority of citizens wanted to leave the South's peculiar institution alone—it was a Southern problem, they said—and the North benefited greatly from the products the slave economy produced and sent north. Mill acknowledged that in his famous article in *Fraser's* magazine. He said: "The North, it seems, have no more objection to Slavery than the South have. . . . They are ready to give it new guarantees; to renounce all that they have been contending for; to win back, if opportunity offers, the South to the Union by surrendering the whole point.[11]

And yet all offers to appease the South over slavery had come to naught. It does seem strange that Southerners, having been offered so many guarantees to protect their slave economies, would go to war when they had won all the battles. The Supreme Court had ruled in favor of the slave owners in the Dred Scott case; Lincoln had said (in his words) "a thousand times"[12] that he had no right to interfere with slavery; and with a new constitutional amendment in the works, why risk civil war and the destruction a war might entail against an obviously superior force? In other words, why be stupid?

But Mill argued that the slave states wanted more than just tolerance and acceptance of their rights as slave owners. That was the problem. He thought he saw that the Southerners wanted to turn the whole world, especially the continents of North and South America and the Caribbean, into one vast "slavocracy." Their ambition was to have slavery extend throughout all of the Americas, all the way down to the bottom of South America, in Mill's words, from "the Potomac to Cape Horn."[13] They were out to reopen the slave trade to provide for this great new world slavery system. Mill didn't know it was not Britain that first abolished the slave trade, but Virginia, in 1778, by a bill introduced by Patrick Henry.

This renewal of the slave trade, wrote Mill, would bring about a war between the Confederate States and Great Britain. Fifty years earlier, Britain had abolished the slave trade and later so had the Americans, under the Constitution. So the Confederate States, in reopening the slave trade, would run into conflict with what had become an international law against trading in slaves, and this would cause naval warfare, for slave traders would be in the category of pirates, and a conviction could carry a death sentence. The world would separate into two great social and economic systems—the free nations and the slave nations. There would be a great Armageddon, with good and evil in mortal combat over the abomination of slavery.

Mill continued with an assault on the tariff interpretation of the war. He noted that when the solid South seceded, the tariff had been moderate, not high (20 percent). The high tariff (50 percent) came months after secession, in March 1861. Surely, then, secession could not have been over the tariff.

And, finally, what about the right to secede in a democratic state? The right of government "by the consent of the governed," as expressed in the Declaration of Independence? Normally, said Mill, this would justify any state withdrawing from a federation it no longer wanted to be a part of. But with the South, no such justification existed, since the South had no real grievance. By rebelling to protect slavery, Southerners had no more right of secession than a band of robbers.

Mill then compares the Confederate States to bands of famous highwaymen and robbers, such as France's notorious Cartouche and England's Turpin, who had plundered the French and English countryside. They were both eventually captured. Turpin was hanged and Cartouche was broken on a wheel. "The only real difference," wrote Mill, "is that the present rebels [the Southerners] are more powerful than Cartouche and Turpin, and may possibly be able to effect their iniquitous purpose."[14] He continues this comparison by likening the Confederates to a band of inmates at Parkhurst Prison on the Isle of Wight. Should the British government recognize a chain gang that had declared itself independent? Of course not, and yet that is the essence of what was happening in America.

No one ever answered Mill's assault on the Southern cause, nor the assertion that slavery was the "one cause" of the Civil War. His article was soon reprinted in *Harper's* magazine in America.[15] It was a shot in the arm for the Northern cause, as Northern apologists had been stumbling around for some honorable explanation for their assault on the South. The war had been highly criticized in European circles—it had no noble purpose, just hard-nosed economics and empire building. And the suggestion that the abolition of slavery was a war objective was never taken too seriously by Europeans. Lincoln's own words proved that point.

But now, here was a leading European philosopher, humanitarian, scholar, political economist, and man of letters giving a noble purpose to the Northern aggression and invasion of the South. If the real motive of the Northern invasion of the South really was to destroy that abominable institution of slavery, then world sympathy would shift from the Southern cause to that of the North.

Mill wrote that slavery was the "one cause" of the Civil War, and that has been Northern gospel ever since. Few in the North have taken the time to carefully scrutinize what the famous philosopher had written, and certainly no one in the North reproduced Charles Dickens's interpretation of the war's objective. Mill became the man of the hour for the North, providing much needed virtue for the Northern cause. He gave more of a boost to the Northern war effort than a dozen battlefield victories would have achieved. North-erners could now sing "Glory, Glory, Hallelujah!" And Lincoln would pick up on that theme some months later with his Emancipation Proclamation and his second inaugural address. And in matters of international law, war would have another justification—the abolition of slavery. The North would now evolve from the bad guys into the good guys on the world stage.

What makes the success and acclaim of Mill's viewpoint on the Civil War so amazing is the outlandishness of his thinking and his faulty research and investigation, for instance, his remarks on the reopening of the slave trade. This had been an issue for the drafting of the Confederate constitu-tion a year before Mill's article in *Fraser's* magazine. That constitution clearly and expressly prohibited the slave trade: "Congress [Confederate] is required to pass such laws as shall effectively prevent the same"[16] (Article 1, section 9). With a constitution prohibiting a reopening of the slave trade and insufficient naval forces to repel the British navy, the whole argument that Mill makes about the South being out to extend slavery throughout the Americas all the way down to Cape Horn is just utter nonsense.

As for Mill's assertion that the South was "fighting for slavery," here he gets the facts of who started the war, and why, all mixed up. The supreme commander of the Confederate forces, Robert E. Lee, hated slavery and said so. He was offered command of all the Union armies but turned it down be-cause these armies were to be used to invade his homeland of Virginia, and other states. But he accepted command of a much smaller force, the Armies of Northern Virginia, to defend his native land from invasion. That, Mr. Mill, is what the Southern armies were fighting for—to expel a foreign invader.

On the tariff/tax issue, what the Southerners called paying "tribute" to the North, Mill is correct in pointing out that when the solid South seceded, a moderate tariff was in place; the ultra-high Morrill Tariff was not put in place until March 1861, after the main seceding states had left the Union and formed the Confederate States of America. But here again Mill had not done any research. You could say he hadn't done his homework (in con-trast to Dickens, who had). A major plank in the platform of the Republi-can party back in August 1860 was to adopt a high protective tariff as a so-lution to a moderate recession that had hit Northern manufacturers. Even many Northern Democrats (e.g., President Buchanan) favored a high tar-iff, with Buchanan actually signing the Morrill Tariff two days before Lin-coln took office.

Many of the prominent newspapers in the South, months before the elec-tion of Lincoln, noted that if he were elected the Republicans would intro-duce a high tariff, just as they had said at their August convention. On 11 Oc-tober 1860, the outspoken *Charleston Mercury,* commenting on the election of a Republican administration, charged that the Republicans would "plunder the South for the benefit of the North, by a new Protective Tariff." South Carolina seceded because Carolinians knew what was in store for them, what they called in that editorial "sectional schemes of appropriation."

When the Morrill Tariff came up for vote in the Congress, there was no opposition from the floor—the Southerners had left Congress. The tariff became a formidable barrier to any Southern return to the Union, and it made enforcement of the tariff an absolute necessity for the Lincoln administration. Lincoln himself had said that a free trade tax law would be a social disaster for the country, as well as an economic disaster. This bizarre thinking shows just how forceful and powerful the protective tariff forces were in the North. Not unlike anti–free traders are today, they painted pictures of disastrous unemployment in the nation, which, of course, did not happen.

Two days before the election in November 1860, an editorial in the *Charleston Mercury* summed up the reason why South Carolina should secede: "The real causes of dissatisfaction in the South with the North, are in the unjust taxation and expenditure of the taxes by the Government of the United States, and in the revolution the North has effected in this government, from a confederated republic, to a national sectional despotism."[17] What gives this editorial special significance are the words "the real causes," implying that there were other not-so-real causes, "paper-weight" rhetoric. Thus when you get down to the nuts and bolts of the conflict, when you boil off all the fat, you find "unjust taxation and expenditure," and the revolution in the general government from "a confederated republic to a national sectional [Northern] despotism." In other words, away with the pretense of protecting slavery.

On 21 January 1861, five days before Louisiana withdrew from the Union, *The New Orleans Daily Crescent* published this remarkable editorial, explaining the causes of secession:

> They [the South] know that it is their import trade that draws from the people's pockets sixty or seventy millions of dollars per annum, in the shape of duties, to be expended mainly in the North, and in the protection and encouragement of Northern interests. . . . These are the reasons why these people do not wish the South to secede from the Union. They [the North] are enraged at the prospect of being despoiled of the rich feast upon which they have so long fed and fattened, and which they were just getting ready to enjoy with still greater *gout* and gusto. They are as mad as hornets because the prize slips them just as they are ready to grasp it.[18]

If Mill had taken the time to read almost any Southern newspaper, going back over a year before his article in *Fraser's* magazine, he would never have written that the only thing the South was concerned about was protecting slavery; he would have seen written time and again that a Republican victory would mean the end of the South as an equal in the Union, that now Northern politics would control the federal government, putting the South in great jeopardy economically, beginning with a high tariff and the expansion of the power of the national government over the states. Mill's thesis that slavery was the one cause of the Civil War did not attract a lot of followers in Europe. The economic and tax issues were too obvious to ignore.

John Stuart Mill may have grown up in the same country and even the same city as Dickens, but other than that, no two men could have been more different in their upbringing. Mill's father decided to raise his son in a cloistered environment, removed from the real world. Mill learned Greek, Latin, and a host of languages at an age not much beyond that of today's elementary school student. He was to be a kind of superintellectual and rise above all the learned of his day. In the end, a brilliant mind was produced, and he had a commanding position and respect in his day as a thinker. Yet, except for his *Autobiography* and his essay *On Liberty,* his writings have no recognition today, and most of his ideas and philosophy are no longer considered valid. Dickens, by contrast, has become immortal.

Why did Dickens and Mill differ so intensely on their analysis of the "American disunion"? This is not hard to explain, since they were mortal enemies of the pen and had been feuding for well over a decade before their contrasting articles appeared in London's periodicals. Dickens, with his background in London's poverty, had a superior insight into what makes society tick. Mill's specious scholarship on the Civil War may not have come from an inability to think but from his rage against Dickens.

Unfortunately, for the cause of accurate history, it was Mill's faulty thinking that found its way into the Northern press, which was hungry for just about anything that would excuse their war on the South. Mill's "slavery, the one cause of the civil war" became a falsehood that lives on to this day, especially among historians, who, like Mill, live in an economically cloistered world that minimizes the role money plays in human affairs.

Mill was right in focusing on the slave issue, not as a cause of the war, which it wasn't, but as a race problem tied up with the institution of slavery. Both Mill and Dickens raise the question, Was this a just war? If Mill was right, if freeing the slaves was the objective, then the war would have had considerable justification in the eyes of the world, especially among Europeans. But if Dickens was right, then democracy in America was a failure, and the American people had descended into the realm of barbarism as a means of settling political disputes. In a sense, the Civil War gave democracy a black eye from which it has never recovered. Even democracy, the rage of our time, does not guarantee that its leaders and people will behave in a civilized manner.

7

How British Cartoonists Saw the War

The Star-spangled banner that blows broad and brave,
O'er the home of the free, o'er the hut of the slave—

Whose folds every year, broad and broader have grown,
Till they shadow both arctic and tropical zone,
From the Sierra Nevada to Florida's shore
And, like Oliver Twist, are still asking for more—

Punch, 15 December 1860

Ralph Waldo Emerson wrote that "caricatures are often the truest history of the times." And that is certainly true of the British cartoons that focused on the American Civil War. While modern cartoons seem to have been invented by the Dutch, the word itself was invented by the founders of London's *Punch* magazine in 1843. That remarkable magazine, even to this day, has no rival for its wit, sarcastic designs, and wisdom. It has always been free from party bias and has done much to cause the English to laugh at their various fads, forms of British ostentation, and political chicanery. From 1860 to 1865, the *Punch* cartoonists, from week to week, told a story about the American war, and they were able to put in caricatures what writers even today have been unable to say in words. As they drew Lincoln's countenance, they painted a picture of Lincoln's inner world—his frustrations, his anguish, and even his caesarism—not possible in words or modern photography. Perhaps most important, they showed the follies and falsehoods of the war, something no American periodical would have dared to present to its readers. It is quite probable that if *Punch* had been published in America at the time, it would have been shut down by military force. And even today, these cartoonists show the war for what it painfully was without the cover-ups and distorted scholarship our historians seem compelled to resort to in the interest of preserving legends and myths of that tragic era.

98   *Chapter 7*

A FAMILY QUARREL.

Figure 7.1. "A Family Quarrel."

Figure 7.1, the 28 September 1861 cartoon, "A Family Quarrel," depicts the political-constitutional issue as States versus Union, with a black man dancing in the background—the real issue? The armies of the North and South had already taken to the field. Figure 7.2 shows the blockade's binding of "King Cotton."

During 1862 the war was not going well for Lincoln, and the cartoons in Figures 7.3 through 7.6 pinpoint some of his dilemmas.

In the caricature in Figure 7.7, a black man is shown appealing for help from Lincoln, who turns the other way; this was New York's problem, not his. Enforcing the draft was a state undertaking.

By the end of 1863, with the unbelievable number of casualties at Gettysburg and elsewhere, the Europeans began to see the war for its horrors in the hundreds of thousands dead. The humanitarian idea to intervene and put an end to the slaughter continued to be discussed in the press and in the halls of government. But in the end, the Europeans stayed away, not wanting to end up victims in the American juggernaut.

In 1864 the interesting caricature with Britannia and Columbia

KING COTTON BOUND;
Or, The Modern Prometheus.

Figure 7.2. "King Cotton Bound." For years Southern writers had extolled the power of cotton. "Cotton is King," was the battle cry from the South, which meant that Britain, France, and certainly Northern industries would have to yield to the demands of their cotton-based industries. But the Northern blockade soon ended that Southern weapon, as shown in this cartoon with King Cotton bound and helpless by the blockade. King Cotton turned out to be just one of a number of Southern delusions.

LINCOLN'S TWO DIFFICULTIES.

Lin. "WHAT? NO MONEY! NO MEN!"

Figure 7.3. "Lincoln's Two Difficulties."

THE NEW ORLEANS PLUM.

BIG LINCOLN HORNER,
UP IN A CORNER,
THINKING OF HUMBLE PIE;

FOUND UNDER HIS THUMB,
A NEW ORLEANS PLUM,
AND SAID, WHAT A 'CUTE YANKEE AM I!

Figure 7.4. The first great Northern victory of the war came at New Orleans in April 1862. A happy Lincoln has pulled out a plum. At last, a win for our side!

ONE GOOD TURN DESERVES ANOTHER.

Old Abe. "WHY I DU DECLARE IT'S MY DEAR OLD FRIEND SAMBO! COURSE YOU'LL FIGHT FOR
US, SAMBO. LEND US A HAND, OLD HOSS, DU!"

Figure 7.5. With a shortage of soldiers, Lincoln turned to the blacks to volunteer but did not find many takers.

JOHN BULL'S NEUTRALITY.

"LOOK HERE, BOYS, I DON'T CARE TWOPENCE FOR YOUR NOISE; BUT IF YOU THROW STONES
AT MY WINDOWS, I MUST *THRASH YOU BOTH*."

Figure 7.6. British neutrality is shown with strong and mighty John Bull looking down at the pip-squeak Americans as a bunch of rowdy boys. As often happens in war, the war policy of the combatants interferes with a neutral country's right to trade. British ports in the Bahamas, for example, were used by blockade runners. Intercepting British ships on the high seas to examine their cargo was within the rights of the combatants, and what could or could not be seized was not always easy to determine. War materials—no, foods—yes.

"ROWDY" NOTIONS OF EMANCIPATION.

" THE mob on the corner, below my house, had hung up a negro to the lamp-post. In mockery, a cigar was placed in his mouth. * * * For hours these scared negroes poured up Twenty-seventh Street, passing my house. * * * One old negro, 70 years old, blind as a bat, and such a cripple that he could hardly move, was led along by his equally aged wife with a few rags they had saved, trembling with fright, and not knowing where to go."—MANHATTAN's *Letter in the Standard, July 30th.*

Figure 7.7. There were terrible riots, especially in New York City, where blacks were lynched because New Yorkers blamed them for the war. In this caricature, a black man is shown appealing for help from Lincoln, who turns the other way. This was New York's problem, not his. Enforcing the draft was a state undertaking.

(America) shows a map of America torn into Northern states and Southern states (Figure 7.8). Britannia notes: "But I'm afraid you'll find it difficult to join *that* neatly." As time was to prove—how true!

Finally, the most significant caricature of all (fig. 7.11). In December 1864, cartoonists saw a new nation rising out of the ashes of the old. Lincoln is the head of a phoenix, a mythical bird of ancient Egypt, which was consumed voluntarily by fire and rose again from its own ashes to a youthful life.

But the blazing fire was consuming the timbers of the older order in the federal system: of "commerce" with the low tariff and world trade; of the "United States Constitution" and its format for limited government; of a "free press," which Lincoln destroyed; of "states rights," where sovereignty once resided; of habeas corpus, the once sacred right against arbitrary arrests, trials, and imprisonment by executive power, lettres de ca-

COLUMBIA'S SEWING-MACHINE.

Mrs. Britannia. "AH, MY DEAR COLUMBIA, IT'S ALL VERY WELL; BUT I'M AFRAID YOU'LL FIND IT DIFFICULT TO JOIN *THAT* NEATLY."

Figure 7.8. This interesting caricature with Britannia and Columbia (America) shows a map of America torn into Northern states and Southern states. Britannia notes, "But I'm afraid you'll find it difficult to join that neatly." As time was to prove—how true!

chet; and credit, the end of a government free from debt, now based on paper money. The older order, like the phoenix, was consumed by the fire of war, induced by Lincoln the great bird.

As shown by these astute caricaturists, the old Union was gone; the new Union was no "union" at all but a new nation with federal central authority in command at all levels of life. Cicero lamented 2,000 years ago that "our beloved republic is gone forever." Americans could lament that their beloved Union was gone as well. Only the walls remained.

Unfortunately, Lincoln's "malice toward none and charity for all" was not to be. The Civil War was to continue with armies of occupation, a disenfranchised Southern society, and invading carpetbaggers who assured the continuation of hostilities, the hatreds, and the de facto secession of the Southern people. Even the ex-slaves were to come up on the short end of the pole of liberty.

MRS. NORTH AND HER ATTORNEY.

Mrs. North. " YOU SEE, MR. LINCOLN, WE HAVE FAILED UTTERLY IN OUR COURSE OF ACTION; I WANT PEACE, AND SO, IF YOU CANNOT
EFFECT AN AMICABLE ARRANGEMENT, I MUST PUT THE CASE INTO OTHER HANDS."

Figure 7.9. "Mrs. North," wearing a black dress and mourning the dead (symbolizing bereaved mothers, wives, and female relatives), urges Lincoln to arrange for peace. He had no such intention, however.

BRITANNIA SYMPATHISES WITH COLUMBIA.

Figure 7.10. As the war ends in May 1865, this cartoon shows a sympathetic Britannia at the bedside of the sick and injured Columbia, giving a wreath of flowers. The black man at the side of the bed has his chains removed but his head is down, like the distraught figure with an American flag on the left.

THE FEDERAL PHŒNIX.

Figure 7.11. "The Federal Phoenix." A nation state arises out of the destruction of the constitutional compact among the states: free commerce is replaced with extreme protectionism; sound money is replaced with credit; the Bill of Rights with press censorship and arbitrary imprisonment—the end of the Union "as it was."

8

A Just War?

Abraham Lincoln, in order to maintain the unity of the United States . . . resorted to the use of force. . . . so, I think Abraham Lincoln, president, is a model, is an example.

Chinese premier Zhu Rongii, on Taiwan, at a news conference
with President Clinton, 8 April 1999

In the summer of 1862, Prince Napoleon and his companions traveled to the United States, first visiting the North and having conversations with Lincoln, Seward, and General Scott. They visited Northern military camps and noticed a large number of foreigners in the ranks—recent immigrants who had been attracted to the pay, many of whom could not speak English. Then the visitors traveled to Virginia, first under a Union escort and then by Confederate cavalry to the camps of Generals Johnston and Beauregard. Mingling with young confederate soldiers, they asked for their thoughts on the war.

First, a soldier mentioned defending his homeland, Virginia, from foreign invaders: "We do not want to have anything to do with the Yankees, neither will we suffer a single Yankee foot on our territory; and they having once violated it, it is all over between us." Another remarked, "Have we not the right of separation, since we possess the right of union? They very well know that, without us, their commerce is ruined for we are the cultivators. But we will no longer be cheated. We will continue the war two years—four, if necessary. . . . we will have nothing more to do with the Yankees."[1]

These "young Confederate soldiers," as they were described, had the issues of the war in good focus, from the South's point of view. Defense—repelling foreign invaders—was the primary motive for these soldiers, and they "vowed a mortal hatred for the Yankees." And then came the economics, which even these young soldiers were aware of: "Without us their commerce is ruined," and "we will no longer be cheated."[2]

They also discussed the slave issue, which these soldiers believed was really a nonissue. They then set forth the proslavery view: The slaves were happy, well fed, and well housed, wanting nothing; they were much better off than the blacks in the North, who had liberty but "liberty to die of hunger." But, of course, in the summer of 1862, emancipation was not an object of the war.

Northern soldiers sang a ballad expressing what they were fighting for: "Union Forever, Union Hurrah!" Certainly not a known justification for war. Wars had been fought by people trying to withdraw from an imperial power, but this was a federation of sovereign states, a compact, or so the Founders said, and that makes "preserving the Union" by violence and war a unique problem in the history of the justification for war. Could this motive make for a just war? This was bothersome to many Americans in the North, but to Europeans even more so. They watched the savagery of the conflict with horror. And even to this day, the American Civil War has to be one of the worst blights on the history of democracy.

To the world, the great American experiment in democracy had turned into a great tragedy, with the nation split and engaged in a great civil war, and for what? And how justified was it?

"When the people of eight states," said one British editorial, "containing many millions of inhabitants, unanimously determine to leave the Union, is it not a contradiction of that principle [democracy] to employ force to compel them to remain? The right to use such force has been expressly repudiated by great American authorities." The editor now quotes Madison and Hamilton: "The use of force against a State would be more like a declaration of war than an infliction of punishment, and would probably be considered by the party attacked as a dissolution of all previous compacts" (James Madison);[3] "to coerce a State would be one of the maddest projects ever devised: no State would ever suffer itself to be used as the instrument of coercing another" (Alexander Hamilton).[4]

The secession of the four border states after the call by Lincoln for troops to invade the South was a recognition of Hamilton's and Madison's views. Where was the constitutional authority for such unthinkable action? Actually, there wasn't any.

But setting aside the views of America's Founders, what principles of international law are at issue in the Civil War? Most academic historians, without legal training, have played down the war crimes issue, as if it has no bearing on those who win a war. It does.

In the early seventeenth century, Hugo Grotius, a Dutch lawyer, came forth with *The Law of War and Peace,* which was translated into English in 1646. It immediately became the bible of the law of nations and found its way into the courts, libraries, and governments of Europe. Grotius soon became "the father of modern international law." Grotius held that states, like people, are bound by a code of law, with duties and prohibitions that are universal, reasonable, and unchangeable. One nation, for example, may not attack another. After reviewing the practices of ancient nations, philosophers and legists, Grotius concluded that "authorities generally assign to wars three justifiable causes: defence, recovery of property, and punishment."[5]

Grotius noted that the German barbarians of the north had a strong code and "were the most just: they refrained from war unless attacked." The Roman lawyer Cicero would have been the father of ancient international law. In his *De Republica* (30.23) he set forth the principle that "wars undertaken without reason are unjust wars. Except for the purpose of avenging or repulsing an enemy, no just war can be waged."

By the nineteenth century, the concept of a just war became a part of the law of nations even though it had been an unwritten rule of society since the Middle Ages. Many of the tax rebellions in Europe, Spain, and England were resisting revenue demands of unjust wars, wars that were not for the defense of the realms. That same principle became part of the U.S. Constitution, which restricted tax expenditures for "the common Defense."

At West Point cadets were taught the principles of Grotius and international law under General Order no. 12, by none other than Lincoln's top commander, General Henry Halleck, who wrote the book. No general during the Civil War can claim ignorance of the laws of wars, especially the laws against the plunder and devastation of private property. Here is an excerpt from General Order no. 12, written by Halleck on the wanton plunder of private property: "The inevitable consequences . . . are universal pillage and a total relaxation of discipline; the loss of private property, and the violation of individual rights . . . and the ordinary peaceful and noncombatants are converted into bitter and implacable enemies. The system is, therefore, regarded as both impolitic and unjust, and is coming into general disuse among the most civilized nations."[6]

But Halleck's book and teachings weren't the only condemnation of plunder of civilian property. On 24 April 1863, under Lincoln's signature, the army promulgated to its officers General Order no. 100, which came to be known as the Lieber Code and eventually received acclaim throughout the military in the Western world. Halleck was a close friend of its author, Professor Francis Lieber of Columbia University. A month after this order was given to the officers in the Union army, Professor Lieber wrote to the top commander, General Halleck:

I know by letters . . . that the wanton destruction of property by our men is alarming. It does incalculable injury. It demoralizes our troops, it annihilates wealth irrevocably and makes a return to a state of peace and peaceful minds more and more difficult. Your order [to the officers] . . . with reference to the Code, and pointing out the disastrous consequences of reckless devastation, in a manner that it might not furnish our reckless enemy with new arguments for his savagery.

Halleck remained general in chief until Lincoln fired him in 1864 and appointed Grant as top commander. It was under Grant that the Lieber Code, now in the hands of all leading officers, was disregarded, and pillage and plunder became the general order of the final year of the war. Sherman and Sheridan could not possibly have undertaken their devastation of the South if they had followed this new military code on the laws of war. They also turned away from their education at West Point and the laws of war they had learned there under Halleck.

Years after the war Sherman wrote a letter to a friend in which he acknowledged that he knew better—that at West Point he had been taught

Figure 8.1. Sherman's troops burn a farmhouse in Georgia while the woman of the house looks on with a few of her furnishings that the soldiers permitted her to keep.

Generals William T. Sherman, Ulysses S. Grant and Philip H. Sheridan

Figure 8.2. U.S. postage stamp from 1936 to 1937 honoring three well-known generals who led Northern armies at the end of the war. All three were schooled in the laws of war at West Point. Sherman even acknowledged that the decimation of civilian property was a war crime that was, as he had been taught, punishable by death.

that the pillage he brought to the South was a crime, punishable by death: "I know that in the beginning I, too, had the old West Point notion that pillage was a capital crime, and punished it by shooting."[7]

American generals were fully aware that Napoleon was punished and banished from Europe for engaging in aggressive wars over a twenty-year period. The law of warfare was being enforced for the first time against a loser. But winners need not worry, then or now, as war crimes, by and large, are only committed by defeated leaders. In the Civil War, Lincoln and his generals were immune from the laws of war—because they won.

Unfortunately, during the nineteenth century, Americans seemed to believe that they had a divine right to aggression. It was the destiny of the American people and government to rule over North America—all of it. And this was God's plan. This made the war against Mexico justified, even though in General Grant's memoirs he condemned the war as one of aggression, and so did Lincoln as a congressman at the time. This may explain why so much has been written about who fired the first shot of the Civil War, as if that justifies the total war that engulfed America, even though that Fourth of July display of cannon at Fort Sumter didn't hurt anyone. It was not Pearl Harbor.

The laws of war not only focused on the aggressor-defender issue, they also set forth rules about how armies and especially its leaders and generals had to conduct themselves. Historians with a strongly Northern

Lincoln-idolizing viewpoint do not realize the criminal element in the way the war was conducted—criminal by the laws of nations. The end clearly justified the means. Consider this observation by a prominent historian, Stephen Oates, who describes Lincoln's method of warfare in glowing terms: "Lincoln's armies were mopping up the Confederacy in all directions, waging scorched-earth warfare against the Rebel economy and civilian morale with ruthless efficiency. . . . Lincoln fully endorsed Sheridan's burning of the Shenandoah Valley, Sherman's brutal March to the Sea through Georgia, and the Carolina's Brigadier General James H. Wilson's destructive raid across Alabama. Such warfare earned Lincoln and his generals undying hatred in Dixie, but it brought victory."[8]

Lincoln and his generals violated the laws of nations, and Northern historians seem unaware of that. Another famous historian from Princeton, James M. McPherson, goes even further than Oates. He doesn't hesitate to call Lincoln's war strategy brilliant, even using the term "genius,"[9] and Sherman, with Lincoln's adoration, is a great noble general for his devastation of civilian property in his march to the sea. When a Southerner called Sherman a barbarian for what he was doing, Sherman replied that a commander "may take your house, your fields, your everything, and turn you out helpless to starve. It may be wrong, but that don't alter the case."

His acknowledgment that "it may be wrong" may have come from his education at West Point, and contrary to the famous general's excuse, it does alter the case—it makes Sherman a war criminal. Writing to General Halleck in September 1864, amid his infamous destruction of civilian property and life, Sherman again excused himself: "If people [civilians] raise a howl against my barbarity and cruelty I will answer them that war is war." This is the same general who later, in the Indian wars, used the same philosophy when he said, "The only good Indian is a dead Indian," which he meant literally. Incidentally, I am not the only historian to see the commission of war crimes by Sherman and his confederates in arms. Otto Eisenschiml, writing in the January 1964 issue of *Civil War Times,* less than twenty years after the Nuremberg war crimes trials, asserted that Sherman should have been hanged as a war criminal.[10]

While the generals were quite pleased with themselves over their barbarism and war crimes, the soldiers who had to carry out these orders were not so pleased with the work. Robert Shaw, a student at Harvard who had risen through the ranks to be promoted to colonel in early 1863, was commanded by a superior officer to burn the city of Darien, Georgia. He wrote to his wife that "for myself, I have gone through the war so far without dishonor, and I do not like to degenerate into a plunderer and robber,—and the same applies to every officer in my regiment."[11]

Figure 8.3. Here in the Shenandoah Valley, a farm wife weeps as Northern troops slaughter her live-stock. Smoke from burning farm buildings often arose against the lovely mountain backdrop. This destruction of civilian property was Sheridan's doing, and he also knew better.

Too bad the top gun, General Sherman, didn't feel that way. Sherman lived, but Shaw, this remarkable officer, was killed in action on Morris Island, South Carolina, a month after writing the above letter.

Another Union officer, Joshua Chamberlain (a brigadier general who later became governor of Maine), wrote in a letter to his sister after having burned out women and children from their homes near Petersburg, Virginia, on order from General Grant: "I am willing to fight men in arms, but not *babes in arms*" (14 December 1864).[12]

When General Sheridan cut his swath of destruction through the Shenandoah Valley, Lincoln conveyed the "thanks of the Nation and my own personal admiration and gratitude."

Finally, as a postscript to Sherman and Sheridan's barbarism toward the South, Sherman wrote to Sheridan in 1868 concerning Sheridan's assaults on the Indians, telling him to act with all the vigor he had shown in the Shenandoah Valley during the final months of the Civil War. And Sherman promised to cover for him if the press starting writing about "atrocities."

Sherman, as commander over the forces against the Indians, after the Civil War, sent a letter to President Grant: "We must act with vindictive earnestness against the Sioux, even to their extermination, men, women, and children. Nothing else will reach the root of this case." Sherman was to call the massacre of all American Indians his "final solution to the Indian problem," a phrase the Nazis were to use for the Holocaust. Just before Sherman died in 1891 he complained bitterly about civilian interference in his Indian policies, which had prevented him from getting "rid of them all."[13]

Ulysses S. Grant, as commander of all Union armies, sent an order to General Sheridan on 16 July 1864 concerning the Confederate colonel John Mosby, whose raids behind Union lines diverted as many as 30,000 Union troops trying to track him down. Ordered Grant, "Where any of Mosby's men are caught, hang them without a trial."

Ten days later, Grant issued another war crimes–type order to Sheridan: "If the war is to last another year, we want the Shenandoah Valley to remain a barren waste." Sheridan had already burned everything in sight.

It might be tempting to compare Northerners, in their barbarism toward the South, with the Nazis, although that would be absurd. Yet a government and its leaders can be guilty of war crimes without reaching the depths of Nazi barbarism. Distinguished military historian B. H. Liddell Hart observed that the code of civilized warfare which had ruled Europe for over two hundred years was first broken by Lincoln's policy of directing the destruction of civilian life in the South. "This policy" he wrote, "was in many ways the prototype of modern total war."

In the last years of the war, after Grant replaced Halleck, Northern generals decided that victory was more important than keeping the war within civilized bounds, and Confederate generals and officers started expressing alarm at this turn to barbarism. When General Sherman gave his order to burn Atlanta, with the option for the local residents to leave and avoid cremation, confederate General Hood, under a flag of truce, sent a letter to Sherman protesting the order: "And now, sir, permit me to say that the unprecedented measure you propose transcends, in studied and ingenious cruelty, all acts ever before brought to my attention in the dark history of war. In the name of God and humanity I protest" (9 September 1864).

Sherman replied that the Southerners were the bad guys and they had done a lot of bad things, like commissioning privateers, seizing federal forts and arsenals, confiscating all debts due Northern merchants for goods had and received, trying to force Missouri and Kentucky into the Confederacy, and falsifying the voting in Louisiana, so Southerners should not make "hypocritical appeals to God and humanity."[14] Sherman seemed to be saying that in a war the good guys do not have to observe the laws of civilized warfare; otherwise, why the laundry list of Confederate sins? Sherman's absurd thinking was taken up by George Bush when he said that he would not apologize to the Japanese for the atomic bombing of Japanese cities, for similar reasons.

There were voices in the North protesting the inhumanity of Sheridan and Sherman's war policy. A Northern general, Don Buell, resigned the army in protest: "I believe that the policy and means with which the war was being prosecuted were discreditable to the nation and a stain on civilization." Even a Northern Washington newspaper, writing to Union troops in 1864, voiced alarm:

> Old men and women and children—the infirm, the sick and the innocent—driven from their blazing homes, gathering in hopeless misery around some dying camp fire, shivering, starving, shelterless, did you feel an impulse prompting you to aid in carrying anguish and desolation and extermination throughout . . . the South, merely to give immediate emancipation to a race who were a thousand times happier as you found them than as you would leave them?[15]

As Sherman and Sheridan were undertaking the devastation of civilian life and property, sixteen European nations met in Geneva, Switzerland, to codify the laws of war in what we call the first Geneva Convention on War. Three other such conventions were held, the last in 1949 after World War II. These conventions did not really create any new law; they simply codified the laws of war, as our codes centralize common law.

The civilized world was motivated by the suffering of injured soldiers during the Crimean War, which had just recently ended. They were equally motivated by what the Northern armies in America were doing to the civilian population in the South. There were many editorials written in Europe about the need for European intervention to put an end to the carnage and destruction that was taking place. The Civil War in America had turned into a war that shocked the civilized world. To this day, the names of Generals Grant, Sherman, and Sheridan are spoken of with hatred and contempt by the descendants of the civilian population who experienced the modern Western world's first massive ethnic cleansing and plunder of a civilian population, contrary to the morality as well as the laws of nations.

The conventions codifying the century-old laws of war at Geneva (1863) and The Hague (1899) decreed:

1. Attacking defenseless cities and towns was a war crime.
2. Plundering and wantonly destroying civilian property was a war crime.
3. Only necessities could be taken from a civilian population, and they had to be paid for.

These rules, when applied to the Northern generals, made their behavior criminal by the laws of nations. Like the subsequent Geneva Conventions that followed, these provisions were codifying international law—the law of war and the basis for the prosecution of war crimes.

You could argue as a Northern apologist that these conventions, which codified the laws of war against the wanton destruction of civilian property, were not binding on the American generals, and furthermore, America was not a signatory to these codifications. But West Point cadets were taught what these conventions codified. This is the same argument Hitler used to justify his mistreatment of Russian prisoners of war—the Soviet Union was not a signatory to the 1925 Geneva Protocol, hence Germany was not required to treat Russian prisoners humanely. Fortunately, that thin argument never held up at Nuremberg and would not hold up for the Civil War.

In *The Laws of War* (1994), three American scholars commented on this line of thinking: "Most of the actions today outlawed by the Geneva Conventions have been condemned in the West for at least four centuries."[16] "These laws of war that condemned what Sherman and Sheridan did were 'self-evident and unalterable' features of the laws of war that crystallized in early modern Europe and survived virtually intact down to our day," wrote Geoffrey Parker, professor of military and naval history at Yale University. Even in Shakespeare's time the laws were well-known. In his play *Henry V,* after the battle of Agincourt, wanton cruelty was taken against an unarmed group of noncombatants. Notes Shakespeare: "'Tis expressly against the law of arms, 'tis as errant a piece of knavery, mark you now, as can be offert, in your conscience, now, is it not?"[17]

An Oxford professor of International Law, Adam Roberts, who specializes in the use of force in war, said that "the convictions in the Nuremberg and Tokyo trials were in the end not so much about the initiation or conduct of the military hostilities as about the treatment of largely defenseless people in the hands of the adversary."[18]

The American Revolutionary War set civilized examples that Sherman and Sheridan could have followed. That war too was a war for secession, this time from the British empire, and the purpose of the war from the British standpoint was to bring the colonies back into the empire. The British, like the Northerners, called the Americans "rebels" at all stages, and they added to that the "traitor and conspiracy" charge as well. In short, both of these uprisings and revolts were wars for the same purposes.

The head of the British forces, General Sir William Howe, unlike the Northern generals, made it Britain's policy to avoid atrocities and devastation of civilian property. Such uncivilized conduct would implant undying hatred in the hearts of the colonists for the Mother Country. The British wanted the colonists to return to the empire as willing subjects, not a crushed and devastated people. This long-term objective made Sherman and Sheridan's type of civilian devastation counterproductive, even if successful. To this day, the South's hatred of "Yankees" stems from the barbarism of these generals—a hatred that justifiably lives.

The object then of the British military leadership in the Revolutionary War was to effect a reconciliation between the mother country and the colonies. Massive destruction of homes, farms, livestock, food, towns, and cities, as undertaken by the Northern generals, would work against reconciliation. Since that destruction was Northern military policy, it is no surprise that a reconciliation has not been achieved.

These Northern generals could also have learned from General Washington. When faced with the urge to retaliate against British forces that had burned the house and laid waste the farm of one of his officers (Sherman style), Washington said that lawful warfare "forbids such a measure," that is, reprisals. "Experience proves," said Washington, "that their wanton cruelty [burning down the farm] injures rather than benefits their cause; that with our forbearance, justly secures to us the attachment of all good men."[19] Sherman and Sheridan obviously had no regard for the opinions of "all good men."

Atrocities were committed by both sides during the Revolutionary War, but the difference between the atrocities in that war and the war between the states was that the policy of "wanton cruelty" expressed by Washington was not the policy of the commanders on either side during the

Revolutionary War. In the American Civil War, "wanton cruelty" was policy for the generals and all the way up to the commander in chief. That helps explain why the reconciliation of the South to the Union was never achieved by that generation or following ones.

Reconciliation was one war objective that the Union lost, setting the stage for the guerrilla tactics that were to be employed by the Ku Klux Klan and other underground paramilitary organizations that took over de facto control of Southern society. The South did not obtain its objective of withdrawing from the Union, being forced back by overwhelming military and naval forces coupled with wanton cruelty toward civilian life and property. But in the end, after a decade or so, Southerners expelled the Yankees from their homeland. They were the first to say, "Yankee go home," and they meant it. In the final analysis, both sides lost the war.

Historians who glorify Lincoln's scorched-earth policy should learn something of international law and the law of war, for they have unwittingly branded Lincoln and his generals as war criminals. As time and honest scholarship take over, future generations will not judge Lincoln well. In fact, it will be hard to not call what he did a crime against the laws of war and nations, making Lincoln, as painful as it may be, a war criminal. And even if his military had behaved according to civilized decency, his purpose of "preserving the Union" finds no support in the laws of war as a just cause.

Western Europeans' need to codify the laws of war developed from the experiences of war as a devil's enterprise, for war turns the moral world upside down and sanctions a temporary suspension of all respect for the sacredness of "life, property, and truth." The insanity of war prompted Immanuel Kant, one of the great philosophers of all time, to argue that war was so stupid that even a race of devils would avoid it and seek out another way to resolve their disputes, provided only that the devils were "intelligent." A critique of war as a great evil, as developed in the nineteenth century, involved five principles:

1. War is organized destruction of the harvest of civilization and those who produce it.
2. Its greatest tragedy is the destruction of the best and brightest as the casualty of war. The Greeks (antedating Darwin by 2,000 years) reasoned that nature was a struggle for the survival of the fittest. War results in the destruction of the fittest.
3. A soldier in fighting reverts to a subhuman level.
4. War makes an appalling addition to the miseries of the human lot.
5. War, when looked on as a whole, is a gigantic evil. Even a just war sets the heart of a nation aflame with hatred, malice, and revenge.[20]

St. Augustine said it best of all: "War? Veritable games in honor of the devils." Hans Kelsen's great classic, *General Theory of Law and State* (1945), noted that states resorting to war have always tried to justify their actions to their own people as well as to the world at large. That wars should only be undertaken for defensive reasons has been a moral tenet of Western civilization since Cicero, so it is only to be expected that most nations undertake aggression with some kind of a phony excuse.

It is no surprise that the invasion of the South by Lincoln's military forces needed justification on some ground. The Southern assault on Fort Sumter would have justified an amphibious operation to recover the fort, and Lincoln made that his policy in his first inaugural address, but that would hardly have justified raising a million-man army to invade and destroy eleven states in the South—like using a Big Bertha to kill a Chihuahua.

Lincoln had to find another excuse for his military assault on the South besides the Sumter episode. The only way he could do that with some semblance of lawfulness was to deny these states their sovereignty, to deny any right to withdraw from the Union, and to deny their right to "the consent of the governed" in their affairs with the Union. They were not freedom fighters, fighting for their independence—they were traitors and conspirators, and he was merely putting down an unlawful rebellion. He could ignore their constitutional processes of secession by popular vote and popular will. He could even maintain falsely that they were planning to invade the North and destroy Northern civilization, but he knew no invasion was planned or even contemplated.

Lincoln was on the horns of a dilemma. To acknowledge that the laws of war and international law were on his side is an absurdity. He had to find new ground—some new theory to justify his military action. Again we have to look to Hans Kelsen: "Never has a government declared that it was resorting to war only because it felt at liberty to do so, or because such a step seemed advantageous." Lincoln came up with his "preserving the Union," and Northerners bought the idea since they didn't have any better excuse. In reality, Lincoln and the Northerners invaded the South and sought to destroy Southerners' right of self-determination because it was a good idea, politically and economically. They were preserving the Union but for whom? For what? And why? Certainly not for the citizens of the Southern states and their best interests. It was Northern commercial interests that demanded Union, on their terms. That is why ordinary civilians during the war years said it was a "rich man's war, and the poor man's fight."[21]

Lincoln resorted to calling the war a "rebellion," like John Brown's attempted rebellion at Harpers Ferry, Virginia. John Brown hoped to start a major slave revolt that would spread throughout the South and end slavery—a harebrained idea, far removed from reality with no chance of success. In the end, seventeen died at the scene, and John Brown was hanged.

The war for Southern independence was not the act of a few fanatics—not even a large number of fanatics. It was the will of 6–7 million people acting through democratic processes. To say that it was a rebellion, or *just* a rebellion, is to stretch credulity to the breaking point. There would be not seventeen dead, but 630,000 dead.

But Lincoln had no choice. He had to hold fast to the rebellion interpretation of the conflict unless he wanted to admit that it was a war of conquest to force the Southern states to stay in the federal compact against their will. If he called it a war, he had to then excuse his suspension of the Constitution—that way he could rule by decree under the president's "war powers," which gave him the rights of a dictator to fight a "war." But as the aggressor in the war, he was violating the laws of nations. Thus it had to be a rebellion, for otherwise he was in trouble, ethically and legally. His years as a frontier lawyer had taught him that much. A lawyer defending a guilty client builds a case on whatever evidence and legal theories are available and hopes a court and jury will be dumb enough to believe it.

There wasn't much morality in the Lincoln cabinet on the laws of war and of nations. As noted, Secretary of State Seward suggested that the nation could be united by starting a war in the North to add Canada to the nation and in the South to annex Mexico and Cuba. This suggestion found its way to the world's press and the British and Canadians were outraged. The idea did not die, however. As the American Civil War was coming to an end in 1865, the prospect of an American invasion of Canada resurfaced, resulting in fortifications and canals in Ontario, Canada, finally ending politically in the formation of the Canadian Confederation in 1867 to defend against Yankee aggression.[22]

Many historians today, trying to excuse the "preserve the Union" justification for the war, cite the nineteenth-century belief of the Americans in what was called "Manifest Destiny." Manifest Destiny was the belief that God was behind the American nation and its people and that the Americans were destined to rule over North America—all of it and then some. This was God's plan and Lincoln was only carrying out God's purpose. Consequently, the Civil War was a holy war to fulfill divine providence and had to be won at all costs; if the rules of civilized warfare had to be ignored, so be it. Lincoln seemed to have this in mind to excuse the slaughter and even to excuse his wholesale imprisonment of anyone suspected of harboring secessionist sympathies. It was all right to lock up anyone who might have the wrong thoughts or speak the wrong ideas. He was justified in order to save the Union. He used the analogy of amputating a diseased limb in order to save the whole body.

In the sixteenth century one more justification for war was added to the just-war doctrines of Cicero and of Western civilization. It was lawful to engage in war to Christianize heathens, which at that time included the Indians in America. Amazingly, in the nineteenth century Lincoln added three more justifications for war. First, it was lawful to go to war to prevent a state or commonwealth from withdrawing from a federal union the state had voluntarily entered into. Second, it was lawful to go to war to prevent the division of the American Union and thus carry out its great mission of Manifest Destiny to spread its principles of government over the world—so they would not "perish from the earth." Third, it was lawful to go to war to carry out God's vengeance against the American people for having tolerated slavery. In other words, as Lincoln said in his second inaugural address, this war was God's punishment for the sins of the American people. He, Lincoln, being God's instrument in that endeavor, had driven the nation into war. He could have ended it any time, but God had other plans. He (God) wanted to punish the American people, and Lincoln became God's servant to carry out God's will.

Whereas Hugo Grotius set forth three justifiable reasons for war—defense, recovery of property, and punishment—Lincoln added three more; he also had Grotius's recovery of property and punishment to fall back on. The South could justifiably be punished for firing on Fort Sumter, and even though Confederate cannon didn't hurt anyone, that was enough to justify total war. But this excuse doesn't stand up. It was used to justify the conquest of Mexico when the Mexicans supposedly fired on Americans in disputed territory, and later it was used when the Spanish supposedly blew up the battleship *Maine* in Havana (they didn't). But a rumor is as good as the truth when you are seeking some excuse for war. Even in Vietnam, the Tonkin Bay resolution wouldn't pass the smell test. The moral problem here is best shown by the rules of law that govern individuals. If someone rudely bumps another person, the use of deadly force in response is not warranted.

Lincoln enticed the South to start the war—to fire on the flag—in order to rally the North. But in Europe, that excuse for total war was ridiculed, especially since the South sent envoys and offered to pay damages for taking over other federal properties. Is that not the way civilized people settle their differences?

WAR: A NOBLE ENDEAVOR?

American leaders have been in love with war since the Revolution. In the War of 1812, some of the war's strongest supporters, like Benjamin Harrison and Andrew Jackson, saw the opportunity to acquire more territory—Canada—as both Jefferson and Madison acknowledged. But American forces were defeated in their attempts to invade and conquer upper Canada (Ontario). The British general Brock captured Detroit and defeated the Americans north of Buffalo. The war ended after a stalemate and no new territory was acquired. But the Mexican War, fought some thirty years later, was different. It was a war of aggression to take California and what is today Utah, New Mexico, and Arizona. The United States wanted to buy the lands but Mexico refused. President Polk persuaded Congress to declare war after news that Mexican forces had fired on American troops on American soil (Texas). General Grant later acknowledged that it was a war of aggression—an unjust war. But, as President Reagan said about Panama, "We stole it, fair and square."

The use of military force to achieve political ends had become American policy by the time of the Civil War, and both the North and the South seemed anxious to use war to achieve desired political objectives. The Constitution provided for settling disputes between the federal government and state governments, yet the thought of using the courts to decide the right of secession never seemed to enter anyone's mind. Lincoln largely ignored the Court, and the Southerners made no effort to have the High Court decide the issue of secession. An interesting question remains. If the Supreme Court had rendered a decision on the secession issue, would the parties have accepted the decision? Probably not.

The use of war continued on the American frontier as Native Americans and their rights under treaty came into conflict with the zeal of settlers moving west. So war was used again, this time to herd Native Americans onto reservations and, when desirable, to break treaties and move them from desirable lands to lands no one else wanted.

Theodore Roosevelt stood for America's feelings about war—it builds character and courage and is a most worthwhile endeavor. The Spanish American War greatly added to America's overseas empire by annexing Puerto Rico, the Philippines, and Guam, and it established hegemony over Cuba with less than six hundred casualties. How could such an achievement be criticized? Was it not in keeping with the Manifest Destiny of the American people, which now extended throughout North America and included the Caribbean and the Far East.

Perhaps William Gladstone best expressed the view of the nineteenth century. Man was a war-prone animal that loved war. But the Almighty made a check on this rather despicable endeavor. Wars required taxes, and men hated taxes, so that would subdue man's passion for war. Unfortunately, Gladstone's analysis, while probably true for his time, never worked. When the passion for war is raging, as it was during Civil War times, the burden of taxes never quells the zeal for violence, on either side.

After more than 2,000 years of historical debate over what amounts to a just war, the apologists for the North developed two new theories of justification. First, that the war was to preserve the Union. As we shall see, this was based upon a rather strained interpretation of the words in the Articles of Confederation and the Constitution, ignoring what the Framers had said and also ignoring the more fundamental right of self-determination as expressed in the Declaration of Independence—the consent of the governed. The second and more appealing justification was that the war was to free the slaves, at a time when emancipation was sweeping throughout Western civilization, even Russia. But that justification became transparent when the black man's bid for freedom and equality was nipped in the bud.

At the root of this abandonment of the cause of freedom for the black man was the issue of racism, which supported American slavery. The real, more fundamental problem was not slavery—a Southern problem—but the more national problem of what could be called Negrophobia. Except for the slave owners, the belief that slavery was immoral and un-Christian was growing throughout America, as in the rest of the world. At the same time, however, counteracting this belief was the fear of what the black race might do to American society, North and South, if emancipated. This was the dilemma that turned most Americans away from abolitionism. Tolerating slavery in 1861 seemed to most Americans to be the lesser of the two evils.

9

Negrophobia

The most formidable of all the ills which threaten the future existence of the Union arises from the presence of a black population upon its territory.
Alexis de Tocqueville, *Democracy in America* (1838)

The abolition of slavery was probably the most important social event of the nineteenth century in civilized society. In 1800, slavery existed throughout the colonial empires of the European nations; by 1900, slavery was nowhere to be found. The strong zeal to abolish slavery began in Europe during the Enlightenment, which insisted that reason must be the foundation for all matters, including government. Using reason, Baron de Montesquieu, whose writings inspired the U.S. Constitution, found it easy to abhor slavery:

> But in moderate states, it is a point of the highest importance, that there should be no slaves. The political liberty of those states, adds to the value of civil liberty; and he who is deprived of the latter, is also deprived of the former. He sees the happiness of a society, of which he is not a member. . . . He sees his master has a soul, that can enlarge itself; while his own is constrained to submit to a continual depression. Nothing more assimilates a man to a beast, than living among freemen, himself a slave. Such people as these are the natural enemies of society, and their number must be dangerous.[1]

By the mid-nineteenth century Europeans universally believed that slavery was barbaric and not proper for a civilized society. This view soon crossed the Atlantic and started to take root in America. In the United States, however, there was no strong political move to abolish slavery even after European nations had done so. This seems strange, since the idea of equality under the law, and personal freedom, had been part of America from its earliest days.

But America had a problem. Slaves had been brought to America almost with the first colonists and became a part of the fabric of American society. It was easy for Western Europeans to abolish slavery because it only existed in the colonies. There were no repercussions at home when the British West Indies colonies were emancipated; no fear that hordes of freed slaves would descend on English society. However, Russia had the same problem that America had—the slaves (serfs) were right at home. The Russian government spent a decade figuring out how to emancipate without creating chaotic conditions. In fact, Tsar Alexander II's decree of emancipation has been called by historians "the greatest legislative act in history."[2] No one says that about Lincoln's Emancipation Proclamation. Americans did not spend any time figuring out how to emancipate and did create chaotic conditions. As emancipation spread throughout Europe's colonies, the question arose, what was holding America back?

The time for the end of slavery in America had come, but only a few were aware of it, certainly not the masses in the North or in the South. It was the slaves themselves who seem to have been aware of the times, of a force for emancipation that was at work and would soon take over the American conflict. In 1861, however, that didn't seem possible. Lincoln spoke to the South in his inaugural address to reassure them that their "peculiar institution" was not in any way in jeopardy: "I have no purpose directly or indirectly, to interfere with the institution of slavery in the States where it exists. I believe I have no lawful right to do so, and I have no inclination to do so."

He went on to note that Congress had just passed a new constitutional amendment—ironically to be number thirteen—protecting slavery. That amendment had Lincoln's approval: "To the effect that the Federal Government shall never interfere with the domestic institutions of the States, including that of persons held to service . . . I have no objection to its being made express and irrevocable."

Although Americans, North and South, did not want to bring the institution of slavery into the conflict, the British sensed the Civil War's impact on slavery. As early as November 1861, the British journal *Once a Week* made this observation about what was happening:

> The planters are restless about their homes and property, as winter approaches. The slaves have been left quite long enough to the care of women and old men and boys; and every week adds to the alarms about negro-risings, as more of them disappear from the estates, and as newspapers vanish from the tables of country houses, and tidings from the seat of war spread through the negro quarter almost before they are known in the mansion. In the expectation of a great day coming, numbers of negroes have secretly learned to read. . . . Every in-

telligent slave tells of preparations making by his late comrades to join the Federal army as soon as it appears.[3]

In a sense, the emancipation of the slaves in America came from the slaves themselves, not from the whites, Lincoln, or the North. It was a grassroots movement of an unusual kind. As the African slaves lost their native language and ways (including slavery in Africa) and absorbed Western ways, they also acquired the Western longing for freedom from servitude. The yearning to be free was gaining strength and energy just as the whites in the North and the South were engaging each other in mortal combat. The disruption of the slave system was taking place whether or not the North or the South wanted it. Slavery was doomed. The emancipation of the slaves had become the "sign of the times," and no society could hold back the force for emancipation any more than it could hold back the Mississippi River.

But a serious drawback in America was what Professor Don Livingston of Emory University calls "Negrophobia," which infected the North as well as the South, judging by the Northern black codes. If emancipated slaves stayed in the South and continued as paid workers and farmhands, that was fine, but as free citizens there was nothing to prevent them from emigrating North. The Dred Scott decision pointed out all the unacceptable consequences of freeing the black population, especially their having the right to bear arms, as provided in the Second Amendment to the Constitution. Freed slaves with arms had butchered whites in the West Indies to the point of extermination. Furthermore, how would states along the Southern border cope with such a massive influx of poor, illiterate former slaves? Would they destroy free labor? Pillage and plunder the countryside? This fear turned most Northerners away from the abolitionist movement.

Negrophobia was not entirely irrational. The slaughter of whites by blacks had often accompanied slave uprisings in the Americas, not far from home. There were over eighty such uprisings in the Caribbean alone from 1805 to 1850, including eleven in Cuba. But the worst were in Haiti, where the French Revolution brought liberty, equality, and fraternity to black slaves. Once freedom was announced, the ex-slaves sought revenge. A British naval officer who witnessed the Haitian Revolution, as it was called, reported that these angry slaves raped, tortured, and killed whites and destroyed their property, houses, and plantations. The leader of the vengeful blacks ordered his men to kill white men in any fashion they chose: "Some they shot having tied them from fifteen to twenty together. Some they pricked to death with their bayonets, and others they tortured in such a manner too horrid to describe."[4] When this report made it to the Americas, the federal government declared an embargo on all goods from Haiti.

Napoleon responded with 45,000 troops to restore order in Haiti and to restore white rule. When his troops failed to stop the revolution, they too suffered death, from disease as well as from enraged freed slaves. After slaughtering Napoleon's forces, the angry blacks sought out any remaining whites. When it was all over, the 20,000 whites living on the island were dead—the modern world's first genocide, a super antiwhite ethnic cleansing. It paved the way for a pure black society, which, for a time, was the hope of enslaved blacks everywhere.

This servile revolution and its outrageous slaughter of the whites made a bad mark for emancipation everywhere, and it was almost thirty years before the abolition movement got started again, beginning in Britain. De Tocqueville, a Frenchman, knew too well what had happened in Haiti and wrote that when the blacks are in the majority, the whites will be exterminated.

Violent slave uprisings continued to occur throughout the Caribbean islands, but they were nothing like the Haitian event. Granted that emancipation must take place, as more and more people in Western civilization believed, how could the horrors of Haiti be guarded against? In time, experience showed the way, as black insurrections disappeared after emancipation in all the British West Indies. But that didn't quiet the rabble rousers, nor the fears of white Americans, Northern and Southern.

The following etching (fig. 9.1) vividly depicts what the blacks did to Napoleon's 45,000 troops that tried to restore order to Haiti and reinstate the white planter class. Was there a message for America?

To protect themselves from the dangers posed by free blacks, nonslave states began early in the nineteenth century to pass laws against black immigrants from slave states. These black codes, as they were called, showed up in the South after the Civil War, but they began in the North. Indiana and Ohio's statutes were typical: No free Negroes were allowed to enter the state or own property in the state. Illinois used a different approach. Blacks could come if they posted a $1,000 bond. There were laws against blacks assembling "for the purpose of dancing or reveling" that carried a $20 fine. Illinois had a tradition, dating back to its territorial period, of restrictive and exclusionary legislation against blacks, culminating in the 1853 black law that in effect barred black people from residing in the state, the "most severe anti-Negro measure passed in a free state."[5] Lincoln never spoke out against this law. Oregon, a latecomer to the Union, in its 1859 constitution prohibited blacks from coming into the state, holding property, even making contracts or filing a lawsuit. Since these prohibitions were provisions in the Oregon Constitution, the legislature could not repeal them. The prohibitions included mulattos as well as blacks.

It wasn't just the border states that suffered from Negrophobia. In Con-

Figure 9.1. Revenge taken by the emancipated blacks against Napoleon's French army sent to reconquer Haiti. French troops failed and the former slaves slaughtered all the whites remaining on the island. Any zeal for the emancipation of blacks anywhere died for decades to follow.

necticut, Prudence Crandall, a Quaker, set up a small school to educate black children. It was against the law to do so, and she went to jail. When the leader of the abolition movement, William Garrison, held a meeting in Boston and distributed his publication, the *Liberator,* a lynch mob formed and he barely escaped with his life. In Illinois, another abolitionist, Elijah Lovejoy, was not so lucky. Four times his abolitionist newspaper was attacked and his presses destroyed. The mob finally got fed up with his persistent advocacy of the abolitionist cause. The last time they wrecked Lovejoy's newspaper they also murdered him.

Throughout the North where blacks were able to reside they were not permitted to attend the theater, be admitted to hospitals, or attend school. The death rate for blacks in Philadelphia from 1820 to 1830 was twice as high as for whites. Free blacks were shunned with much more pertinacity than in the South, where blacks mixed more freely with whites. De Tocqueville wrote in 1830, after his travels and study of American society, that the Southern people were "much more tolerant and compassionate" toward blacks than were Northerners. In the words of the *North British Review* in 1862, "free Negroes are treated like lepers" in the North.[6] Another British correspondent, who traveled to America to learn about the attitudes in both the North and South toward the conflict, wrote in an article entitled "The Outlook of the War"[7]:

> Everybody still professes to disapprove of slavery. "Of course," so the cant of the day runs, "slavery is a very dreadful thing, and everybody, the South above all, would be glad to see it abolished; but slavery has nothing to do with the present war. The North dislikes the negro even more than the South does. . . . He is out of court, and any attempt to get up sympathy on his behalf is irrelevant to the present question."

Negrophobia also found expression among the leaders of the North, including Abraham Lincoln. This racial fear can be traced to the Founders. Jefferson expressed what most Americans believed: "Nothing is more clearly written in the book of destiny than the emancipation of the blacks, and it is equally certain that the two races will never live in a state of equal freedom under the same government, so insurmountable are the barriers which nature, habit, and opinion have established between them."[8] This point of view was dominant when the Civil War started. Like Jefferson, Lincoln did not believe in racial mixing, nor in the ability of the races to live with one another in harmony. The solution? Expulsion.

British writers all condemned expulsion partly because it deprived Southern agriculture of workers, slave or free. But what this radical scheme does show is the intensity of Negrophobia in the North—of the belief in the impossibility of the two races living together as citizens with equal rights and freedoms. The plight of the free blacks in the North since the founding of the republic confirms this belief and fear. Ironically, contemporary support for the separation of the races comes from a black movement, the Nation of Islam, and its leader, Louis Farrakhan.

Many black leaders in America during the nineteenth century favored emigration to a place where blacks could develop their own nation and society and ennoble the black race. It had become clear that in America they had no future in the North or the South. For a time Frederick Douglass was attracted to the idea of a massive black emigration to Haiti, and the Haitian government offered to accept America's blacks. It was at this time that the Mormons, who could find no justice or acceptance in the Northern states, left for the wilderness of what was Mexican territory in 1846, far removed from a hostile United States. The blacks had similar hopes long before the Mormons.

One prominent black leader, James Holly, wrote a remarkable book trying to promote the emigration of blacks to Haiti. Faced with overwhelming inequality in all of America, the black man, he said, had lost confidence in himself: "And the result is, that many of the race themselves, are almost persuaded that they are a brood of inferior beings."[9]

The prospects for blacks to emigrate to a new land without white domination provided a chance to revive the black man's confidence in himself, a confidence stolen from him during the three hundred years of enslavement. America offered no such hope, and even the abolitionists failed to stand up and be counted among those advocating full equality. There was, in short, no hope in the lifetime of America's blacks in the nineteenth century to ever achieve these ends. Emigration, however, did offer hope within the lifetime of the current generation. Thus some blacks wanted to leave American society, just as the whites wanted them to go. Hardly a setting for goodwill and racial assimilation. A massive emigration of almost 4 million people, however, was not feasible. A few thousand Mormons could pack their belongings in wagon trains and go west; millions of blacks had no place to go. A few could and did, but 99 percent were stuck in America's racial gulag.

Emancipation in the Northern states came easy—too easy. In 1788, New York prohibited the importation of slaves. Eleven years later, in 1799, a more decisive measure was taken to eliminate slavery. All children born to slaves after July 4, 1799, were to be free. Sounds like a good idea; Jefferson thought so. Except there was one catch. By declaring that the children of slaves were free, slaves lost a large percentage of their market value, since their posterity was no longer part of the bargain. The Northern slave owner had to ship his slaves to the auctions in the South in order to receive full value. This policy of emancipation throughout the North had the effect of sending all the blacks to the South and draining Northern societies of future black citizens. It was also in these early postrevolutionary times that black codes were adopted to promote a kind of nineteenth-century "racial cleansing." Massive emancipation, as proposed by the abolitionists, obviously threatened the status of whites in the North. No wonder William

Garrison and his small but vociferous abolitionist group were mobbed and murdered. They were persona non grata in the extreme. Lincoln had to live with this, and his crackpot emigration scheme no doubt was what the majority of Americans in the North wanted. No Negroes welcome here.

One British periodical (1 February 1862) carried an article about Lincoln's colonization scheme:

> He [Lincoln] tries to accommodate himself to the vulgar prejudice of colour by taking for granted that the negroes must all go away somewhere. He openly declares that he hopes the free blacks will go away with the slaves, and he holds this out as the great recommendation of the [emancipation] plan to the citizens of the North. . . . The people are, by Congress, to give money to buy a territory somewhere, outside of their own country; and there the four millions of slaves are to be transported, with as many free blacks as can be induced or compelled to go with them. There they are to be colonised, at the expense, and by the care of the people of the United States. Such is Mr. Lincoln's pretended scheme. . . . The four millions of negroes would be carried away from shelter and food, to be set down in a wilderness to starve. . . . [This] looks like insanity.[10]

The attitude in the North explains correspondence that Lincoln received from his commander of the armies, "Fighting Joe" Hooker, on the Emancipation Proclamation. Wrote General Hooker, "A large element of the army had taken sides against it, declaring that they would never have embarked in the war had they anticipated this action of the government." The army, observed one historian, "which was strongly anti-abolition, was demoralized."[11]

General Hooker wasn't the only military man to speak out against emancipation as an objective of the war. All accounts from the army uniformly indicate that the soldiers who fought the battles had no stomach for the emancipation of slaves. "Let it be understood," said an educated and respected colonel of a regiment that had seen hard service, "let it be understood that [if] this is a war for emancipation of the Negro, instead of a war in defense of the Constitution, three quarters of the army would lay down their arms."[12]

This Northern hostility to emancipation explains Lincoln's rebuke of General Fremont in August 1861, when Fremont emancipated the slaves in his theater of operations, Missouri. Fremont also ordered any civilian found with arms to be tried by a military tribunal and then shot. Lincoln had to cancel both orders and return the slaves to their masters. Fremont immediately went to Washington and sent his wife to the White House late one evening to demand an immediate audience with the president. Lincoln expressed to her his disapproval of Fremont's attempted emancipation order: "It was a war for a great national idea—the Union, and General Fremont should not have dragged the Negro into it."[13] Lincoln had enough problems with stirring up Negrophobia in the North, which Fremont's order would have stimulated. Fremont was relieved of his command.

Fremont wasn't the only general to attempt emancipation. Simon Cameron, secretary of war, wanted to arm blacks. Lincoln objected because, in his words, "I did not yet think it an indispensable necessity." Later, in May 1862, General David Hunter attempted another emancipation in the states of Georgia, Florida, and South Carolina. Again Lincoln forbade it.[14] The American ambassador to France wrote home to Secretary of State Seward, explaining the negative impact of Lincoln's firing of Fremont and of the canceling of his emancipation order. No doubt this found its way to the president's ear, and he then realized that notwithstanding Northern apathy and opposition, emancipation as an objective of the war would do much to enhance the Northern cause abroad and undermine the cause of the South.

In September 1862, Lincoln promulgated the Emancipation Proclamation as a war measure. Emancipation would take place only in the rebel states, if after one hundred days the South didn't surrender. He limited this to the rebel states, thus giving the border states the right to work out their own emancipation, preferably with compensation, European style. Throughout history from ancient slavery to recent serfdom, the process of emancipation had been a process known as *manumission*—the grant or purchase of freedom. Lincoln, like most sensible abolitionists, accepted the requirement of compensation. In Britain's colonies, compensation was paid, and slave labor became free market labor. When Lincoln finally named unqualified emancipation as an object of the war in his 1864 re-election campaign, support from Europe increased and the Southern cause was doomed.

THE ABOLITIONIST

Some historians have difficulty with Lincoln's less-than-enthusiastic support for the Abolitionists. When asked if it was all right to have Abolitionists in the Republican party, he replied in the affirmative, "as long as I am not painted with the Abolitionist brush."[15] If Lincoln abhorred slavery, and he did, why repudiate those wanting to root it out of the nation? Yet it is no small wonder Lincoln did not want to be "painted with the Abolitionist brush." The Abolitionist organization was extremely harmful to the cause of emancipation. A few year before, Daniel Webster and Supreme Court Justice Joseph Story, and others, condemned the Abolition Society, and so did the powerful abolition societies and movements in Europe. What was wrong with America's movement? According to Webster and Story the Abolitionists worsened the plight of the slaves and created hostility and distrust among both Northern and Southern peoples.[16]

Worst of all, the Abolitionists in America can be blamed for destroying any chance of Southern support for emancipation and did much to add fuel to the fire of secession. It was impossible to persuade the planters to teach their slaves to read when the Northern Abolitionists were smuggling into the South inflammatory tracts urging slaves to slit the throats of their masters, as well as other criminal acts and violence. Even the demand for immediate emancipation was insane—turning millions of slaves loose on society without any thought of how they were to survive, let alone be accepted in a free society. No compensation was provided either, as the Europeans had done.

The leaders of the Abolition Society were fanatics of the worst sort who advocated getting rid of slavery by slaughtering every person in the South. John Brown was typical. Over a period of five years, he had made a number of violent attacks on proslavery forces in turbulent Kansas Territory. A few deaths were attributable to him. Finally, in the summer of 1859, he developed his scheme to seize the federal arsenal at Harpers Ferry. He expected the slaves to rise up in a great rebellion that would spread throughout the South, but they didn't. Most people at the time considered Brown mad. There was an attempt to have his murder charges dropped on the grounds of insanity, but a jury found him guilty and he was hanged on 2 December 1859.

Once the Civil War took up the cause of emancipation, Brown became a martyr and the "Battle Hymn of the Republic" acquired new verses: "John Brown's body lies a-mouldering in his grave, But his soul is marching on." In New York, a minister, Reverend W. J. Sloane, pastor of the Third Reformed Presbyterian Church, was reported in the newspapers to have said, "That it was better that the six millions of white men, women and children in the South should be slaughtered than that slavery should not be extinguished."[17]

In reply to the newspaper editor who condemned the good Reverend for promoting such an atrocity, Reverend Sloane replied, "I affirm that it is better, far better, that every man, woman, and child in every rebel State should perish in one widespread, bloody, and indiscriminate slaughter; better that the land should be a Sahara; be as when God destroyed the Canaanites, or overthrew Sodom and Gomorrah, than that this rebellion should be successful."[18] Numerous other Christian ministers expressed the same genocidal fervor.[19] Such fanatical thinking was far removed from Lincoln's moderate view, when he said, "I will proclaim emancipation entirely, or partially, or not at all, according to whichever of these measures shall seem to me best for the Union."[20]

Shortly thereafter Lincoln issued his Emancipation Proclamation, commenting, "I can only trust in God I have made no mistake." Nine days before, he obviously had serious doubts when he made this strange remark to a representative from the city of Chicago. He objected to issuing an emancipation order on the grounds "that the whole world would see it to be necessarily as inoperative as the Pope's bull against a comet."[21]

The abolition movement took form in 1833, when the British were abolishing slavery throughout the British empire. The American Anti-Slavery Society was founded in Philadelphia, led by William Lloyd Garrison. A weekly newspaper was circulated from 1835 to 1865. The paper denounced even the Constitution. In 1854, an angry group of abolitionists in Massachusetts called that revered document "a covenant with death and an agreement with hell." The group then burned the Constitution (reminiscent of modern flag burners). Garrison then proclaimed, "So perish all compromises with tyranny." Remember, this occurred during a time when America had great reverence for both the flag and the Constitution, so the abolitionists were easily repudiated and held in contempt by most Americans, North or South.

The reader should not look upon the abolitionists as favoring equal rights for blacks. Getting rid of slavery was fine, but then what? One abolitionist, Hinton Helper, wrote of a solution in his *The Impending Crisis of the South: How to Meet It* (New York, 1857). He suggested chartering every vessel in America, herding all blacks onto those vessels after abolition, and shipping them off to Africa in one vast armada. It did not occur to Helper that many would not want to go. And what would happen to them? What would they do, how would they live when dumped on Africa's coast? And what about the Africans who were there—would they receive them? Tolerate them? But with American whites and American laws treating the blacks as an inferior race, what other solutions were there?

How was the emancipation of approximately 800,000 slaves by the British in 1834 received in America? And why didn't America see the signs of the times? Editorials in the *New York Herald* claimed that "Jamaica is ruined" and "Negro unfit for freedom," and that "the downfall of prosperity and the loss of trade" from the former British slave colonies was inevitable. After all, the only other emancipation in the West Indies was in Haiti, and look at what happened there. Once the most prosperous island in all the West Indies, the economic jewel of France, Haiti moved from being the most economically advanced and the most prosperous of all the West Indies to being the poorest and the most tyrannical, as black strongmen battled for the right to rule and exploit their own black brothers. Americans had good reason to believe that "Jamaica is ruined."

Jamaica, as it turned out, was not ruined. Blacks did not rise up and slaughter whites in revenge but formed a free society; soon blacks made up the majority of civil servants in the British colonial government. Land was opened up for the blacks to own. In one year, 40,000 land patents were issued to them for from ten to one hundred acres. Schools were introduced. But most important, unlike Haiti, the whole country was redeemed from slave insurrections, and a reign of slave terror ceased. Jamaica, not Haiti, became the example for the Americans. With land, education, and opportunities in the civil service, blacks transcended slavery and ran society as well as the whites did. But America did not take notice, or did not want to.

Contrast the American abolitionist movement with the British movement, which successfully lobbied emancipation through Parliament in 1833—emancipation legislation that ended all slavery in the British colonies. The movement was mainstream and was willing to compensate the slave owners, at great expense to the taxpayers; provide land for the ex-slave; and provide education. All America had to do was follow the British example but didn't. Lincoln hoped to have the same policy effect emancipation in America as he urged the border states in 1862 to end slavery by compensating the owners. But America's abolitionists wanted no such thing. When Lincoln made his appeal for the compensation of slave owners, he was bucking his powerful secretary of state, William Seward, who had been expected to be the Republican candidate for the presidency. After he was appointed to the most powerful cabinet post, he thought that he would really run the government—that Lincoln's presidency would be like the British monarchy run by the prime minister. As a powerful senator, he addressed the Southern senators angrily:

> Compensation to slaveowners for their negroes! Preposterous idea! The suggestion is criminal—the demand wicked, unjust, monstrous, damnable! Shall we pat the bloodhound for the sake of doing them a favour? Shall we feed the curs of slavery to make them rich at our expense? Pay *these welps* for the privilege of converting them into decent, honest upright men?[22]

The abolitionists attacked the slave owners as barbarians, torturers, and Simon Legrees (from *Uncle Tom's Cabin*). Again, William Seward, as a senator, said to the senators from the South:

Frown, sirs! fret, foam, prepare your weapons, threat, strike, shoot, stab, bring on civil war, dissolve the Union! dissolve the Union! nay, annihilate the solar system, if you will! Do all this — more, less, worse, better, anything — do what you will sirs, you can neither foil nor intimidate us: our purpose is as fixed as the eternal pillars of heaven; we have determined to abolish slavery, and, so help us God! abolish it we will![23]

Lincoln was for ending slavery, but not by the call to arms that the abolitionists were demanding. He appears to be very much in tune with the European approach — moderate, sensible, and fully aware that emancipation required introducing the former slaves into society in an atmosphere conducive to their being accepted and being capable of taking care of themselves. The key to this, Lincoln knew, would be the slaves' former masters, who now would become their employers. Goodwill was necessary, and, like it or not, just compensation would be required to achieve that end. In February 1865, at an attempted peace conference in Hampton Roads, Lincoln told the Confederate vice president, Alexander Stephens, that the "people of the North were as responsible for slavery as the people of the South." If the war should cease with the voluntary abolition of slavery, he would be willing to institute a tax on the nation to compensate slave owners — "a fair indemnity."[24] Lincoln's assassination ended that.

The abolitionists were so blind in their hatred that they enthusiastically endorsed secession, which was everything Lincoln was against. It is no small wonder Lincoln didn't want to be "painted with the Abolitionist brush."

Whereas Lincoln was a realist, the abolitionists were on the lunatic fringe. It was this fanaticism that so angered and enraged the South, and it also drove most Northerners away from the serious matter of working out a prudent emancipation policy. Unfortunately, the South wasn't at all interested in any massive plan of emancipation, and the North wasn't up to any help in that regard — and that meant trouble. Yet slavery was doomed.

The reaction of the Southerners was polarized by the superradical abolitionists, and America began to develop an excess of fanatics on the slave issue, unlike the rest of the world that quietly set about abolishing slavery without any great conflict, violence, or call to arms. These rational and peaceful abolition movements were effective throughout the European world as slavery slipped into history. But in America the North and the South were not up to the task. Chided one British newspaper, the *Ashton and Stalybridge Reporter* (21 January 1863), "It was anything for Union and nothing for the slave with President Lincoln, as shown by his desire to restore the Union even with slaves in the South. If they loved the Negroes so strongly in the Northern States, why not allow them to travel, eat or worship with them?"

The editor was apparently unaware that in some of the states, blacks were not even permitted to take up residence. But such antiresidency laws would not be very effective if 100,000 ex-slaves suddenly poured across the border. In January 1861, Texas congressman John Reagan raised this sobering question about abolition, speaking to the Congress:

> Suppose these slaves were liberated; suppose the people of the South would today voluntarily surrender $3,000,000,000 of slave property, and send their slaves at their expense into the free States, would you accept them as freemen and citizens of your States? You dare not answer me that you would. You would fight us with all your energy and power for twenty years, before you would submit to it. And yet you demand us to liberate them, to surrender this $3,000,000,000 of slave property, to ruin our commercial and political prospects for the future.

Few were willing to support emancipation without some solution to the many problems it raised. The Texas congressman addressed the Negrophobia problem as well: "Now, suppose you succeed in striking down African slavery in the United States: you strike down not only our prosperity in the South, and inaugurate instead all the horrors of Africanized barbarism under which the French and British West India colonies now suffer."[25]

These words and their warning did not go unnoticed in the North and explain why most Northerners wanted no part of the South's slavery problem. The cure to them seemed worse than the disease—and it was, for the moment.

EMANCIPATION PROCLAMATION

On 20 February 1863, the *Manchester Guardian* condemned the Emancipation Proclamation: "To the few surviving chiefs of that great anti-slavery struggle in England [1834], and the representatives of those who are gone, will have nothing to do with the hypocritical adoption of their cherished principles as a pretext in the last resort for further shedding of human blood."

In 1963, the U.S. Postal Service issued a five-cent stamp for regular postage, which commemorated the Emancipation Proclamation of President Lincoln, as if it had ended slavery in the United States. Unfortunately, it was not the glorious civil rights document it was held up to be by later generations. On 22 September 1862, Lincoln warned the world that on 1 January 1863, emancipation would go into effect. He thus gave the Confederacy a little over three months to surrender and keep their slaves or face enforced emancipation if they continued their war for secession from the Union. Although the Constitution left the matter of slavery for the states and thus denied the federal government the right to interfere, Lincoln felt that he could bypass the Constitution by emancipating under his power as commander in chief of the military. This was within his war powers, or so he believed. Many lawyers and scholars disagreed. Here are the exact words of the Proclamation:

> I, Abraham Lincoln, President of the United States of America, and Commander-in-Chief of the Army and Navy thereof, do hereby proclaim and declare that hereafter, as heretofore, the war will be prosecuted for the object of practically restoring the constitutional relation between the United States and the people thereof, in which States that relation is, or may be, suspended or disturbed; and that, with this object, "on the 1st day of January, 1863, all persons held as slaves within any State, or any designated part of a State, the people whereof shall then be in rebellion against the United States, shall be then, thenceforward, and for ever, free."

Secretary Seward spoke for the Emancipation Proclamation: "All the good and wise men of all countries," would approve of the proclamation as "a just and proper military act." In fact, there were few if any "wise men" in Europe who saw it that way, and just as few in the North. The abolitionists saw it as a fraud, as it only applied to the territory over which the North had no control. It was, thus, an illusion. The army hated it and it is a wonder there was no mutiny. The Democratic leadership hated it, even though they strongly supported the war and its objective of preserving the Union at all costs. And in Europe, it was looked upon with utter horror, even though all Europeans favored emancipation. Why did this document, which is so revered today, stir up such a hornet's nest of anger in 1862–1863? What was wrong with it?

The November 1862 issue of London's *Blackwood's Magazine* (p. 640) had this explanation: "It was the most atrocious act of war-policy ever adopted by a civilized state." And yet this magazine, like all periodicals in Europe, was strongly for emancipation. Why the contempt?

As early as December 1861, after General Fremont issued the first such proclamation, Charles Dickens explained the reason for condemnation. It would set off a slave uprising: "Such a servile war would be indeed, if

Figure 9.2. A critical view of the Emancipation Proclamation in an etching by Adalbert Volck in 1864. With his foot on the Constitution, Lincoln nevertheless signs the document that the Constitution would not permit. On the wall is a picture of the slave insurrection in Haiti that exterminated the white population. Also on the wall is a picture of John Brown with a halo. The proclamation was a war measure designed to promote a slave rebellion in the South. Or at least that is how most foreigners saw it. Its humanitarianism, as well as its legality, was doubtful under the circumstances.

successfully instituted, too dreadful to be deliberately thought of. . . . Arms, if put in their hands, might possibly be turned against their masters in a way little short of extermination." General McClellan, who became the Democratic candidate for president in 1864, said he could not be a party to "such an accursed doctrine of servile insurrection." It appeared to most observers to call for the arming of the black population throughout the South. With the farms and plantations in the charge of women, juveniles, and old folks, the prospects of putting down such an insurrection were small indeed. Lincoln, facing the wrath and disapproval of a large segment of civilized thinking, deleted from his early draft of the proclamation language calling for a violent uprising.

In Europe, the proclamation encouraged talk of intervention because of the fear of the human slaughter a massive slave uprising could produce. Lincoln justified his emancipation as a war policy to disrupt the Southern economy and war effort. Obviously, a slave uprising, with its conse-

Slaves revolt, massacre owners, and sack plantations of the North. *Library of Congress*

Figure 9.3. Servile Insurrection. This etching in the Library of Congress depicts a slave uprising with blacks slaughtering whites. Southerners and many Northerners, as well as Europeans, were concerned that this could possibly be one of the dangerous consequences of uncontrolled emancipation, especially when Lincoln's proclamation included no controls. It was fraught with terrible dangers to Southern whites.

quences, would do just that. The toning down of the wording came in anticipation of the growing condemnation by European writers and their governments, as well as among many Americans. Emancipation? Yes. A slave uprising? No. Slave uprisings were not a figment of the imagination, as Haiti had proved. John Brown's effort to incite a violent uprising was still fresh in Southern minds, as was the 1831 uprising led by Nat Turner in Virginia; Nat Turner and his band of five members soon grew to fifty-three members. They massacred twenty-four white children, eighteen women, and thirteen men before finally being put to flight by local militiamen.

There were harsh critics of the proclamation in the Democratic party. In Albany, New York, Horatio Seymour, in a speech on the eve of his election as governor of New York, called the proclamation an act of unparalleled atrocity. After sarcastically exposing the hypocrisy of the abolitionists, he acknowledged that Lincoln had now joined their ranks. At least the

Southerners would have the Africans live in America, but the abolitionists, and even Lincoln, wanted them to leave America and live elsewhere. Said the governor to be:

> The scheme for an immediate emancipation and general arming of the slaves throughout the South is a proposal for the butchery of women and children, for scenes of lust and rapine, arson and murder, unparalleled in the history of the world. Its effect would not be confined to the walls of cities, but there would be a widespread scene of horror over the vast expanse of great States, involving alike the loyal and the seditious. Such malignity and cowardice would invoke the interference of civilized Europe. History tells of the fires kindled in the name of religion, of atrocities committed under the pretext of order or liberty; it is now urged that scenes bloodier than the world has yet witnessed shall be enacted in the name of philanthropy.[26]

Governor Seymour was a fanatical Unionist. He was for the Union on any terms and at almost any military cost, but not if it meant a slave uprising with horrendous consequences. Shortly after this speech, he was elected governor of New York; in 1868 he ran as the Democratic candidate for president against Ulysses S. Grant, and lost.

As the war dragged on and its horrible consequences were brought home to the North, many Northerners began to look with favor on anything that would help defeat the tenacious South, even a slave insurrection. As usually happens in wars, hatred for the enemy escalates—especially as the military endeavors drag on and the misery and suffering of the rank and file come home to a civilian population. On the eve of the much expected proclamation, in October 1862, the *North American Review* of Boston reiterated the suffering of Union soldiers and the losses to Boston families; if a servile insurrection took place in the South, so be it:

> It may be that the slaves thus armed will commit some atrocities. We shall regret it. But we repeat, this war has been forced upon us. We have sent to the field our bravest and our best. The idols of happy homes have fallen by hardship, disease, and battle, and deep anguish has come to many a Northern household. . . . We hesitate not to say, that it will be better, immeasurably better, that the rebellion should be crushed, even with the incidental consequences attendant on a servile insurrection, than that the hopes of the world in the capacity of mankind to maintain free institutions should expire with American liberty.[27]

The last sentence is reminiscent of the Gettysburg Address, with Lincoln's concern that government of the people would "perish from the

Earth" if the South seceded. If there ever was a non sequitur in the annals of human warfare, that was it. All the South wanted was to withdraw from the Union and be left alone. How could that threaten the political institutions of the North, or the right of free government? Nevertheless, that fallacious line of thinking persisted. Even a generation after the war, the illusion lived on. In 1881, a popular author of the North wrote a large, six-hundred-page volume on the war and its purposes. He ended the narrative by saying: "The Rebellion was an attempt to suppress Truth and Justice by tyranny."[28]

Eighty years later, in the 1960s, the chancellor of Boston University, Daniel L. Marsh (commenting on an article in *Life* magazine) continued the good guy–bad guy theme from a Northern point of view: "In the Civil War, more nearly than in any other war in all of history, the Right was on one side, and the Wrong was on the other."[29] According to the learned chancellor, the North was right because it was fighting for "liberty and justice for all," whereas the South was fighting for slavocracy and the dissolution of the Union. Falsehoods born of war die hard, if at all.

"WE HAD ABOUT PLAYED OUR LAST CARD"

On the eve of the Emancipation Proclamation, *Punch* magazine published a cartoon (18 October 1862) depicting the proclamation as a desperate last trump card. Lincoln faces Jefferson Davis and plays a black spade bearing the countenance of a black man. Some months later Lincoln picked up on the theme of the British periodicals, and explained his reasons for the proclamation: "Things had gone from bad to worse, until I felt we had reached the end of our rope on the plan we were pursuing; that we had about played our last card, and must change our tactics or lose the game. I now determined upon the adoption of the emancipation policy."[30]

Emancipation, to be successful, requires the will of the dominant class to integrate into society a people who lack even the most basic means of taking care of themselves. In America's emancipation, a minimum of effort was provided by the conquerors, and they were outsiders and bitter enemies of the people. No wonder emancipation was such a disaster. Even Lincoln had no awareness of what his proclamation would produce. At an unsuccessful peace conference in February 1865, the vice president of the Confederacy, Alexander Stephens, asked Lincoln what was to become of the emancipated slaves in the absence of education, wealth, or land. Lincoln replied with a story—a wonderful talent he had to illustrate any point he wanted to make—about an Illinois pig farmer who was telling a neigh-

PUNCH, OR THE LONDON CHARIVARI.— October 18, 1862.

ABE LINCOLN'S LAST CARD; OR, ROUGE-ET-NOIR.

Figure 9.4. A famous *Punch* cartoon showing Lincoln playing his black ace of spaces—the last card he held in his struggle with Jefferson Davis. Lincoln actually referred to his emancipation policy as his "last card."

bor about a great discovery he had made. He'd found a way to economize on the time and labor spent on the food crops for his pigs, which would also feed them in the winter.

"What is it?" asked the neighbor.

"Why, it is," said the pig farmer, "to plant plenty of potatoes, and when they are mature, without either digging or housing them, turn the pigs loose in the field and let them get their own food."

"But," said the neighbor, "how will they do when the winter comes and the ground is hard frozen?"

"Well," said the farmer, "let 'em root!"[31]

Alexander Stephens replied to Lincoln, "That, Mr. President, must be the origin of the adage, 'Root, pig, or perish.' "[32] Hardly a wise or even civilized solution to the problem of emancipating 3.5 million slaves and releasing them into the social order. Contrast Lincoln's "root, pig, or perish" advice on how to deal with emancipated slaves with Robert E. Lee's wisdom on this issue, after the war and after sudden emancipation: "The best men in the South have long desired to do away with the institution, and were quite willing to see it abolished. But with them in relation to this subject the question has been: What will you do with the freed people? That is a serious question today. Unless some humane course, based on wisdom and Christian principles, is adopted, you do them a great injustice in setting them free."[33]

The alternative to starving was pillage, thievery, or a return to the workforce of the former slave economy. Within less than a year after the slaves were freed, the chaos of sudden, unplanned emancipation began to show its ugly results. Hundreds of thousands of black men, most of them without land, without food, without money, and without skills or trades of any kind, did not know what to do. Then came the Republican carpetbaggers. They had the answers. Vote for us. Hate the Southern whites, your former masters, and we will make you masters over them. After all, your labor built the South, and now you can reap the rewards of your labors if you will let us be your guide, your new masters. So went the sales pitch, and it is no wonder the ex-slaves bought it. For a time, it succeeded. But, in the end, not much would change. The Ku Klux Klan would make sure of that.

10

The Ku Klux Klan

I expect to murder every Yankee I ever meet when I can do so with impunity if I live a hundred years and peace is made in six months. Peace will never be made between me and any Yankee if I can kill him without too great risk.

Sergeant Edwin Fay, Confederate cavalry
10 July 1863, letter to his wife

Historians have noticed that the seeds of the next war are often planted by the army of occupation of the last war. This is easy to understand. An enemy force runs amok among a conquered people. Rape, pillage, and theft are almost unrestrained. Seldom have the officers of an occupying army been able to restrain their troops from plunder. Then follows an alien bureaucracy to rule over the conquered people, and hatred seethes among those defeated, for here is the enemy that devastated your homeland and killed your friends and relatives. In such a hostile atmosphere there is little chance for civilized behavior. Martial law rules, and army officers with no appreciation for due process of law are quick to maintain order with summary trials often based on faulty evidence or trumped-up charges. In this explosive state, the old conflict can erupt into a new war. History is full of such examples that help us to understand the Ku Klux Klan and to put the Klan in proper perspective.

An underground organization opposed to rule by Northern Republicans and their cohorts was inevitable. Once you disenfranchise a ruling population and superimpose a new government composed of enemy aliens of the past, an underground will develop to frustrate the alien rules and to set the stage for a new uprising, if necessary, to return to power those who had ruled in the past. A conquered people seldom remain conquered for long. Sometimes they do rise up in revolt a second time and a third time, and even again, in their struggle for independence, but often, as with the South, they work out an accommodation and return to power, making an uprising unnecessary.

The South was a scene of devastation. Cities lay in ruins, banks were gone, Confederate money was worthless, railways had been torn up, crops and farms destroyed, and, worst of all, the labor force was in a state of chaos. The women of the South mourned the loss of their husbands, brothers, and sons, and the streets were filled with disabled veterans as well as those who were still able but had no place to go, nothing to do. Desperation was everywhere. The emancipation of slaves meant that there were hundreds of thousands of black men without land, without food, without money, and without skills and trades of any kind. They too were at a loss to know where to go and what to do. Some went back to their old plantations and masters, wanting work and sustenance. Many loafed about their old cabins while others gathered around Yankee military posts, living on scraps of food, garbage, and rations; still others roamed about the countryside, scavenging for food and beginning to realize that their freedom looked more like a freedom to starve.

Then there was the plight of slaves who had fled the South and joined the Federal armies and fought against the Confederacy. It would have been better for everyone if they had gone North with the withdrawing Union army, but that wasn't an option because of the black codes that forbade their residency in many Northern states; besides, their homes and families were in the South. So they went back to the South, over 100,000 of them. To the ex-Confederates, these men who had waged war against the South were marked men, who in time would be hunted down for punishment and lynching. Like the Russians who joined Vlasov's army in World War II and fought against Russia, they were despised traitors. The Soviets summarily executed most of their traitors, and even the civilian Russian society held them in utter contempt. Southerners who had tolerated blacks for centuries had no tolerance for those who had joined the Federal army and fought and killed Southerners.

One group of ex-Confederate soldiers, while executing vengeance against an ex-slave (a member of what was called the USCT—United States Colored Troops), "swore they meant to kill every black son-of-a-bitch they could find that had ever fought against them."[1] And they did. There were more lynchings in 1866 than in any other year.[2]

The defeat of the South was so complete and the devastation, physically and economically, was so extensive that there was no chance of its rebuilding its military forces. There was no chance that the South could go to war again and fight for its independence.

There are many historical examples that have surprising similarities with the defeat of the South and military occupation by the conquerors. In the zenith of Roman rule, there arose secret underground societies that set off major revolts within the Roman Empire — revolts for independence. We do not have many facts concerning the revolts in Britain and in Gaul (France), but we know much more about the underground zealots in Judea, who preyed on the conquering Romans and their carpetbaggers, and finally took over the country. More Jewish uprisings followed, but the rebels lost in the end. In the American colonies the Sons of Liberty threatened British loyalists with death and carried out wanton destruction of government and private property. They are esteemed as heroes today, but they were terrorists in their time. Cartoons in London often depicted them as fiends. Lawlessness, assaults (tar and feathering), and death threats were their stock in trade, and in the end they drove thousands of loyalists to emigrate to Canada and abandon their farms, lands, houses, and businesses.

The name Sons of Liberty showed up during the Whiskey Rebellion in 1794, and even in the Civil War, but we cannot equate the Civil War Sons of Liberty with the Revolutionary group, just as we cannot equate the Ku Klux Klan of our century with the Klan of the Reconstruction era.

The guerrilla organizations that were organized by the defeated Southerners never had any serious thoughts about organizing a military force to fight for independence. The horrors of the war and the devastation and loss of life were so extensive that another war for independence clearly would not succeed.

In the South the underground secret society that soon came into being was the Ku Klux Klan, but there were other similar underground societies, such as the Knights of the White Camellia and the White League, all carrying a strong message of white supremacy, which was under threat by the conquering forces in the North. The white population in the South saw the incoming Northern occupying forces and bureaucrats as hell-bent on destroying the establishment in the South and instituting a new government with the ex-slaves providing the voting power to make that possible, and they saw and feared that these ex-slaves, with the help of Northern carpetbaggers, would gain control of Southern society, as the final lasting defeat of the war. To the white population this was an intolerable prospect, and one of the main purposes of these underground societies was to keep that scenario from ever playing itself out.

The Ku Klux Klan happened by chance. It came into being as a kind of fraternal group organized by a small group of Confederate veterans on Christmas Eve, 1865. They adopted a Greek style of name, as is common with college fraternities, *Kuklos* meaning a circle that has no beginning or end. Their Scottish heritage taught them reverence for one's clan, and they substituted a K for the C. At that time in America there were many secret orders, with secret hand shakes, signs, and passwords, and often with blood-curdling oaths to keep the secrets and never reveal them, even under threat of death. The mountain people of Appalachia had their signs and oaths to protect themselves from the Confederate military draft. Other societies of a religious nature, like the Masons and even the Mormon Church, had similar secret signs to create a solidarity within their society.

The Klan developed some fancy names for its leaders and required an oath of allegiance that set forth a statement of principles:

> This is an institution of Chivalry, Humanity, Mercy, and Patriotism; embodying in its genius and its principles all that is chivalric in conduct, noble in sentiment, generous in manhood, and patriotic in purpose; its peculiar objects being
>
> First: To protect the weak, the innocent, and the defenseless, from the indignities, wrongs, and outrages of the lawless, the violent, and the brutal; to relieve the injured and oppressed; to succor the suffering and unfortunate, and especially the widows and orphans of Confederate soldiers.
>
> Second: To protect and defend the Constitution of the United States, and all laws passed in conformity thereto, and to protect the States and the people thereof from all invasions from any source whatever.
>
> Third: To aid and assist in the execution of all constitutional laws, and to protect the people from unlawful seizure, and from trial except by their peers in conformity to the laws of the land.

In the beginning, the Klan was organized to have fun, and the young ex-soldiers raided their linen closets and masqueraded in simple costumes. They then rode on their horses to the houses of family and sweethearts in a night serenade. Black people who saw these strange horsemen thought they were the ghosts of Confederate soldiers from nearby battlefields and cemeteries. This intimidation was great fun, but it also caused many blacks to turn away from lawlessness, and many of the idle ones returned to the fields in which they had once worked. Superstition and fear often go hand in hand, and in this instance it was not men they feared but ghosts.

Within a year after the Klan organized as a fraternal society with recreational and social ends, men from the North with hostile ideas and plans were flocking into the South, even before the war ended, on the heels of Union armies. After the war they came first as tax collectors. This prompted the Klan's first political venture—to defeat the hated cotton tax and the thieves masquerading as federal tax agents. Then came the Union League, an organization based in Philadelphia and New York, with political ambitions. Without much success in the North, they decided to switch their efforts to the South and achieve power through the black vote and with former black Union soldiers, who had been fully indoctrinated to hate Southerners, whites, or blacks loyal to Southern society. It was a marriage that would make the KKK a necessity for the survival of Southern civilization.

These Union Leaguers—supported by a new militia of ex-black Union soldiers—moved into the plantations, cities, towns, and villages, seeking out blacks. The illiterate and simple-minded freedmen were easy victims of their guile. Hate the whites. Hate your former masters. Vote for us and we will divide the spoils of the South with you. The blacks were incited to treat the whites with contempt. One black speaker said to a group that within ten years the problem would be what the blacks would do with the Southern whites. The game plan was to establish secret clubs "in every township in the South" for the ex-slaves to rise to political power over the Southern whites. There followed night meetings, flamboyant ceremonies, solemn oaths, and passwords, to arouse the blacks. Then followed incendiary speeches from the Northern politicians promising to confiscate the white man's land for the blacks and telling them they had a perfect right to take any foodstuffs they needed. In the end, many of those enticed by the Union Leaguers refused to work and pillaged the countryside, meandering about threatening passing whites. Soon the whites became gravely fearful. A lady from a Georgia plantation saw nothing but tragedy ahead by the carpetbaggers "exciting the negroes to every kind of insolent lawlessness."[3] Servile insurrections had a history of erupting after emancipation. The ex-slaves began threatening whites, for they had discovered that freedom wasn't of much value if you were hungry and homeless. And since no real plan had been developed to raise the blacks from servitude to self-sufficiency, it is no wonder that a spirit of arrogance was awakened, even a spirit of revolution.

In North Carolina alone, the clubs of the Union League of ex-slaves had 80,000 members, in Louisiana 57,300 members. Some organized into military companies, drilling by day and night. They were armed, and white people lived in constant fear. Thus by 1867 ex-slaves had consolidated all over the South, with Yankee leadership and enticements to turn on their former masters with the plan and expectation that the wealth and power of the South would be in their hands—those on the top a few years ago would be on the bottom, or so it was anticipated.

The Union Leaguers, supported by black militiamen, started an intraracial war between the black militia and black Democrats. The sign in an 1878 polling booth, "Death to Colored Democrats," was no idle threat. At a political meeting in the 1868 presidential campaign in Georgia, the following banner was displayed: "every man [negro] that didn't vote the Radical [Republican] ticket, this is the way we want to serve him: hang him by his neck."[4]

Daniel Goodloe, U.S. Marshal for North Carolina for three and a half years, wrote, "I have also heard of combinations of negroes calling themselves Ku Klux and committing outrages [against negroes]. . . . It has been charged that they have mobbed negroes for the [Democratic] ticket."[5] In Mississippi in 1870, the state passed an anti–Ku Klux Klan law, offering a $500 reward for conviction of any person guilty of violent crimes in a disguise. The first claim grew out of the Ku Kluxing of a Democratic negro named Adam Kennard by a group of negroes in Ku Klux disguise.[6]

The most destructive force for the ex-slaves was the conduct of the returning black soldiers in Yankee uniforms. They did more to turn Southern whites against all blacks than did the carpetbaggers and conquering armies of occupation. Few Confederate veterans were able to stomach armed black soldiers patrolling the streets of their hometown, jostling their wives and daughters from the sidewalks and claiming authority over all. One pro-Northern writer had to admit that "the catalogue of 'atrocities' and 'daily outrages' for which black soldiers were responsible seemed endless."[7] A white man who had been arrested and was in jail in Victoria, Texas, was dragged from the jail and lynched; another, in South Carolina, also in jail, was taken by black soldiers, shot, and buried after a "drumhead court-martial" by the black lynch mob. A Georgia woman, Eliza Andrews, said that what appalled her most was not that black soldiers cursed and threatened whites on public streets but that they did so "while hundreds of idle negroes stood around, laughing and applauding it."[8]

In short, by insulting whites in the presence of ex-slaves, black Union soldiers created a dangerous illusion of power and even superiority that would infect the observing ex-slaves. By telling them that they would soon obtain the lands of their former masters, these black soldiers encouraged false expectations and furnished a disincentive to work. Why work when a glorious day of black rule and wealth was just around the corner? This seemed inevitable, with the carpetbaggers telling them so, the black soldiers with military power telling them so, and Union generals and armies camped in their midst. The evidence was everywhere, and they would be fools not to believe it, at least, so it seemed.

The once proud Southerners swallowed these insults and assertions of power—but only for a short season; then the tables would turn and whites would once again return to power. In the meantime, the Klan would come to the aid of the whites and foretell of things to come—the doom of the blacks' expectation of ruling Southern society.

Out of this threat to the white establishment, the Ku Klux Klan turned into a militant, guerrilla order, and its purpose became to reestablish and preserve white rule in the South, and to protect themselves from militant ex-slaves, hell-bent for revenge for generations of servitude. The ex-slaves demanded property rights. Said one Virginia black, "We has a right to the land . . . didn't we clear the land, and raise de crops?" Said a Virginia scalawag, urging the blacks to pillage: "There is corn and wheat and flour and bacon and turkeys and chickens and wood and coal in the State and the colored people will have it before they will starve." The audience of blacks "cheered wildly."[9]

The Klan's violence soon caught the attention of the Congress, and in 1870 a committee investigated its activities. Their report covers thirteen volumes. While condemning the Klan in no uncertain terms, a minority report (seven of the twenty members) put the blame for the lawlessness of the Klan on Northern Reconstruction practices, especially the Union League:

1. The Ku Klux Klan arose as an inescapable consequence of the Union League's brutality.
2. Many of the crimes against black people were committed by Union League men disguised as Klansmen.
3. Had there been no wanton oppression in the South, there would have been no Ku Kluxism. Had there been no rule of the tyrannical, corrupt carpet-bagger or Scalawag (white Southerners supporting Reconstruction for personal gain) rule, there would have been no secret organization.
4. From the oppression and corruption of the one sprang the vice and outrage of the other.

The Congressional report continues with this indictment of Republican rule over the conquered South:

> [The Union League] hatred of the white race was instilled into the minds of these ignorant people by every art and vile that bad men could devise; when the negroes were formed into military organizations and the white people of these states were denied the use of arms; when arson, rape, robbery and murder were things of daily occurrence; when the great mass of the most intelligent whites were disenfranchised and the ballot was put into the hands of the negro by the government in Washington . . . when even the courts were closed and Federal officers, who were by Congress absolute rulers and dispensors of what they called justice, ignored, insulted and trampled upon the rights of the ostracized and disenfranchised white men while the officials pandered to the enfranchised negro on whose vote they rallied, in short, when the people saw that they had no rights which were respected, no protection from insult, no security even for their wives and children, and that what little they had saved from the ravages of war

was being confiscated by taxation . . . many of them took the law into their own hands and did deeds of violence which we neither justify or excuse. But all history shows that bad government will make bad citizens.[10]

Fifty years after the war, a Southern leader who had made his peace with the Union looked back at his years under the Reconstruction governments: "The Freedman's Bureau, established by the Federal Government and supported by the military, officered by the very worst element of [illegible] who had drifted in the wake of the armies under the guise of feeding, clothing and educating the darkies, was sustaining them in all their arrogant pretensions and encouraging them to make issues with the whites, all of which were sustained in favor of the negroes by the powers that were: no courts whatsoever were in existence at which even this form of justice could be secured to a white Southerner."[11]

It did not take long for the Southerners to realize the danger they were in. Troops arrived to rule over the South. The few newspapers that sought to criticize the generals and Northern Reconstruction policy were shut down and locked up, just as Lincoln had done during the days of the war. Then in 1867 Congress took away from all of the South and its people the constitutional right of habeas corpus. Freedom of the press died, and there wasn't even a war or a rebellion.

The tragic story goes on and on, but we need only tell enough to let you understand the apparent hopelessness for the cause of the whites in the South, with no political base or power to work from. With an enemy military force taking over society and providing public patronage to local ex-slaves and foreign carpetbaggers—it was because of this hopeless situation that an underground, secret, terrorist response was made to combat the foreign invaders and their local compatriots, especially the militant and arrogant blacks expecting to be top dog in a new revolutionized Southern society. It was war on a new level, but a war nevertheless in which a lot of innocent people would get hurt. Sherman and the generals in the war had set the stage for illegal and dishonorable plunder and devastation. The emerging secret societies of the disenfranchised South would, perhaps with equal injustice, work the same violence against their enemies.

The Klan became the leading underground society for resistance. Klansman would punish and kill the conquerors, reassert control and dominion over Southern society in a clandestine fashion, and eventually succeed through political machinations to once again lawfully control their society.

The game plan of the Yankees was to use the ex-slaves to take over Southern society and wealth. It was easy to entice the ex-slaves with

Figure 10.1. A nineteenth-century caricature showing the South as a woman chained to Yankee sol-diers. She is staggering under the weight of a huge carpetbag carrying a federal bureaucrat and rifles and weapons. The smug bureaucrat appears to be dressed like Napoleon the conqueror, with his sword and a general's cloak.

promises of glory—that they would soon be masters over the whites if they would only do as they were told. Unfortunately, they did.

But a terrible tragedy for the ex-slaves occurred, which wasn't in the game plan. The invaders from the North, with their awesome military power over the South, along with local scalawags, packed up their bags and went home. The blacks were left alone to face the wrath of an angry

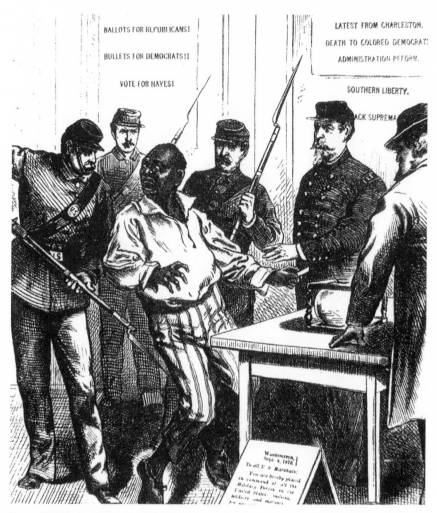

Figure 10.2. "In the Polling Booth." This caricature in a German history of the Civil War shows one reason why Republicans were hated in the South for over 100 years. Northern troops, probably blacks, with fixed bayonet, prod a black voter to vote for the Republican candidate (Hayes, 1878). On the wall is written: BALLOTS FOR REPUBLICANS! BULLETS FOR DEMOCRATS! DEATH TO COLORED DEMOCRATS.

populace. The South had won by playing its cards well in Washington politics. In a close presidential election in 1876, which the Democrat candidate Tilden had initially won, disputed electoral votes from three Southern states went for the Republican candidate Hayes in a political deal—Northern military and bureaucratic forces would withdraw from the South without truly helping the blacks, which they hardly intended to do anyway. Southern whites of Confederate vintage would rule once again, and the blacks who had joined forces with the enemy—the Yankees—would suffer the consequences of their disloyalty to the Southern whites—they would once again be under the boot of Southern white society—not as slaves, but with very limited rights and freedoms.

Now the threat of a black–Yankee takeover of the South was over. The Klan continued because the Yankees did not completely disappear. They had revenue to collect from an excise tax on whiskey, and a war between moonshiners and federal revenuers continued with much violence on both sides. But that is another story.

WHITE SUPREMACY

The Ku Klux Klan and the other underground organizations in the South after the Civil War were decidedly racist by today's thinking. We view white supremacy with disdain and contempt as a great evil. Yet in 1860 white supremacy thinking existed in the North and the South. It seemed almost self-evident that the blacks were an inferior race, even to ardent abolitionists.

Lincoln believed in white supremacy, as did Thomas Jefferson and just about everyone else. In his last year as president, Lincoln told a group of ex-slaves that there was no place in America for free blacks and that repatriation to Africa was the only solution to the dilemma that emancipation would soon pose for both races. His racist view illustrates not only Lincoln's thinking but that of the vast majority of Northerners. Lincoln knew that blacks would not be accepted as equal citizens in the Northern states. A half-century of mistreatment of freed blacks had proved that.[12]

Racism is everywhere, even to this day, even if white supremacy is unfashionable. The belief in Anglo-Saxon superiority was brought to the Americas and was tied to American imperialism during the last century. The Japanese have taught and they believe that they are a superior race, which formed part of their Greater East Asia Policy in the Pacific War, an excuse for their conquest and control over all of Asia. Racism pervades many religious groups who believe they are favored by God and thus are better than anyone else.

American racism, which focuses on black people, has much deeper and even more bizarre roots than racism in other places. But why is racism such a problem for Americans when it exists everywhere, among all peoples? Why are Americans so sensitive about it?

Figure 10.3. A nineteenth-century caricature showing the Ku Klux Klan and another white supremacy society, which created a new brand of servitude and degradation for blacks in the South. Their emancipation having come at the end of the bayonets of the hated conquerors from the North, blacks had little chance of realizing even the barest aspects of civil rights. When the carpetbaggers withdrew and returned the South to the embittered Southern whites, the black man's bid for freedom was nipped in the bud.

It seems that America's racism has its roots in the book of Genesis and in the Adam and Eve story, as well as the creation story vis à vis modern science. Religious scholars in the eighteenth and nineteenth centuries had to explain the black race and their primitive condition. How did that happen to these descendants of Adam and Eve? Remember that the creation, by biblical calculations (Bishop Usher's chronology), took place at around 4000 B.C., meaning that in a short span of time, these children of Adam and Eve, through Noah, degenerated into savages, while the other children, who were white, were advancing in culture, with written language, and many advanced tools to build great cities and ships to explore the world. The blacks, by contrast, were savages, themselves practicing slavery, and engaging in constant intertribal warfare. Did this not indicate an obviously inferior race of man, and suggest a curse by God for this lower human state? This was a Christian belief up until modern science proved otherwise. Racism was the inevitable result that was reflected in laws and customs of the white culture, making white supremacy the natural order of things, even God's order. While blacks were physically well endowed, it was their souls that were inherently below the superior race. While this may sound shocking today, it was social and religious gospel in the not too distant past.

The supposed biblical condemnation of the black race came from the story in the book of Genesis about Noah, who was the only man, with his family, to survive the great flood. All the races of man descended from the three sons of Noah: Ham, Shem, and Japheth. But Noah cursed his son Ham, decreeing that Ham's son, Canaan, should be a "servant of servants" under his brothers, essentially a slave. Most preachers in the South and even some in the North used this story to explain and justify slavery.[13] It also found favor in the North. The popular and now respected Mormon Church, through its founder Joseph Smith, expounded on this curse, and in his inspired version of the Bible, he wrote that a blackness came over the descendants of Canaan, and "they were despised among all people."[14]

This same view was expressed almost a century before by the great sage of the Enlightenment, Baron de Montesquieu, in his *The Spirit of Laws:* "It is hard to believe that God, who is a wise Being, should place a soul, especially a good soul, in such a black ugly body."[15] These views reflect the attitude of Western society, especially American society, in the eighteenth and nineteenth centuries, where blacks were despised for their physical features. This explains to some extent the numerous laws in both the North and the South that condemned the blacks to second-class citizenship, even after the abolition of slavery, and gave them little opportunity for education or to rise above the status of common laborer.

The Northern states all abolished slavery during the first seventy years of nationhood, but they did not give up their disdain for black people. As Alexis de Tocqueville wrote in *Democracy in America* (1838), "the prejudice of the race appears to be stronger in the States that have abolished slavery, than in those where it still exists; and nowhere is it so intolerant as in those States where servitude has never been known."[16]

Science, of course, has destroyed the biblical case for slavery and white supremacy. The Anglo-Saxons, who were by and far the vast majority of whites in both the North and especially the South, also came from savage stock. They did not invent written language, nor did they invent the engineering for building great cities and ships. Nor did they create the art, politics, and philosophy that made civilization possible. Aristotle was not of English stock, nor were any of the Greeks, Romans, Phoenicians, or Egyptians. The Romans brought civilization to Britain, just as the Europeans brought civilization to the Africans, Americans, and Asians. So, at this stage of our knowledge, the lowly savage was not a unique man—we all lived in a stone-age culture for at least 100,000 years. Black people cannot lay claim to having invented the unique tools that made civilization possible, but neither can the Anglo-Saxons. They are both in the same boat, so to speak, when it comes to being civilized. If the Romans had moved into Africa instead of Europe, then Europeans may have been the last to be civilized, the last of the lowly savages. So much for Anglo-Saxon white supremacy. Mankind owes civilization to the people of Semitic, Egyptian, Greek and Roman stock, with the Chinese not to be overlooked.

Unfortunately, science only recently put forth overwhelming evidence that the earth is more than 6,000 years old, and man has been around for tens of thousands of years. The Anglo-Saxons were in the Stone Age while the blacks were, and they had been there since evolving from truly subhuman ancestors.

In the nineteenth century, without science to provide accurate knowledge about the races and their universal Stone Age past, fanatical racism infected everyone, even most abolitionists, and this is why emancipation in America was such a disappointment, not just the emancipation in the South, as a war measure, but emancipation everywhere in the nation long before the Civil War. Northern states bordering the South set up all kinds of laws to keep the blacks out. They were not just inferior, they were persona non grata.[17]

Lincoln made some effort to provide compensation for slave owners, but there never was any solid planning for the ex-slaves as had been done in other countries, and Lincoln's "root, hog, or starve," was hardly an intelligent response to a serious problem. As it turned out, the only plan came from Reconstruction aimed at destroying the rule of the former Confederates and exploiting the South by a carpetbagger/ex-slave partnership. It failed. *One of the strange ironies of the Civil War and its aftermath is this: The Confederate military cause against vastly superior Northern armies was hopeless from the start; and the Republican cause to rule over the South after the war was equally a hopeless endeavor.* In the end, Lincoln's objective to preserve the Union was achieved at a cost in money, blood, and a social calamity that has survived to this day.

Is the Klan and its acts of violence against the South's enemies and their compatriots to be excused? Not easily, but they can be explained and understood. This was war on a guerrilla level, but war nevertheless, against an invading foreign force and those who allied themselves with the invaders. War is a great evil, and "even a just war sets the hearts of a nation aflame with hatred, malice and revenge." That is what was behind the Klan and provided the force for violence they unleashed on their enemies. It was war's aftermath—predictable, understandable, and perhaps most of all, inevitable.

Guerrilla units fighting invading and occupying armies have a long history going back to the Zealots in ancient Judea who carried out raids against the occupying Romans after the abortive Jewish attempt to secede from the Roman Empire around A.D. 66. Their violence and crimes caused the Romans to send in their best legions to put down the Zealots who had taken refuge in a natural fortress on Masada. The final defeat of the Zealots is well-known and was the subject of a motion picture. The Romans built an enormous earthen ramp to breach the fortress, only to find the Jews dead, having committed suicide. In World War II, the occupying Germans in Russia had to deal with the partisans, whose history went back to the days of the tsars. The partisans also carried out violence against Russians who worked for, or even associated with, the Germans. Russian girls, often just teenagers, were lynched, like the ex-slaves in the South who fought against the Confederacy or even associated with the occupying enemy.

With the Klan the stakes were high. Their guerrilla operations were more important than Lee's army. The war had been for independence from Washington and those limited areas of federal power they objected to. In the Union, before the war, the Southerners would still retain control over their destiny. But with defeat and Reconstruction, the South was now ruled by the conquerors, who were determined to remake Southern society and to not only disenfranchise, but to dispossess and even destroy the ruling establishment. The occupying conquerors were a far greater threat to the Southern people than were Lincoln's Republicans. In short, the Southerners' very existence was "on the line." It was a fight for survival, and in the end they won. But what would have been the consequences if the carpetbaggers had won? With the use of ex-slaves, the Southerners would have ended up just like one former slave owner whose ex-slave was guarding him in a POW camp. The ex-slave said to his master: "Hello, massa; bottom rail top dis time!"[18] Of course, that state of affairs didn't last for long.

It could be argued, with some merit, that the Klan saved the Southern society from destruction, and there seems little question that that is what the Yankee invaders had in mind. Looking at the Klan from that standpoint, and from the history of similar guerrilla organizations, it would seem to cover a multitude of their sins and crimes. Were they white terrorists or Southern patriots? Or both?

Thus a rational case can be made to understand the Klan during the Reconstruction years—better described as the years of occupation and rule by the South's enemies who had brought so much devastation and death. To gain a perspective of the severity of the slaughter of Southern men (and boys), on a proportionate basis to population only the Russians in World War II suffered comparable deaths in their military forces. After the war, hatred for the enemy continued, perhaps even more intensely than during the war years.

In 1878, things changed dramatically. The Northern conquerors went home and any need for guerrilla operations ceased, as the defeated Southerners reasserted control over their society. The Klan should have returned to being a social organization, with the patriotic purposes expressed in their oath. Any justification for the Klan's existence as a paramilitary organization ended. Unfortunately, the violence and lawlessness of the past ten years continued against the weak and defenseless minority of ex-slaves who were not welcome to emigrate north with the withdrawing Yankees because of the Northern black codes.

It was then that the Klan became a criminal conspiracy against law and civilized order. The ex-slaves' bid for freedom and equality disappeared. As the illustration on page 160 shows, the life that they had was even worse than slavery (Figure 10.3). If one wants to make out a convincing case against war, the American Civil War and its aftermath is all the convincing one needs. The Union was preserved, but at what a horrible price.

Racism took a turn for the worse. In the antebellum period, for example, mammies would often wet-nurse white babies, and would love and nurture them as their own and with their own; but, in the post–Civil War period, all of that ceased, as the black wet nurse became suspect of adulterating the blood of the whites. So much so, that an elderly South Carolinian, in 1885, said that this practice was evil, as it "thus poisoned the blood of our children, and made them *cowards*. . . . it will take five hundred years, if not longer, by the infusion of new [white] blood to eradicate the hereditary vices imbibed with the blood of black wet nurses."[19] Thus it is easy to see how the segregation of the races became so all-important and overriding in the South up to the era of desegregation in the late twentieth century. This same pseudoscience idea formed the rationale for the laws making intermarriage a crime; like incest, it would endanger the human species with this crossbreeding. In 1955, twenty-nine states had these antimiscegenation laws on the books, not just in the South.

Lincoln's assassination was the worst thing that could have happened for both the North and the South. A young private from Massachusetts saw the folly of the assassination: "In killing the President the South has lost their best friend."[20] And that turned out to be so true, as radicals with fanatical hatred for the South took over the reins of government. For Lincoln had had no intention of reconstructing the South as the radicals did. With these hate mongers, it was not "malice toward none," but rather "malice toward all" in the South. Northern armies would make sure of that. Unlike the radicals, Lincoln envisioned the seceding states returning to the Union with a minimum show of loyalty. Although he went to the extreme to win the war, he showed a strong inclination to go to the other extreme to win the peace and restore the goodwill of the South toward the Union. The radicals who took over after his death did everything possible to destroy any reconciliation. Even to this day, as a result of their malice, hatred for the North still lives in the South, as does the Klan. Lincoln's war was a tragedy for all, and so was his death. Is this not the great irony of this whole tragic era?

11

The Peacemakers

Blessed are the peacemakers: for they shall be called the children of God.

Sermon on the Mount

If America was a Christian nation in the nineteenth century, one would hardly know it, considering the zeal for conquest it showed as a way of settling disputes and expanding the nation. Vast expanses of land from the Pacific to the Mississippi were stolen from the Mexicans by war, probably because the land was not for sale and could not be acquired by peaceful means. Within the nation, even larger territories were taken from Native Americans by conquest and subterfuge.

This was a period of empire building in which war and imperialism were the most admired of national activities. Building an empire and colonizing required war and violence against the weaker society, for no people volunteer to become colonials, subject to the rule of alien invaders. The guiding principle of the Declaration of Independence, that governments derive the just powers from the "consent of the governed," had not yet been accepted by civilization, nor by the American governments. The so-called self-determination of peoples had to wait for the twentieth century to have meaning in international and domestic affairs. America at that time was no different from the imperialistic British or Germans or any other European power. Indeed, it was believed that it was the destiny of the American people to rule over North America from the Arctic to Panama. This was God's will, and military force for God, as during the Crusades, was fully justified. But even that was a rationalization, for the root of the problem seems to be nothing other than the need to conquer, almost as if it were inherent in the psyche of the human race.

I am a child of the twentieth century who abhors war and imperialism. The horrors of the world wars and the debacle in Vietnam are shining examples of what war is all about.

It is hard to understand why any man would want to go to war when death, disease, and crippling disabilities are the lot of so many soldiers. Why did a million or more men in the North rally around the flag to conquer the Southern states and coerce an unwilling population to stay in a federal arrangement that no longer appealed to them? Today, such a war for such a cause would bring even greater public outcry than Vietnam, when so many men evaded the war in one way or another. We even elected a president who had evaded the draft, and there was little condemnation for his unpatriotic actions. But what about the thousands of young Canadians who joined our military to fight in Vietnam, and the few thousand of them who came back in body bags?

No doubt the thrill of adventure and the romanticizing of war enticed young men to enlist, go to war, and go to an early grave. But what blinded Civil War–era young men to the horrors of the battlefield? Southerners had a cause—independence and repelling an invading foreign army—a just cause like the American Revolution. But Northerners had no correspondingly noble cause. Preserving the Union can be translated into conquering the South and imposing Northern will on the Southern people. Hardly a rallying cause to die for. Unless, of course, the need to conquer and dominate others was justification, as with so many wars in the history of Western civilization. Thus conquest alone becomes justification for imperialism, and leaders easily adopt noble reasons to justify conquest. Lincoln did this at Gettysburg, and most Americans have been mesmerized by his logic, which was that democratic government would "perish from the earth" if the North lost the war. Now that's downright absurd, but we still worship the words as if they had great merit and truth, when in fact they don't have either. As one Northern commentator in 1863 called Lincoln's address at Gettysburg: "The silly remarks of the President."

Aside from the nonsense that the South was out to destroy democracy in the world, Republican leaders reiterated another alarm for decades after the war—that there was a vast, organized conspiracy by Southern-minded Northerners, who were traitors out to destroy America and the Constitution, and so on. Modern scholarship and research has proven it to be without foundation in fact.

To understand this propaganda, we can look at a similar event not too long ago in the McCarthy era in which there was another vast conspiracy in the government; a witch hunt pervaded the nation, looking for Communists hiding and infiltrating everywhere. According to the John Birch Society, even President Eisenhower was a Communist stooge, groomed for the job of president. There followed all kinds of "investigations" by the Congress and Hoover's FBI, and a batch of laws to punish these so-called

Communist sympathizers filled the law books. Since that also looks silly, so we should not judge Northern political leaders too harshly. The difference, however, was with the way these imaginary traitors were dealt with. During the McCarthy hysteria over Communists, the Bill of Rights remained in force and no one was imprisoned without compliance with those rights. Not so in the Civil War era when there were no constitutional rights—no right to a trial by a jury of your peers, no right to due process in even its most basic fundamentals. It was America's reign of terror, without the guillotine. In France there was the Revolutionary Tribunal administering brutal judgments; in America there were the generals and the military court-martials condemning many to death, and many thousands, perhaps more than 14,000, to prisons for as long as the generals thought necessary. Lincoln as the commander in chief had the power to prevent all this, and on occasion he would free someone whose innocence was unquestionable. But for the "crime" of voicing disapproval of his war and his war policies, Lincoln stood by his generals.

As in the McCarthy era, name-calling was an effective way of destroying the reputation of many a good citizen. Copperhead is the name of a venomous snake common in the East. It is often found in shadowy places, hiding from detection and able to striking without warning. It is hard to understand how the name of this creature came to be applied to those in favor of peace. Peacemakers were called the children of God by the Prince of Peace 2,000 years ago. The Copperheads were peace advocates, properly called the "Peace Democrats," not unlike the antiwar movement in the Vietnam era. Northern prowar advocates, especially the Republicans, excused Lincoln's massive arrests and imprisonments without a civilian trial by maintaining that these peace advocates were like the dangerous copperhead and that they were well organized and ready to strike at the government's war program.

The Copperheads were not Southern sympathizers nor were they traitors, aiding and abetting the Southern cause. They were peacemakers, and there is no evidence that they were anything more than victims of Northern Republican propaganda. The Copperheads were led in the East by the governor of New York, Horatio Seymour, and in the West by Congressman Clement Vallandigham, with the objective of saving the Union by negotiation, not by force of arms. They professed a strong devotion to states' rights and the Constitution, and they opposed the destruction of civil liberties by Lincoln through arbitrary arrests and the suspension of the right of habeas corpus. They opposed conscription and, like the majority of Northerners, opposed the Emancipation Proclamation, primarily because it would produce a flood of ex-slaves, especially into states like Ohio,

Figure 11.1. Northerners for peace were called "Copperheads," named for a poisonous snake that inhabits much of the eastern and midwestern regions of the United States. Unlike a rattlesnake, a copperhead strikes without warning. It seems strange that peacemakers would be branded as venomous serpents in a Christian nation. Yet to the Northern war hawks, they were dangerous, for peace meant a negotiated peace and may have meant the division of the United States into two confederacies and the end of one nation "indivisible" whose destiny as a world leader and world power would be impaired.

Indiana, and Illinois, which bordered on slave states.[1] They even sided with the South over tariff issues, as the farmers in the West suffered from a high tariff that profited Northern industrialists.

The Copperheads were strong in the West, which at that time comprised the farming states of Ohio, Indiana, and Illinois. The war hurt them as Mississippi trade ceased, farm prices plummeted, and farm products had to be transported long distances to the East at high costs. The tariff also increased prices for the manufactured goods they needed. There were strong economic reasons to favor peaceful negotiations to settle the secession of the Southern states. Amazingly, they were not in favor of secession—they wanted to preserve the Union—but through peaceful means, not the destruction and horrors of war. As the casualty lists continued to grow, the peace movement gained its strength despite the Copperhead epithet.

But looking at the peace advocates from the condemnation of Northern propaganda—that the nation was in grave danger because of them—it is easy to understand why so many in the North supported the war and were willing to sacrifice so much blood and money. Tossing the Constitution out the window in order to save the nation was justifiable, so it was believed. Locking up innocent citizens in time of war has been an acceptable practice ever since the Civil War period. In World War I, over seven hundred people were convicted of publicly disapproving of the war and received sentences of up to twenty years in prison.

History, tragically, has confirmed that the peacemakers were right; we should never become involved in the wars fought among Europe's empire builders. In World War II it was not necessary to oppose the war to be imprisoned in concentration camps; you only needed to have the wrong ancestors. In the Vietnam era there were no laws on the books against verbally opposing the war, and there was no president with the nerve of a Lincoln to suspend the right of habeas corpus and lock up civilians through military tribunals. It was an unpopular war and that is what made it different from the Civil War, which had great popular support in both the North and the South. This popularity permitted the governments to do as they pleased when dealing with dissidents.

The wholesale destruction of civil liberties and the Bill of Rights in the North, and the war policy itself, did not go unchallenged—the military tyranny that gripped the country notwithstanding. But the peacemakers had to face the wrath of an enraged populace, fed by the propaganda that if you are not with us you are a traitor. The former governor of Connecticut had his portrait removed from the capitol building because he advocated peace and negotiations with the seceding states.

Some of the first peacemakers following the war measures introduced by Lincoln after Fort Sumter were the Marylanders, especially a majority of the members of the state legislature. The Maryland legislature, not unlike the governors of the border states still in the Union, responded to Lincoln's call for four regiments from that state by passing the following resolution on 16 May 1861, after debating the issue of Civil War:

> Whereas the war against the Confederate States is unconstitutional and repugnant to Civilization, and will result in bloody and shameful overthrow of our institutions; and while recognizing the obligations of Maryland to the Union, we sympathize with the South in the struggle for their rights—for the sake of humanity we are for peace and reconciliation, and solemnly protest against this war, and will take no part in it;
>
> Resolved, that Maryland implores the President, in the name of God, to cease this unholy war, *at least until Congress assembles;* that Maryland desires and consents to the recognition of the independence

of the Confederate States. The military occupation of Maryland is unconstitutional, and she protests against it, though the violent interference with the transit of federal troops is discountenanced, that the vindication of her rights be left to time and reason, and that a Convention,
under existing circumstances, is inexpedient. [Emphasis added]

It was resolutions like this one, opposed to war but favoring Union by
peaceful means, that set the stage for the harsh military action against the
legislators of Maryland—their arbitrary arrest and imprisonment to prevent any possible opposition to Lincoln's war efforts. The famous Merryman case involved the arrest of someone who criticized the call to arms,
which was the view of the people's representatives. Merryman simply had
been the man in a vast crowd who spoke the loudest.

The most famous and notorious of the Copperheads was Clement Vallandigham, whose story became the subject of a book and a motion picture,
The Man without a Country. He had been a thorn in Lincoln's side for almost two years, attacking his war policies while a member of the House of
Representatives and even introducing a bill in the House to "imprison" the
president if he continued making illegal arrests and imprisonments through
military tribunals. His antiwar views appeared in many of the Democratic
newspapers in the North, but when Lincoln shut down most of these periodicals, Vallandigham went on a speaking tour. He just wouldn't stop talking. In the House the prowar crowd introduced seven resolutions calling
for his expulsion from the Congress. They were all defeated, however. He
called Lincoln "wicked" for usurping power and holding the Constitution
in contempt, which took a lot of courage at the time.

In the elections of 1862, the pro-Lincoln legislature in Ohio redefined
the district Vallandigham was in (what we now call gerrymandering) by
adding staunchly Republican Warren County to his district. He was defeated, but he still remained in Congress as a lame duck member and continued his verbal assaults on Lincoln's war policies. With the war going
badly at this time, Vallandigham openly opposed the war on the floor of
the House of Representatives. This was followed by peace resolutions by
the state legislatures of Illinois and Indiana, Copperhead country. Although Congress passed no law making it illegal to oppose the war (as it
did in 1917–1918), that was not a problem, as military generals could rule
by decree and make opposition to the war or sympathy for the South a violation of military, general-made law. Congress was not necessary. By-
passing a legislature for lawmaking and ruling by decree is a tyrant's path
to power and dictatorship. Nevertheless, our own Civil War policy of military decrees made Congress unnecessary and the democratic process

nonexistent. A nation does not need a Congress when military generals can make law by decree.

Vallandigham's troubles really began when he returned from Washington to his native Ohio and ran for governor on a peace platform. In a number of speeches throughout Ohio for the Democratic nomination for governor, he said: "The war is a bloody and costly failure. The dead, the dead, and the numerous dead: Think of Fredericksburg. Let us make peace. Let the armies fraternize and go home."[2]

With speeches like this one from the now famous Copperhead, enlistments declined and desertions increased, but so did hostile attacks on Vallandigham. He was hung in effigy and there were placards and flags condemning him as a traitor. As his effigy was dangling with a rope around its neck, Republican zealots kept hacking away with sabers and poking with their bayonets.

You cannot help but admire the courage of this man for speaking out at a time when thousands of other critics of the war—including newspaper men and even members of state governments—were in prison. Surely, Vallandigham had to be silenced for the cause of the war against the South. His courage to speak out against the war is even more amazing when you consider his reference to Fredericksburg. The leader of the Northern armies in that military disaster was none other than the recently appointed military commander over Ohio, Major General Ambrose Burnside, who had been responsible for a tactical blunder that routed Burnside's army and left a battlefield strewn with vast numbers of dead and wounded Northern soldiers. The general was obviously rather sensitive about his misdeeds and follies as a general. He decided to go after Vallandigham, and on 13 April 1863, he issued Military Order no. 38, aimed specifically at Vallandigham: "All persons found without our lines who commit acts for the benefit of the enemies of our country will be tried as spies or traitors and, if convicted will suffer death."[3] Burnside also warned that "the habit of declaring sympathy for the enemy will not be allowed in this department."

Vallandigham was undaunted and tore up a copy of the order with the comment, "I have the most supreme contempt for General Order no. 38," and "I have the most supreme contempt for King Lincoln."[4] Vallandigham should not have been surprised when soldiers battered down the door of his Dayton, Ohio, home and took him to Cincinnati for trial where the General resided and where a military tribune could quickly convict him and put an end to his critical speeches. A nine-member military court convened on May 6 and took no time convicting Vallandigham. In his defense, Vallandigham referred to the Constitution and his right to freely speak and to criticize the government. He even asserted and affirmed his loyalty, stating that he was for the Union, the Constitution, and liberty. The general ordered his confinement in a prison for the duration of the war. Protest swept through much of the nation, especially among the Democrats, for here was a man running for political office who was destroyed by a phony court martial when a civil trial was his constitutional right. This was no war zone.

General Burnside had acted shrewdly for the Republican cause and the war cause. Arresting and silencing a candidate for the governorship of Ohio was to be tolerated, but to have had to arrest and imprison a duly elected governor may have been too much for even the all-powerful Republican administration and its generals.

The Republican administration in Washington seems to have played a behind-the-scenes role in the Vallandigham affair. Lincoln had put Secretary of State Seward in charge of Internal Security, the nineteenth-century equivalent of secret police. Seward bragged about his ability to lock up people at his whim, shut down newspapers, and silence an outspoken antiwar Democratic candidate for the governorship. By 1863, any possibility of a judge issuing a writ of habeas corpus was no longer a threat, as judges had been told and threatened if they would dare to issue such a writ. Nevertheless, a writ was submitted to the Supreme Court—a rubber stamp operation after Justice Taney retired, like the Congress. Naturally the writ was denied (*In re Vallandigham,* 1 Wall. 243 [1864]), citing the Lieber Code as authority. They should have cited "the Constitution according to Lincoln." In all fairness to the Court, they ruled that the Supreme Court had no jurisdiction over military tribunals, paving the way for the judicial murders that were to follow Lincoln's assassination. They, in effect, said that the military was above the Constitution, above the Bill of Rights, a law unto itself, with no restraints, limitations, or due process to be followed.

Secretary Seward was behind this era of totalitarianism in America. He was drunk with power, bragging to the British ambassador that he was more powerful than the Queen of England. (By this time in British constitutional history the queen was a mere figurehead.)

In response to Seward's boasting of his powers, the caricature on page 175 appeared (Figure 11.2). It seems to indicate that it was Seward and not Burnside on his own who was behind the arrest of Vallandigham.

No honest court could possibly have convicted Vallandigham of anything whatsoever. So his arrest by Seward's military henchmen, and being tried by a selected group of military officers for the crime of "sympathy for the enemy," was an outrage. Under Lincoln's signature, he was banished from the United States, not unlike the Soviet Union banishing Solzhenitsyn for criticizing the policies of that government. Just think, the Soviet

Figure 11.2. "My Lord," said Seward, "I can touch a bell on my right hand, and order the arrest of a citizen of Ohio (Vallandigham); I can touch the bell again, and order the imprisonment of a citizen of New York; and no power on earth, except that of the President, can release them. Can the Queen of England do so much?"

Union could have used Abraham Lincoln to justify deporting Russian dissidents. Another crime justifying arrest and arbitrary imprisonment was "expressing treasonable sentiments," which meant recognizing the right of a state to secede from the federal union.

But Vallandigham wasn't even expressing treasonable sentiments (i.e., the right to secede). No, he was only expressing a desire for peace and to maintain the Union by peaceful means. Since he made his position clear to the military tribunal, about all they could come up with was "sympathy for the enemy." What kind of a crime was that?

Modern Northern scholars have no difficulty whitewashing the Republican dictatorship. So what if over 14,000 people were imprisoned? So what if over three hundred newspapers were shut down? Those thousands imprisoned by military tribunals probably deserved what they got.[5] This same kind of justification would excuse most lynchings. These scholars are proud of their "professorial detachment," which makes all these evil deeds sound tolerable. They overlook the ugly facts, such as the fact that Lincoln signed the order deporting Vallandigham to the South, although he was reminded by his attorney general that he was punishing a man for exercising his right of free speech. Today, that would be a flagrant violation of the civil rights acts and would surely lead to impeachment and removal from office. The real criminals were not those persons expressing disapproval of the war, but those locking them up for doing so.

But today, all the academic acclaim lavished on those who whitewash the crimes of the Lincoln administration notwithstanding, there are a growing number of scholars and historians like Frank van der Linden (*Lincoln: The Road to War*) who will not stop talking, and sooner or later those of Northern persuasion will have to face the realities of the war against Southern secession. The whitewash, with time and honest scholarship, is wearing off.

12

The Trial of the Century
That Never Was: The United States
versus Jefferson Davis

During the second week of May 1865, President Johnson and his cabinet received exciting news. Jefferson Davis had been captured in Georgia on May 10, less than a month after the government had offered a $100,000 reward for his capture. The cabinet cheered the news and immediately made plans to try the leader of the Confederacy for treason in a great public state trial—the trial of the century. They'd hang the rascal by the neck to show the world how traitors should be dealt with. Hanging old Jeff Davis would drive the final nail into the coffin of the Confederate cause. It was indeed a time to celebrate, and the news quickly spread throughout the country. In Iowa City three men offered the federal government $300,000 for the right to travel around the country and exhibit Davis in a dress—the disguise Davis was supposed to have used to avoid capture.[1]

The press was jubilant as well. The *New York Times* ran this editorial on the captured leader of the South. He was "a murderer, a cruel slave owner whose servants all ran away, a liar, a boaster, a fanatic, a confessed failure, a hater, a political adventurer, a supporter of outcasts and outlaws, a drunkard, an atrocious misrepresenter, an assassin, an incendiary, a criminal who was gratified by the assassination of Lincoln, a henpecked husband, a man so shameless that he would try to escape capture by disguising himself as a woman, a supporter of murder plots, an insubordinate soldier, an unwholesome sleeper, and a malingerer."[2]

Jefferson Davis, of course, was never tried, and to this day Northern historians assert that Davis was lucky. He would surely have been convicted and hanged. A recent biography of Davis by a popular Civil War historian, William C. Davis, who reviews books on the war for the History Book Club and movies on the History Channel, wrote in 1991 that "it is well for him that he never went to trial, however, for *certainly* he would not have prevailed" [emphasis added].[3]

Any lawyer with criminal trial experience would not agree with this, especially if Jefferson Davis would have been given a fair trial as guaranteed by the Bill of Rights. In 1987, another historian, Professor Edward K. Eckert, took the opposite view: "But the trial would never be held. The federal government knew that it could not try Davis for treason without raising the constitutional issue of secession. . . . Since any trial would have to take place in Virginia, where the 'crime' had been committed, the federal government wisely recognized that it would never be able to convict Jefferson Davis for treason in a Southern court."[4]

The federal government dropped the case because it became increasingly clear that it could not win. As time passed and reason replaced war passion, it became obvious that Jefferson Davis had a formidable defense, both in the substance of his defense and perhaps, even more important, in the great criminal defense lawyers who would defend him. For four years the government had been shouting from the housetops that secessionists were "traitors and conspirators," and to silence any contrary expression, the military had been throwing people into prison and closing down newspapers that dared challenge their view or even suggest that there was such a thing as a right of secession. But now, with the Constitution restored — with the end of military trials of civilians for "crimes" manufactured by the generals — the issues of the war would now have to be decided by legal analysis and by history, not by force of arms. The traitor verbiage might not hold up in a bona fide court of law.

The many great lawyers who were willing to come to the defense of Jefferson Davis had a score to settle with the federal government. The bar in the North was angry at the government over the way it had ridden roughshod over the Bill of Rights and the Constitution for four years. Lawyers were angry at having their clients locked up in prison with no civil rights as guaranteed by the Constitution. They were frustrated at having civilians tried by military courts for crimes that never existed in any law book. They were angry at a government that ignored the Supreme Court and set itself above the constitutional scheme of checks and balances. They didn't like having to beg the president for justice for clients convicted by phony court-martials or locked up without any trial. This had been a government of oriental despotism, not a free and constitutional society.

Consequently, the best lawyers were willing to volunteer to defend Davis. Davis's trial would indeed have been the trial of the century. Even lawyers who didn't believe in secession found the conduct of the Republican administration and the military disgraceful, to say the least. The lawyers were aware of that most of all, and they had a score to settle even if it meant vindicating the Confederate leader.

One of the most famous trial lawyers of this era was Charles O'Connor of New York. He volunteered to be Davis's counsel. O'Connor's stature was on a par with that of Salmon P. Chase, Chief Justice of the Supreme Court, who would act as trial judge. The trial would have to take place in Virginia and as that was the circuit over which Chase presided, he would have to act as trial judge.

The attorney general's staff of lawyers was delighted that Chase would be acting in this capacity. His stature and high office would provide international focus and truly make this the trial of the century. A trial and a conviction under the wise direction of the chief justice followed by an unsuccessful appeal to the Supreme Court finally declaring secession to be treason would make a victorious ending to the war and put the stamp of judicial approval on the Northern conquest of the South. This was the game

Figure 12.1. Jefferson Davis was imprisoned at Fort Henry for almost two years. Guards watched him around the clock but were not permitted to speak to him. Initially he was bound in irons and was allowed no visitors; a light was kept burning day and night. His only reading material was a Bible. This outrageous treatment, in clear violation of the Bill of Rights, caused many in the North to change their opinion of Davis from an archtraitor to the fallen leader of a lost cause.

Radicals in the Congress wanted to try Davis before a military tribunal where, as throughout the war, a verdict of guilty was rendered no matter what the evidence. But after the war the Supreme Court asserted itself and held that these military trials were illegal and could not take place when the civilian courts were open. In a sense, the Constitution saved Davis's skin (and neck). His remarkable wife, Varina, went North and persuaded a large number of influential people to demand justice for Davis—a fair trial and release from military custody.

plan that the president and his cabinet had unanimously, and very enthusiastically, agreed upon.

The enthusiasm in the North over trying Davis probably stemmed from the fact that all secessionist thinking had been stamped out by military courts, and these same courts had been grinding out convictions with little or no due process of law, the most famous trial being the court-martial of civilians accused of conspiring to assassinate Lincoln. Mary Surratt, who ran a boardinghouse that Booth visited, was tried, convicted, and hanged within a few weeks after the assassination, although she had nothing to do with it.[5] The military considered bringing Jefferson Davis into this conspiracy trial, with perjured testimony that would not have held up in a bona fide law court. But why try Davis with the conspirators, when he could easily be tried and hanged for treason by almost any military court?

But with the passing of only a few months, the use of military courts in peacetime became impossible. And this speaks highly of the deeply rooted tradition of the Bill of Rights in American society. Throughout most of history, democratic and free societies have not recovered from wartime military dictatorships. But in America, the Constitution was resurrected in the North soon after the Confederacy collapsed, and that meant an end to military tribunals when civil courts were available. Trying Davis in a bona fide civilian court, with due process, soon sobered up the president and his cabinet. The case against Jefferson Davis had to be examined in the light of history, and upon legal precedents and procedures. And it might show that secessionists weren't traitors after all. Maybe a state and its people, acting through democratic processes, did have the right to withdraw from the Union. What had the Founders said? Jefferson had said while president that if any of the states, alone or in combination, wanted to withdraw, then they should go in peace, as brothers and friends. More recently, on 30 April 1839, there had been a great celebration on the fiftieth anniversary of the inauguration of President Washington. Former president John Quincy Adams gave the jubilee address. He ridiculed the right claimed by South Carolina to nullify a federal law, as had recently been attempted, but then concluded, "If the states ever lost their fraternal affection, gave way to cold and indifference, or a collision of interests should foster hatred, and the bonds of political association should sever, it would be far better for the people of the disunited states, to part in friendship from each other than to be held together by constraint."[6]

Northerners seem to have forgotten or were unaware of a great secessionist tradition in America. Southerners were not alone in their view that each state had the right to determine its own destiny in the Union. The procedure for joining the Union also applied to withdrawing from the Union.

And the Tenth Amendment, which reserved to the states powers not delegated to the federal government, would seem to put the matter of secession with the states and the people. In the North in 1860, many editorials saw the secession issue this way, before the fury of war shut off and shut up any such seditious thinking.

The *Cincinnati Daily Press,* shortly after Lincoln's election, on 21 November 1860, had this to say: "We believe that the right of any member of this confederation [the federal Union] to dissolve its political relationship with the others and to assume an independent position is absolute — that, in other words, if South Carolina wants to go out of the Union, she has the right to do so, and no party or power may justly say her nay."[7]

A daily publication in Springfield, Massachusetts, was even more outspoken on 9 February 1861, and this was a Republican newspaper: "The idea that the free states intend to march armies into the seceding states to force their return to loyalty seems too monstrous for serious denial, and yet this is precisely the thing now declared by the incoming administration."[8]

Another Ohio newspaper, the *Circleville Watchman,* on November 23, 1860, also editorializing before the war, explained the right in democratic terms: "We are quite free to say that, our idea of true Democracy, of the natural and inalienable rights of man, lead us to the opinion that any State of the confederation [Federal Union] has, or at least ought to have, a perfect and undoubted right to withdraw from the Union and to change her form of government whenever a majority of her people shall be of the opinion that their rights are being encroached upon and impaired by the other States."[9]

Even after the war started, some courageous editors were still hammering on the Republican despotism, but not for long. Consider the following editorial printed by an Ohio newspaper, the *Cincinnati Daily Inquirer,* in the summer of 1861, after the "traitor" label was unleashed by the North:

> The Republican papers are great on treason. . . . It is treason to circulate petitions for a compromise or peaceful readjustment of our national troubles . . . to question the constitutional powers of the President to increase the standing army without authority of law . . . to object to squads of military visiting private houses, and to make search and seizures . . . to question the infallibility of the President, and treason not to concur with him. . . . It is treason to talk of hard times . . . to say that the war might have been avoided . . . It is treason to be truthful and faithful to the Constitution.[10]

It seems strange that the impressive and rational analysis of the secession issue in the North, as well as in the South, should be totally overpowered by the traitor philosophy and that the government should be so taken in by its rather shabby thinking. Historically, the main protagonists were not the Founders, but Daniel Webster and Justice Story, who both argued that because the Constitution referred to the "people," it was not a compact of states (despite what Jefferson and Madison and all the Framers had written). They further argued that since the Constitution was silent on the issue of secession, that meant that once a state joined the Union, it was in it forever. And finally, since the Articles of Confederation used the word "perpetual," that meant the later Constitution (after the "perpetual" Articles only lasted seven years) was also perpetual, even if it didn't say so. Therefore, no state could withdraw.

And it is even stranger no new or significant arguments have been developed since then. Lengthy books and multi-volume works on Lincoln and the war pass over the issue in one short paragraph. In short, "preserving the Union" by armed coercion still has no compelling or convincing rational basis. There were a few Northern thinkers of note who did understand the moral implications. Justice George Comstock, a founder of Syracuse University, made this sobering comment: "If Mr. Davis is right as to all the circumstances and results flowing from separation, then the seceded states are the rightful possession of a perfect sovereignty . . . [the Civil War then] was a war of invasion and conquest, for which there is no warrant in the Constitution, but which is condemned by the rules of Christianity, and the law of the civilized world."[11]

It wasn't just Americans who had trouble giving much merit to Daniel Webster's position that the Union was indissoluble, which he thundered from the floor of the Senate. European thinkers had difficulty as well. In 1862, a British quarterly magazine commented that "it does seem the most monstrous of anomalies that a government founded on the 'sacred right of insurrection' should pretend to treat as traitors and rebels six or seven millions of people who withdrew from the Union, and merely asked to be left alone."[12]

Northern antisecession gobbledygook didn't sway European thinkers. When the Supreme Court, after the war, expounded the doctrine of Webster that the Union was indissoluble, James Bryce (whose work ranks with de Tocqueville's) in his famous *The American Commonwealth* (1888) ridiculed the thinking of the Chief Justice and Webster's point of view. In analyzing the arguments that the Union was indissoluble, he labeled the reasoning as "a mass of subtle, so to speak, scholastic metaphysics regarding the nature of government." Unlike all other federations throughout history, the American federation was not a compact between commonwealths "but an instrument of perpetual efficacy."[13] In other words, the reasoning was sophistry at its best. The medieval scholastics couldn't have

Figure 12.2. George Comstock, a founder of Syracuse University and a justice on New York's highest tribunal. He wrote a pamphlet during the Civil War (1864), justifying the war on the South because the Southern states lacked sovereignty. He reasoned, rather dangerously for the cause of the North, that if the Southern states and people were sovereign, then the war for "preserving the Union" was a crime against civilization and Christianity. Photo: Courtesy of the collection of the Court of Appeals for the State of New York.

reasoned any better. Bryce then levels all of the arguments—especially Webster's rambling on and on that the Constitution was not a compact among the states—by noting that the Constitution merely substituted one compact for another. Bryce could have leveled a coup de grace by citing James Madison, who called the Constitution "a compact between the States in their sovereign capacity" or Thomas Jefferson in the Kentucky Resolution, which he framed. It was adopted in 1798 to protest the Alien and Sedition laws. The resolution asked the other states to declare "whether these acts are or are not authorized by the Federal Compact." Was this an oversight by Webster and Chief Justice Chase caused by a lack of research into America's founders, or was Webster the "great deceiver" Bledsoe claimed him to be? Reading Webster's so-called great expounding of the Constitution on the floor of the Senate shows us the craft of a lawyer at work. The object was persuasion, not truth, and he marshaled and repeated over and over again the same worn-out arguments for a perpetual Union.[14]

The argument that the North hung to tenaciously was that the war was a rebellion and thus all Southerners who supported the war were traitors who could all be tried, convicted, and hanged for treason. Once Northerners acknowledged that it was a war, they were in big trouble. But the common man in the North was not always so persuaded with the treason pitch. In October 1861, a Southern privateer, *Savannah,* was captured and its crew put on trial in New York for piracy. If it was a war that was being waged, they would be prisoners of war; if it was only an insurrection or a rebellion, they were guilty of treason and could be tried, convicted, and hanged. Lincoln believed this, as would be expected, but a jury in New York acquitted the crew because to them, this was a war, and the members of the crew were indeed prisoners of war, not pirates. The treason charge failed.

As a result of this case and the Confederacy's threat to hang Yankee sailors in reprisal, Lincoln suspended the sentence of another Confederate sailor and ruled that he was a prisoner of war. Jefferson Davis could also make the plea to any court and jury, even a Northern one, that this had been a war (and by 1867, who could convincingly argue otherwise). In fact, it was a war on a scale almost unknown in modern history.

The substantial case for secession notwithstanding, it was probably a law professor from the University of Virginia, Albert Bledsoe, who took the wind out of the sails of the prosecutors and their zeal to try Davis. In 1866, while Davis was still in prison, Bledsoe published a treatise, *Is Davis a Traitor?* Bledsoe attacked the case against secession, especially its main supporter, Daniel Webster. He called Webster a "great deceiver," not a "great expounder,"[15] and then set forth an impressive array of historical facts and constitutional analysis to make out a solid case for secession. This

Figure 12.3. Daniel Webster, who thundered from the floor of the Senate that the Union was perpetual and no state could secede except by war. This provided the rationale for Lincoln to hold the Union together by force of arms. Webster was heralded in the North as the "Great Expounder." In the South, they called him the "Great Deceiver," with his flawed knowledge of history. He seemed more like a "Great Windbag."

book probably found its way into the reading of the attorney general's staff and must have come as a shock. The North had been so brainwashed by the "traitor" logic that it didn't realize how formidable Jefferson Davis's case was. Shortly thereafter, the prosecutors started dragging their feet, delaying the trial and searching for some way to avoid prosecuting Davis without vindicating the South. One federal judge considered jury tampering once the judiciary realized a Virginian was apt to acquit Davis.[16]

Professor Bledsoe concluded that the issue of secession had indeed been settled by war but that the "final verdict of history has not been heard on the question of secession." Bledsoe lamented that "perhaps no other question of political philosophy, or of international law, pregnant with such unutterable calamities has ever been so partially and so superficially examined as the right of secession from the Federal Union of the United States. . . . The voice of reason, enlightened by the study of history . . . yet remains to be heard."[17]

Shortly after Bledsoe's book came out in 1866, the attorney general decided to bring in outside, independent counsel to try Davis (as in the Watergate case more than a century later). They needed someone of great stature to stand up to the lawyers defending Davis. They chose as their leading trial prosecutor John J. Clifford. But after reviewing the case, Clifford withdrew, arguing that he had "grave doubts" about the case and that the government could "end up having fought a successful war, only to have it declared unlawful by a Virginia jury."[18] The case was, in short, a loser with disastrous consequences for the cause of the war against the South.

President Johnson thought of an easy way out. He would pardon Davis as he had pardoned so many other Confederates. But Davis refused a pardon: "To ask for a pardon would be a confession of guilt." Davis wanted a trial; he wanted the issue of secession decided by a court of law, and while he was waiting and hoping for this, so were many in the South. Bledsoe began his treatise: "I shall proceed to argue the right of secession; because this is the great issue on which the whole Southern people, the dead as well as the living, is about to be tried in the person of their illustrious chief, Jefferson Davis."[19]

A year passed after the withdrawal of John J. Clifford. Another special counsel was appointed to handle the case, the famous author and lawyer Richard Dana of Boston, who had written the great novel *Two Years before the Mast*. But he too decided the case was a loser. He wrote a lengthy brief, given to the president, taking Clifford's position. Dana argued that "a conviction will settle nothing in law or national practice not now settled . . . as a rule of law by war."[20] Thus, as Dana observed, the right to secede from the Union had not been settled by civilized means but by military power and the destruction of much life and property in the South. The North should accept its uncivilized victory, however dirty its hands might be, and not expose the fruits of its carnage to scrutiny by a peaceful court of law. President Johnson then appointed a new attorney general but he wanted no part of the case and left it to the staff already working on it.

THE STAGE IS SET

Now, over two years after Davis's imprisonment and grand jury indictments for treason, the stage was set for the great public trial of the century. Davis had been released from prison on a $100,000 bond, supported by none other than Horace Greeley, the leading abolitionist writer in the North. Greeley and a host of others were outraged at the treatment Davis had received—no speedy trial, incarceration in a dungeon for well over a year with only a Bible to read, a light burning day and night, and sentries constantly walking by, forbidden to talk to the prisoner. Added to that outrage, irons had been put on Davis's legs. The inhumane treatment he had received and the contempt that was shown for the Bill of Rights worked in his favor. The government, continuing its behavior of the past five years, looked once again like an evil despot. It couldn't even offer the fallen ruler a minimum of the so-called guarantees of the Bill of Rights.

Of course, by now, with two famous special counsels telling the government the case was a loser, only the staff of the attorney general's office could try the case, and this worried just about everyone, especially the Chief Justice. He came up with an amazing solution to avoid the trial without vindicating the South. The Fourteenth Amendment had been adopted, which provided that anyone who had engaged in insurrection against the United States and had at one time taken an oath of allegiance (which Davis had done as a U.S. Senator) could not hold public office. The Bill of Rights prevents double jeopardy, and thus Davis, who had already been punished once by the Fourteenth Amendment in not being permitted to hold public office, couldn't be tried and punished again for treason.

Chief Justice Salmon P. Chase secretly passed along his ingenious argument to Davis's counsel, Charles O'Connor, who then made the motion to dismiss. The Court took the motion under consideration and then passed the matter on to the Supreme Court for determination. While this was pending, President Johnson granted amnesty to everyone in the South,

Figure 12.4. Salmon P. Chase, as he appeared on the first greenback (1862), paper money used to finance the war. In 1864 he was appointed to be Chief Justice of the United States and soon had the unpleasant duty of presiding over the trial of Jefferson Davis, which Chase realized was a loser. He developed an ingenious theory to release Davis without vindicating the South.

Later, after the war, Chase got his chance as Chief Justice to write an opinion that would make secession illegal and thus justify the war to prevent any state from withdrawing from the federal union. The logic did not go unnoticed, as it merely reiterated the windbag logic of Daniel Webster. It was criticized by British scholar James Bryce in 1888 as having its roots in the logical process of medieval scholasticism. It may have been more honest for the learned justice to have said "we won the war and that settles it," recognizing that war is the final arbiter of political questions.

including Davis, in late December 1867. The Davis case was still on the docket, however. But in February 1868, at a dinner party attended by the Chief Justice and an attorney for the government, it was agreed that on the following day a motion for nonprosecution would be made that would dismiss the case. A guest overheard the conversation and reported what was on the minds of most Southerners: "I did not consider that he [Davis] was any more guilty of treason than I was, and that a trial should be insisted upon, which could properly only result in a complete vindication of our cause, and of the action of the many thousands who had fought and of the many thousands who had died for what they felt to be right."

Thus ended the case of United States versus Jefferson Davis—a case that was to be the trial of the century, a great state trial, perhaps the most significant trial in the history of the nation. Two outside special prosecutors who examined the case with a sharp legal eye withdrew and washed their hands of the whole affair, understandably.

But besides the secession issue, what other aspects of Davis's defense frightened the prosecution? Surely, Lincoln-appointed Republican justices on the Supreme Court would have ruled against secession, and even Justice Chase may have instructed the jury that no state had a right to secede from the Union.

First, there is the matter of mens rea, or criminal intent. Even assuming a strong hand by the Chief Justice against secession, a good faith belief that the states had the right to withdraw from the Union would be enough to permit a jury to find no criminal intent, hence no crime.

And then there is the duty of a citizen of his state to come to its defense in time of armed invasion, which is what Lincoln's war was all about. These were not revolutionaries but men coming to the aid of their country and certainly to their sovereign state. That also would warrant an acquittal. The lawyers who came to defend Davis knew they had a good case, and when the prosecution began to drag its feet with delaying tactics, they had every reason to be excited about the probability of winning in a court of law. It is no wonder the special prosecutors withdrew.

Bledsoe, in his treatise *Is Jefferson Davis a Traitor?* quoted a speech that Lincoln made on 4 July 1848. He said, "Any people whatsoever have the right to abolish the existing government, and form a new one that suits them better. This is a most valuable, a most sacred right." Why didn't this apply to the South? "The reason is plain," said Bledsoe. "It was, indeed, most perfectly and fully explained by Mr. Lincoln himself. When asked, as President of the United States, 'why not let the South go?' his simple, direct and honest answer revealed one secret of the astute policy of the Washington cabinet. 'Let the South go!' said he, '*where, then, shall we get our revenue?'* There lies the secret." Lincoln and his war party were quite willing to ignore principle and law, and to maintain that secession could not be. Why? asks Professor Bledsoe. Taxes, that's why.[21]

Finally, after over a century, the South does have a judicial decision of some merit that refutes the medieval scholasticism of Justice Chase. In August 1998 the Supreme Court of Canada faced the secession issue of Quebec, initiated by a request from the prime minister and the cabinet for an advisory opinion on secession—something neither the North nor the South considered doing in 1861. Our leaders at that time thought that war was the way to go, ignoring the obligation of a civil society to pursue peaceful means for settling disputes.

The Canadian High Court held that there was no constitutional means or basis for secession, whether unilaterally or by some other process. However, the people of Quebec, according to the Supreme Court of Canada, enjoyed a constitutional right to have a referendum without any interference. If the people of Quebec clearly voted for secession, then the government of Canada had a constitutional duty to negotiate in good faith to accommodate the expressed desire of the people of Quebec. The Court thus repudiated the course taken by Northern Republicans in 1861 but affirmed the essence of the view expressed by President James Buchanan in his 6 December 1860 annual message to the Congress: "Our Union rests upon public opinion, and can never be cemented by the blood of its citizens shed in a civil war. If it cannot live in the affections of the people, it must one day perish. Congress possesses many means of preserving it by conciliation, but the sword was not placed in their hands to preserve it."[22] President Buchanan's view was held by many Northerners, especially the "peace Democrats," or Copperheads.

The similarity between Canada's current secession crisis and America's 1860 crisis arises from constitutions that are silent on the issue but also from the social structure of the nations. The United States was established to accommodate two cultures that, with time, separated into an agrarian society in the South and a growing commercial and industrial society in the North. Slave labor, originally lawful in all the colonies and states in the eighteenth century, began to split the nation's economic system. In addition, there was a growing aversion to slavery throughout Western civilization.

In Canada, the Dominion was established to accommodate two distinct cultures as well, separated by language and national origin. The North and the South in 1860 had evolved into the same kind of separateness, on different issues. Even the great churches came apart—again, similar to

Figure 12.5. Varina Davis, the wife of Jefferson Davis, was a beautiful and brilliant woman. She visited a number of prominent men in the North, even those without any sympathy for the Southern cause, yet she charmed them and motivated them to demand the release of Davis from prison, and even to put up the bonds for his release. She may have done much to eventually have all treason charges against him dropped.

Canada. Anglophones, as they are called in Quebec, have increasingly fled to the English-speaking provinces, and those who remain are forced to use French by the police power of the state.

A few months before the Supreme Court of Canada announced its decision, on New Year's Day 1998, the archbishop of Montreal—the highest ranking cleric in Quebec—alarmed antisecessionists by stating that "the Supreme Court can say what it wants. Even if they say the right [of secession] does not exist, if the people decide to do it, the people are sovereign." Strong words, but not the way Lincoln saw it in 1861.

Granted that there probably will be secession in Canada by the Francophones in Quebec, is it not reasonable to believe that the South will rise again, as so many descendants of the Confederacy maintain and teach their children? The numbers do not add up for this to happen, as the number of those of Confederate descent shrink in a growing population of outsiders, minorities, and especially African-Americans, who look with contempt upon the old South and its progeny. But secession is in the making in America, and it is not in the old South—it is in the Southwest, by the Mexican-Americans, who are not just separate by culture and language but by race as well. As their numbers move them into the majority, secession from the United States to form a Mexican-American nation is not as far-fetched as it may sound. This prospect has been in the vision of Mexican-American leaders as their long-term game plan, and, unlike the Southerners, they do have the numbers. Consider what a Hispanic leader on the Los Angeles City Council said in 1996: "Because our numbers are growing, they're afraid of this great mass of minorities that now live in our communities, they're afraid that we're going to take over the governmental institutions and other institutions. They're right, we will take them over, and we are not going to go away, we are here to stay, and we are saying *ya basta* [enough]."[23]

At the University of Texas (at Arlington), the founder of Chicano nationalism had this to say in January 1995: "We are millions. We just have to survive. We have an aging White America. They are not making babies. They are dying. It's a matter of time. The explosion is in our population."[24]

What makes this potential secession so significant is the racial distinction coupled with language, plus leaders with a vision for secession. When they have the numbers, will they not have every reason to secede, to withdraw from the leviathan in Washington to form a new nation where they will be, like the Southerners tried to be, making their own destiny, free from gringo domination—as the South wanted freedom from Yankee domination?

13

Lincoln's Logic

Lincoln has become one of our national deities and a realistic examination of him is thus no longer possible.

H. L. Mencken, 1931

AT THE GETTYSBURG CEMETERY

Lincoln's mental processes and his logic have fascinated me ever since my university days. In a class in logic, we studied his Gettysburg Address. The analysis showed that this famous speech didn't fit the real world. It was good poetry, perhaps, but was it good thinking? It's chiseled in stone in the Lincoln Memorial in Washington, and it ranks in the minds of most Americans with the Declaration of Independence and the Constitution. This oration was given to dedicate the cemetery at Gettysburg, where tens of thousands of young men died in a battle that was probably the turning point of the war. The address is reminiscent of the funeral oration of Pericles of Athens in the fifth century B.C. But Pericles's oration seemed to fit the real world of his day and the virtues of Athenian democracy. Lincoln's address did not fit the world of his day. It reflected his logic, which was based on a number of errors and falsehoods. That it has survived with such reverence is one of the most bizarre aspects of the war.

"FOUR SCORE AND SEVEN YEARS AGO"

By simple arithmetic that would be 1776, when the Revolutionary War started and the Declaration of Independence was signed. That declaration was written with "decent respect for the opinions of mankind," to explain the reasons for the separation of the thirteen colonies from Great Britain. It contained no endowment of governmental power and created no government. The government came later in 1781 with the Articles of Confederation. The articles stated that this confederation was established by "sovereign states," like many of the leagues of states throughout history. To be accurate, Lincoln should have said "four score and two years ago," or better still, "three score and fourteen years ago." Even the Northern newspapers winced. The *New York World* sharply criticized this historical folly. "*This* United States" was not created by the Declaration of Independence but "the result of the ratification of a compact known as the Constitution," a compact that said nothing about equality. Others accused Lincoln of "gross ignorance or willful misstatement." Yet today, that gross ignorance is chiseled in stone as if it were some great truth like scripture, instead of a willful misstatement.

"OUR FATHERS BROUGHT FORTH ON THIS CONTINENT, A NEW NATION"

The federal compact among the former thirteen colonies, the new "sovereign states," as expressed in the Articles of Confederation in 1781, was not a nation as that term was then and is normally used. That was recently ex-

Figure 13.1. The gathering at the dedication of the cemetery at Gettysburg, 19 November 1863. It was an impressive occasion with many dignitaries from Washington in attendance. The speaker of the day was the prominent Edward Everett of Massachusetts. He spoke for two hours. Lincoln was not even on the program, but protocol dictated that he be invited to say a few words. He spoke for just a few minutes as requested, three hundred words in all. There was a faint applause, unlike the strong ovation given to Edward Everett. It became Lincoln's most noted speech, yet careful analysis shows it to be common prose that did not really fit the occasion.

plained by Carl N. Degler, professor of American history at Stanford University, in a memorial lecture given at Gettysburg College in 1990: "The Civil War, in short, was not a struggle to save a failed union, but to create a nation that until then had not come into being."

Thus Lincoln's "new nation" really came into being by force of arms in the war between the states. Lincoln, according to Professor Degler, had a lot in common with Germany's Otto von Bismarck, who built a united Germany in the nineteenth century and believed that "blood and iron" were the main force for national policy. When it came to blood, Lincoln surpassed them all. The slaughter of Confederate men only matched, on a proportionate basis, the losses incurred by the Russians and the Germans in World War II.

In Lincoln's first inaugural address he used the word "Union" twenty times but "nation" not at all. But once the South seceded, the term began to disappear, and by the time of the Gettysburg Address, it was the American "nation" that was used, and the word "Union" had disappeared completely.

Thus the call from Northern peace Democrats—"the constitution as it is; the Union as it was"—seems to make sense, but as Lincoln took over control of the federal government, he soon wanted no part of it. Although he tried to trace the "new nation" back to 1776, he had to ignore history and the intention and words of the Founders, and create a new "gospel according to Lincoln" on the American commonwealth. Lincoln's new nation had no constitutional basis—no peaceful legal process. It was created by war, by "blood and iron," like Bismarck's Germany, and has survived to this day. In a sense, Lincoln did more to create America than did the Founding Fathers. It is Lincoln who is the father of our present country, not George Washington. Lincoln's Gettysburg reference to the Founders creating a new nation was not true. Just as Julius Caesar created an imperial order out of a republic, so Lincoln created a nation out of a compact among states, and both used their military forces to do so.

"CONCEIVED IN LIBERTY"

A leading man of letters in Britain during the American Revolution, Samuel Johnson, replied to the Americans' claims of tyranny in his book *Taxation Not Tyranny* (1775). He said, "How is it that we hear the loudest *yelps* for liberty among the drivers of negroes?"

The British are still chiding us for the absurdity of the Declaration of Independence. Some years ago, while I was living in a British colony, we Americans got together on the Fourth of July for a barbecue. One of my older English friends asked me what the celebration was all about. I took the bait and told him it was to celebrate the signing of the Declaration of Independence. He replied, "Wasn't that document kind of a farce? All that verbiage about equality of all men and liberty when over a million black people were in bondage for life, and their children and children's children?" Of course I had no answer, for the term "all men" meant all white men. And to make matters worse, it really meant "white guys," as white women weren't much better off. What is not known is that when Lincoln issued his Emancipation Proclamation, many of the early women's rights groups asked, How about us too? Thus the declaration that Lincoln refers to in his address, of four score and seven years ago, was *not* conceived in liberty *nor* was it dedicated to the proposition that all men were created equal. So much for logic and reality.

Lincoln's logic at Gettysburg, as elsewhere, reveals a trial lawyer with a tool of his craft—using the best logic he can muster to support his client's (the North's) case, however bad that case may be. It is also, of course, the craft of a politician, which may explain why so many politicians are lawyers.

"TODAY WE ARE ENGAGED IN A GREAT CIVIL WAR"

Actually, it wasn't a civil war as that term was then, and is now, defined. A civil war is a war that breaks out in a nation between opposing groups for control of the state, for example, in Russia in 1917 with the Red against the Whites or in China in the 1940s.

The War of Rebellion, as the war was called in the North, was really a war for Southern independence. The Southern states had withdrawn from the Union by democratic process—the same process they had followed to join the Union initially. The Northern federation went to war to prevent their secession from the Union just as Britain went to war in 1776 to prevent the colonies from seceding from the British nation. It was the fundamentals of the Revolutionary War, eighty-five years before. It was, if you get down to the nuts and bolts of it, a war of conquest by the North to destroy the Confederacy and to establish a new political leadership over the conquered territories. Illiterate slaves were given the vote, and the rest of the Southern society, the ruling groups, were not permitted to vote. The poor, illiterate blacks were then told by Northern occupation forces to vote as directed, and they did so, infuriating the conquered people and creating a zeal for white supremacy that is only in our time losing its grip on Southern society.

"TESTING WHETHER THAT NATION . . .
CAN LONG ENDURE"

That comment seems to presuppose that the South was out to conquer the Northern federation. That is as absurd as saying that the revolting colonies in 1776 were out to destroy the British nation. The thirteen colonies' withdrawal from the British Empire in 1776 was the same as the attempt of the Southern states to withdraw in 1861 from the 1789 federation. In reality, the 1789 federation was not in any danger. It would have endured with secession. Unlike Grant, Lee was not out to conquer the North. In reality, this logic was as absurd as the rest of Lincoln's funeral oration.

"A FINAL RESTING PLACE FOR THOSE WHO HERE
GAVE THEIR LIVES THAT THAT NATION MIGHT LIVE"

Again, "that nation" was not in danger of dying—that was not Southern Confederate policy and Lincoln knew it. But again, he was only being a good lawyer, arguing his client's case as best he could, and with no rebuttal he was an easy winner.

"AND THAT GOVERNMENT OF THE PEOPLE,
BY THE PEOPLE AND FOR THE PEOPLE SHALL
NOT PERISH FROM THE EARTH"

Why did Lincoln even suggest that secession by the Southern states would mean that democracy would perish from the earth—in America or elsewhere? That was perfect nonsense, and Lincoln knew it, but again, there was no one to rebut his argument.

Lincoln's repeated assertion that secession would amount to a failure of the American experiment with democracy and liberty "just is plain nonsense," wrote Professor Hummel in his refreshing book on the Civil War, *Emancipating Slaves, Enslaving Free Men.*[1] The London *Times* seems to have best understood what was going on in America with the Northern invasion to prevent secession: "If Northerners . . . had peaceably allowed the seceders to depart, the result might fairly have been quoted as illustrating the advantages of Democracy, but when Republicans put empire above liberty, and resorted to political oppression and war . . . It was clear that nature at Washington was precisely the same as nature at St. Petersburg. . . . Democracy broke down. . . . when it was upheld, like any other Empire, by force of arms."[2]

By 1860 democracy was strongly entrenched throughout Western civilization, and certainly in the American states. The democratic process had emerged decades before in Europe—in Britain, France, the Netherlands, Switzerland, and so on. The war in America for Southern independence was in no way a danger to the concept of government "of the people." Strange as it may seem, as it turned out, it was Lincoln who was out to destroy governments of the people in the eleven Southern states. The declaration's assertion that governments derive their "just powers from the consent of the governed" was not an acceptable idea in Lincoln's mind so far as the South was concerned. Like a good lawyer he ignored it.

What makes Lincoln's ending so outrageous is that he didn't believe in the self-determination of peoples, as British writers noted in 1861 and a hundred years later in 1961. (See chap. 1.)

Ordinances of secession had been adopted in the Southern states, often with huge majorities. Their right to govern by consent was not acceptable to Lincoln's thinking—that would undermine his client's case. Yet it was Lincoln who ended up destroying the Union as it was and substituting an all-powerful national government in which the states were relegated to not much more than county status. There emerged the "imperial presidency" that is with us to this day, in which presidents can go to war, without congressional approval, spend money without congressional approval; in fact, they can rule by decree like the consuls of Rome. In other Western democracies, this is not so. Their chief executive must have the permission and approval of their legislature to do such things. Thus Lincoln did more to destroy the Union than preserve it. Is not this irony at its best?

There were many in the North who, upon reading the Gettysburg Address, saw its logical follies. The *New York World* noted the president's "gross ignorance" and reminded him that "*this* United States" was not created by the declaration but by a compact known as "the Constitution," which said nothing about equality. Other newspapers, such as the *Chicago Times* (which Lincoln had shut down) called the address "a perversion of history." Still others referred to "the silly remarks of the president." In this century the logic of the Gettysburg Address has been questioned by none other than H. L. Mencken, a journalist and wit who at times shocked the nation with his strong language as well as logic:

> The Gettysburg speech was at once the shortest and the most famous oration in American history. . . . the highest emotion reduced to a few poetical phrases. Lincoln himself never even remotely approached it. It is genuinely stupendous. But let us not forget that it is poetry, not logic; beauty, not sense. Think of the argument in it. Put it into the cold

words of everyday. The doctrine is simply this: that the Union soldiers who died at Gettysburg sacrificed their lives to the cause of self-determination—that government of the people, by the people, for the people, should not perish from the earth. It is difficult to imagine anything more untrue. The Union soldiers in the battle actually fought against self-determination; it was the Confederates who fought for the right of their people to govern themselves.

Figure 13.2. Lincoln's Gettysburg Address, now immortalized on his monument in Washington, D.C., was far off the mark of reality, not only in what was at issue in the war but in what principles really brought forth this nation and when.

THE SIMPLE-MINDED SOLDIER BOY

The arrest of Clement Vallandigham in 1863, one arbitrary arrest out of thousands, had brought forth anger in the North about the whole matter of military arrests and trials and the suspension of the right of habeas corpus. Such arrests had been going on for two years, and there was some public concern. But Lincoln had been able to avoid the issue since his address to the Congress on 4 July 1861. In that address he excused his apparently unconstitutional arrests on the grounds that "public safety" made the arrests not only necessary but legal. As long as the public safety was endangered, the arrests were constitutional. The Constitution, of course, makes no such justification. In short, this reasoning was the Constitution according to Lincoln. Over the course of two years, any challenges to this thinking were squelched by closing newspapers and arresting exponents, even monitoring and censoring the mails. One man in Ohio, for example, was arrested when someone overheard him saying that he voted the secessionist ticket. Another, while drunk, said he'd like to take a rope to old Abe Lincoln's head. Even shouting "hurrah for Jeff Davis" was enough to warrant an arrest. And there was no exception for women. They were locked up equally with the men. But Vallandigham's case was different, as noted in chapter 11. He was a candidate for governor, giving a political speech at a Democratic rally. To many, his arrest was just too much, and there was a public outcry.

Lincoln signed an order to banish Vallandigham, but the public outcry forced him to justify his actions, not only in the matter of Vallandigham but for the thousands of others languishing in prisons throughout the land. His response and explanation seemed to cool the opposition and put the matter to rest until the end of the war. Lincoln said that Vallandigham's speech was hurting the army by discouraging enlistments, even encouraging desertions. "Must I shoot a simple-minded soldier boy who deserts, while I must not touch a hair of a wily agitator who induces him to desert?" Lincoln asked. In such a case, "to silence the agitator, and save the boy, is not only constitutional, but, withal, a great mercy." The public was impressed.

Lincoln's logic for silencing dissent has been used for centuries by tyrants, and in our age, by Communists and strong-arm dictators. The Soviets had a crime of "slander against the state," which was used to silence dissidents who spoke out against the government. If we had followed Lincoln's logic in Vietnam, we would have had to undertake a massive building program for more jails, courts, and security police. We would have had to put hundreds of thousands into prison and closed down most newspapers in the country. Even Walter Cronkite would have been locked up. The

Vietnam War, like the Civil War, was on shaky constitutional grounds. In Vietnam we didn't execute deserters, something Lincoln might have considered as an alternative to executing his "simple-minded soldier boy."

What had Vallandigham said that was so bad? Plenty. At the Democratic party rally, he called the war "wicked and cruel" and asserted that it was started to "enthrone Republican despotism on America." He called Lincoln "King Lincoln" and charged that Lincoln's tax law was "the like of which has never been seen upon any but a conquered people." All this is just hard-boiled American politics.

Hatred runs almost unchecked during wartime—a kind of lynch mob psychology prevails. German farmers often murdered American airmen shot down over Germany, and the Japanese didn't hesitate to kill Doolittle's raiders over Tokyo. In the United States, citizens who had Japanese ancestors were sent off to internment camps. The logic was similar—they might engage in sabotage, they might be disloyal. So Vallandigham "might" encourage desertion. But as with the Japanese citizens, there was no showing that he did so. It was, like the O. J. Simpson case, a lawyer's makeshift argument that a biased jury might believe, even if it was not much more than a pipe dream. But even if Vallandigham's arguments did encourage deserters or discourage enlistments, that is the price a free society has to pay for free speech and a free press. As it turned out, it was Lincoln's logic that was for the simple-minded.

The simple-minded soldier boy has to be contrasted with the intelligent-minded soldier boy. The assumption behind Lincoln's logic is that any reasonable soldier would be more than willing to die for Lincoln's war, and would not desert. There were millions of Americans who found fault with Lincoln's war—the vast majority did not want war. As it turned out, representative government was a failure at this time in history.

Vallandigham was a well-educated lawyer of considerable stature, not a rabble-rouser. He served in the Ohio legislature and served for two terms in the U.S. Congress. While in exile he was the Democratic candidate for the governor of Ohio. His logic may have made a lot of sense to the intelligent soldier boy as much as to the "simple-minded" one Lincoln wrote about. By 1863, disapproval of the war was rampant in the nation. At more than half of the dinner tables there was talk opposing the war and Lincoln's unconscionable conduct. There was fear in the land to oppose the government. The Republicans never had a united nation behind the war effort. Vallandigham was arrested and tried before a military court because no civilian court would have tried him—no grand jury would have even indicted him. He had committed no crime that could be found on the statute books. The military tribunal simply made up a crime.

Figure 13.3. Lincoln excused his crackdown on free speech whenever his war was criticized or there was even a suggestion that a state had the right to secede from the Union. Such critical expressions might entice a simple-minded soldier boy to desert and end up the victim of a firing squad, as shown above.

THE SOUTH WAS THE AGGRESSOR

In your hands, my dissatisfied fellow-country-men, and not in mine, is the momentous issue of civil war. . . . You can have no conflict without being yourself the aggressors.

Lincoln's first inaugural address, 1861

These words of Lincoln had been edited by Secretary of State Seward. Lincoln's original draft read: "With *you,* and not with *me,* is the solemn question of 'Shall it be peace, or a sword?' "

Some years before, Lincoln as a Whig congressman had blasted President Polk for going to war against Mexico. Behind whatever facade the government tried to create, it was a war of aggression against Mexico for Mexican territory—lots of it, from California to Texas. In the war to come against the South, Lincoln would try to label the South the aggressor. At the time, that seemed important. He promised in his inaugural that there would be no invasion of the South, no use of military force *except to collect taxes and recover federal property*. At the time, there was no federal presence in the seven Confederate states. All federal officers had resigned. How could he collect taxes without invading the South? And how could he recover the forts without invading the South? Lincoln's argument was an absurdity.

The South did fire the first shot at Fort Sumter after having been repeatedly promised by federal officials, including the secretary of state, Seward, that the fort would be abandoned. Lincoln consulted his cabinet on two occasions about the consequences if attempts were made to reinforce Fort Sumter. At first, the cabinet opposed reinforcement—the likelihood of war was too obvious to question. But with the "war of the tariff" (i.e., the government's taxes) the cabinet reversed itself. Just before Lincoln addressed Congress in July 1861, he confided in a close friend, Orville Browning, that he (Lincoln) had "conceived the idea and proposal of sending supplies. . . . The plan succeeded. They attacked Sumter—it fell, and thus did more service than it otherwise could."

The so-called provisioning plan for the fort involved a major naval task force, with eleven warships and twenty-five hundred men, plus 285 cannon. Lincolnite historians seem enraged at the suggestion that Lincoln enticed the South to fire the first shot. After all, this was a relief squadron to provide food to a starving garrison—a garrison that had been purchasing foodstuffs at the markets in Charleston up to a few days before the naval squadron went to sea. Only after Lincoln notified the South that the surrender of the fort was off and that provisioning would take place did the South fire on Sumter. As it turned out, Lincoln had enticed them to fire the first shot. They had taken the bait. The war had been started, just as Lincoln had hoped, by the South.

THE CIVIL WAR: THE OTHER GUY'S FAULT?

Lincoln didn't mind taking credit for the start of the conflict. The nation rallied around the president and accepted his dictatorial powers to avenge the assault on the flag. Doubters now became supporters. But as the war turned into bloody carnage and Union defeats multiplied, support began to wane and Lincoln began to suffer doubt and melancholy. In the North and South hundreds of thousands of families suffered the loss of their sons. Lincoln said that he dreamed of his dead son Willie time and again. What about the tens of thousands of families that also dreamed of their lost sons in a war he could have stopped at any time? The time had arrived for Lincoln to find others in the North to blame for the war.

The ranks of the army were thinning from the carnage. More young men were needed for cannon fodder and to fill dark graves. During one of the many calls of Lincoln for more young men for the army, Joseph Medill of the *Chicago Tribune* went to Washington to urge Lincoln to reduce the quota of troops from Cook County. Lincoln was angered at Medill and the committee that came with him and said:

> Gentlemen, after Boston, Chicago has been the chief instrument in bringing this war on the country. The North-west has opposed the South as New England has opposed the South. It is you who are largely responsible for making blood flow as it has. You called for war until we had it. . . . Now you come here to be let off from the call for men which I have made to carry out the war you have demanded. You ought to be ashamed of yourselves. Go home and raise your 6,000 men. And you Medill, you are acting like a coward. You and your *Tribune* have had more influence than any other paper in the North-west in making this war.[3]

Lincoln was telling the truth. Immediately after the bombardment of Fort Sumter, Medill predicted that if Lincoln went to war, it would be soon over, "within two or three months at the furthest," because "Illinois can whip the South by herself." Without the support and demands of the newspapers, there could have been no war. Here Lincoln's logic made sense. However, there were just as many newspapers opposed to the war, but in a few months Lincoln had shut them down.

THE CIVIL WAR: GOD'S WAR

As the war dragged on and as the casualties escalated to over a quarter of a million dead in the North alone, Lincoln had to find another faulter. Thus it became God's war; it was God's punishment for America's sin of slavery. At first slavery was not an issue. Captured slaves were being returned to their masters, and abolition was repudiated as both a purpose and a cause. It was a war for the Union, with no withdrawals; it was a war for America's God-given destiny, for the American empire in the making.

Lincoln was no longer the leader of the cause of the North, nor was the Union the fundamental factor. Now it was God's war, and God had his purposes. In the second inaugural address, Lincoln quoted the words of Jesus when he condemned those who would offend children and humble believers: "Woe unto the world because of offenses! for it must needs be that offenses come; but woe to that man by whom offenses cometh" (Matthew

18:7; Luke 17:1). Lincoln then applies the biblical passage to the war's carnage: "If we shall suppose that American slavery is one of those offenses which, in the providence of God, must needs come, but which, having continued through his appointed time, he now wills be removed, and that He gives both North and South this terrible war, as the woe due to those by whom the offense came. . . . Yet if God wills that it continue until all the wealth piled by the bondsman's two hundred and fifty years of unrequited toil shall be sunk, and until every drop of blood drawn with the lash shall be paid by another drawn with the sword, so still it must be said, 'The judgements of the Lord are true and righteous altogether.' "

Lincoln's Jehovah complex gave the war a psychopathic Calvinistic fatalism, with God directing the whole affair and punishing both North and South for tolerating slavery. The punishment, being most severe in terms of the slaughter of hundreds of thousands of young men, will continue until God decides the people have been punished enough. As time passed, Lincoln seems to have found comfort in this approach to the war he started and tenaciously pursued. Making it God's war and God's punishment helped keep his psyche in some balance. In a letter to a Kentucky editor, Albert G. Hodges, dated 4 April 1864, he continued this theme: "If God now wills the removal of a great wrong, and wills also that we of the North as well as the South, shall pay fairly for our complicity in that wrong, impartial history will find therein new cause to arrest and revere the justice and goodness of God."[4]

Not even the maddest of religious fanatics ever uttered words to equal Lincoln's second inaugural address. Lincoln tells America that slavery had brought God's wrath on America and had to be paid for with blood and agony but that the debt had to be paid for by those who did not contract the debt. A just God willed this, and his will would require almost two-thirds of a million lives, a devastated land, and a cost in money beyond comprehension at that date. If God was now willing to end slavery, it was his will to do so with men like Lincoln who would give the North and South this terrible war as atonement, and peace efforts to end the suffering were not in God's plan. Lincoln accepts this scenario as the work of a just God, "just and true." as he expressed it. Another interpretation is that Lincoln had to shift the blame and remove his own guilt, and he was quite willing to resort to reasoning more characteristic of a psychotic mind than a healthy mind.

Lincoln's logic may have had some appeal to the religious mind—that God punishes sinners and America's slavery was a sin. But even a passing glance at the world at large in 1864 would force any thinking person to question the "oh ye sinner" scenario: If God was punishing America so severely, with such agony and cruelty, why didn't God punish the rest of the Western world for slavery? How come Great Britain, France, the Netherlands, Denmark, Sweden, and, most of all, Russia got off scot-free and carnage free? And then, of course, there is the Holy Scripture's silence—the extensive discourses and writings of the prophets, of Jesus, of

Figure 13.4. A Confederate teenager, Edwin Francis Jennison, killed at Malvern Hill, Virginia, in 1862. His blood, and the slaughter of hundreds of thousands of teenagers on both sides, was on the hands of those responsible for the war—those who could have stopped the war at any time. According to Lincoln, the war was God's doing, and the slaughter would end when God had had enough of it. Lincoln called this "the justice and goodness of God."

Paul, of almost two thousand years of Old Testament Scriptures, without a word of condemnation for the operation of slavery. If slavery was so bad, why didn't Jesus or Paul or the prophets say something?

The answer, of course, is that Lincoln's war had not gone so well. God had not given any support for the military operations. If the North was on a crusade, even unwittingly, should not God have brought about many victories, as he had done when the Israelites conquered the inhabitants of the land of Canaan? God gave Joshua a tremendous boost and support as he went to battle, even bringing walls down and stopping the sun up in the sky. Why didn't "Fighting Joe" Hooker and the rest of his appointed generals enjoy such divine support? In short, how come the bad guys were doing so well on the battlefield?

To answer that, Lincoln sought solace and inner freedom by bringing God into the fray. In short, Lincoln was guilt-ridden and was close to being mentally ill at this time. He now saw God as the primary force behind the war, thus granting himself absolution and exculpating his actions in driving the nation into war and refusing to promote peace when the opportunity was always there. Increasingly, God's will is brought into play to explain America's most tragic epic and to thus excuse those involved, especially the leaders. Union armies suffered great losses and defeats because God wanted it that way. Over 360,000 young Northern men died, most of them still teenagers, and this was God's will? A whole generation of youth was sacrificed, and only when there was enough slaughter, enough suffering for sin, would God stop the carnage. An angry God was at work in the affairs of America and his newly chosen people to punish them for allowing slavery.

At first, Lincoln's logic showed that the purpose of the war was to preserve the Union because the Constitution didn't provide for secession, and so once a state voluntarily joined the Union, it was in it forever. Then, after two years of military disasters, Lincoln brought out the slavery abolition purpose. Now the war had become God's war of punishment. In reality, all these "purposes" were, as Charles Dickens said, "specious humbug" designed to conceal the North's desire for economic control over the South. Now that's real logic.

On 30 September 1862, Lincoln wrote "The Will of God Prevails": "In great contests each party claims to act in accordance with the will of God. God cannot be for or against the same thing." But God appears to be involved on both sides. Lincoln continues: "In the present civil war it is quite possible that God's purpose is something different from the purposes of either party; and yet the human instrumentalities, working just as they do, are of the best adaption to effect his purpose. I am almost ready to say that this is probably true; that God wills this contest, and wills that it shall not end yet. By his mere great power on the minds of the now contestants, he could have either saved or destroyed the Union without a human contest [i.e., war]. Yet the contest began. And having begun, he could give final victory to either side any day. Yet the contest proceeds."[5]

This Calvinistic fatalism becomes a doctrine to justify the cruelty of the war, the slaughter of 630,000 young men. This was, as one historian observed, "Christian cruelty, which is dishonest and irresponsible." But it shifts the blame from those primarily responsible for starting and perpetuating the carnage to divine will. A not-so-nice deity, like something out of the religion of the ancient Aztecs, who also required blood sacrifice from his mortal offspring, only that was just one bleeding heart a day, not thousands. But it was the young men, the young warrior, whose blood both gods demanded. In the final analysis, however, it was not a deity at all in either case, but the will of the high priests who held in their hands the control over the people. Lincoln early called this the "people's war." Actually, it was Lincoln's war and the war of his cohorts.

Lincoln was unable to even consider negotiating with his adversaries. The Confederates sent many prominent citizens to Washington to discuss the conflict to see if a peaceful solution could be worked out in some fashion. For over four years peace feelers came from the Confederacy. Lincoln rebuked them with the argument that they had no legitimacy and he therefore would not talk with them. This obstinacy simply multiplied the deaths that were to follow. Lincoln might have considered the wisdom of Cicero, who wrote almost two thousand years before: "Then too, in the case of a state in its external relations . . . There are two ways of settling a dispute— first, by discussion; second by physical force—and since the former is characteristic of man, the latter of the brute, we must resort to force only in case we may not avail ourselves of discussion."[6]

The Confederacy sent some of the nation's most respected citizens, former senators and national leaders, for discussion, yet Lincoln would not talk with them or even have his cabinet ministers talk with them. He was for war, hardly in the camp of the "blessed are the peacemakers: for they shall be called the children of God." Lincoln was a war maker, through and through. Who knows what diplomacy may have produced? Why were peaceful means never even tried? Again, to quote Cicero, "Diplomacy in the friendly settlement of controversies is more desirable than courage in settling them on the battlefield."

Time and again civilized decency was repudiated by Lincoln. When prisoner exchanges were offered, both Lincoln and General Grant refused, knowing full well that Union men in Confederate prisons were suffering and dying by the hundreds, almost daily. When medicines were requested by the South, to aid Union prisoners as well as Southern citizens and soldiers, this request was also denied, even knowing full well it was a death warrant to thousands of Union troops. Eventually the South proposed to send in medicine only for Union prisoners and even this was turned down. The horrors of Andersonville, that most notorious of Southern prisons for Union soldiers, can be blamed on Grant and Lincoln when they refused to send medicines and to exchange prisoners. They felt the South would suffer and the inhumanity to Union soldiers was necessary to further punish the South. Nice guys. It is not the commander of the prison in Andersonville who should have been hanged, but the Union policy makers who could have brought these soldiers home.

THE MERCY OF GOD

In November 1861 a Yankee slave trader was captured on the high seas with a boat load of slaves bound for the West Indies. Trading in slaves had been illegal for many years, although the New England slave ships had been carrying on clandestine slave trading with considerable success for Cuba and Brazil but not the South, which was not interested. It is commonly but erroneously assumed that slave trading was a Southern occupation, but in fact almost all slave trading, when it was legal and later illegal, was from ships of New England registry with Northern crews.

The Yankee slave trader Nathanial Gordon, who was originally from Maine, was tried before a federal judge in New York and sentenced to be hanged on 7 February 1862. It was the first and only time such a sentence was handed down and carried out. Realizing the undue harshness of the sentence, 25,000 New Yorkers petitioned Lincoln to commute Gordon's sentence to one of life imprisonment. There was nothing to be lost by Lincoln doing this, but Lincoln refused to commute the sentence. (Later, when another slave trader was caught, Lincoln went to the other extreme and granted a pardon.) There were many vociferous abolitionists who called for the hanging to be carried out, and Lincoln yielded to their demands. He did, however, grant a cruel delay of thirteen days so that the execution would not take place until 20 February. Lincoln explained his course of action in these words: "In granting this respite [thirteen days] it becomes my painful duty to admonish the prisoner that relinquishing all expectation of pardon by human authority, he refer himself alone to the mercy of the common God and Father of all men."[7]

It would seem that mercy from God, to be realistic, would have to come through men, and in this case, Lincoln. Where was the "mercy of the common God" when Lincoln had him hanging from a rope until dead? What is the logic of this cruelty?

Lincoln also participated in the execution of thirty-nine Sioux Indians. The Sioux had rebelled at the starvation they had been experiencing when the government, as usual, breached its promises to them. And with no means of support, the Indians—men, women and children—were starving to death. Lincoln had the rebellious Sioux executed in one grand hanging of all thirty-nine at one time, the only mass hanging on such a scale ever to take place in American history. Even to this day, the descendants of those executed hold Lincoln and his government responsible for this barbaric execution. It would seem that the wrong side was on the gallows.

"IT WAS NOT BELIEVED THAT ANY LAW WAS VIOLATED" (LINCOLN'S MESSAGE TO CONGRESS, 4 JULY 1861)

After Lincoln had made the war an accomplished fact and had prepared war plans to invade the South, he called Congress into session—something by the plain language of the Constitution he should have done immediately after Sumter and before he instituted a bundle of war measures that were the exclusive prerogative of the Congress. In his written address to Congress he tried to explain and excuse what he had done and why. He had summoned the militia, which the Constitution clearly states is a congressional decision. He spent millions without an appropriation from Congress. He suspended the right of habeas corpus and told military officers to arrest anyone they thought might be a problem. If any judicial officer interfered with the arrests and imprisonment, they should resort to force and violence. He authorized the recruiting for the army. He decreed a blockade—an act of war by all known principles of international law. He defied the orders of the Supreme Court, reasoning that he had the right to repudiate any of the Supreme Court's rulings on the Constitution that he didn't like. He even signed a warrant to arrest the chief justice of the United States for rebuking him. When Lincoln had finished his four months of military dictatorship, there wasn't much left of the Constitution and its provisions: its separation of powers, its checks and balances, its protection of civil liberties, its plain and clear language on how the government is to be run.

Then he had the audacity to say that "it was not believed any law was violated." However, in that written message to Congress, he tried to excuse himself: "These measures [like calling the militia], whether strictly legal or not, were ventured upon, under what appeared to be popular demand, and a public necessity." In other words, reasoned Lincoln, there are no constitutional limits or restraints if a noble cause, or popular demand, is taken into account. Lincoln then had to deal with Taney's Supreme Court order against suspending the right of habeas corpus, which Lincoln repudiated. It was perfectly all right to disobey one law in order to save the nation and protect the Constitution.

There are two problems with this logic: First, he didn't disobey just one law, but a whole bundle of laws, creating nothing less than a military dictatorship. Second, there was no showing that the Constitution was being overthrown. That was his interpretation of the crisis; his excuse for actually tossing the whole Constitution out the window, Julius Caesar style. His most dangerous act was not calling the Congress forthwith to debate and decide all these issues. In not doing so, he repudiated the whole scheme of constitutional government, thus making a joke of its three primary provisions: Articles 1, 2, and 3, along with the Bill of Rights. It was not that one little law that had been repudiated but that a new government had been created, a new constitution, in which one man assumes all the powers of government—legislative, executive, and judicial. Lincoln was not violating one little law to preserve the Constitution but, in effect, all the laws.

The Romans had their dictatorships in times of crisis, but they had a constitutional safeguard—no man could be a dictator for longer than six months. By "popular demand," to quote Lincoln's logic, that was extended by the Roman senate for Caesar's lifetime. The whole purpose of a constitution is to prevent "popular demand" from running the nation. Too bad America didn't have the six months dictatorship rule. If we had, then Lincoln's dictatorship would have ended in the fall of 1861.

As for Congress, it had about as much input into the decision to go to war as did the Roman senate after Caesar took over the state. On 4 July 1861, Congress met not to seek peace, not to rebuke the president's usurpations of its powers, and certainly not to debate and deliberate the momentous decision of civil war that Lincoln had decided on his own. Opposition would be silenced by the charge of disloyalty. Everything the president asked for was granted, without delay, without debate. To doubt the president's wisdom—to question his decision for war—was treason. Lincoln's logic became holy writ on stone tablets for the faithful. There were only two classes of citizens—those who followed the president's line and traitors.

14

The High Ground

They [Confederate soldiers] took the high ground, which appeared to them above all discussion or controversy.

Charles Dickens, 1862

A Union that can only be maintained by swords and bayonets, and in which strife and civil war are to take the place of brotherly love and kindness, has no charm for me.

Robert E. Lee, January 1861

Sitting on high ground in Washington, D.C., less than a mile from the Potomac River, is the Lincoln Memorial, a gigantic Greek temple honoring the president who led the nation during the Civil War. The memorial is clearly visible from Virginia, less than a mile away. I have often thought that the memorial should have faced south toward Virginia, for it was in this direction Lincoln devoted his energies—the direction of his foes. The speeches engraved in stone on that monument were also directed at the South, the wicked Confederacy, which Lincoln and his compatriots branded as "traitors and conspirators."

It was the Army of Northern Virginia, led by Robert E. Lee, that was Lincoln's most formidable foe. Lee too had to be a major "traitor and conspirator," for his military skills brought the armies of the North to their knees, more often than not, and prolonged the war and greatly increased the casualties and slaughter of Union soldiers. Yet this great leader of the Confederate forces was seldom called a traitor, and he has somehow been on higher ground than the political leaders who directed the South's failed struggle for independence. For many, he is even on higher ground than his political adversary in the North, even though there is no similar memorial for Lee.

There is a statue of Lee in the main floor of the nation's capitol building in what is commonly called Statuary Hall. Each state was to have the right to provide a statue of two of its most distinguished citizens. Lee was chosen as the second great Virginian. The other? George Washington.

Some Northerners erroneously believe that Lee was fighting to perpetuate slavery. They don't know he was against slavery; that he opposed secession and loved the Union. After secession got rolling, he told his son that he was not pleased with this course of action. As a colonel in the Union army in Texas, he was present when Texas seceded. He refused to aid the secessionists and returned to his native Virginia, which at that time was still in the Union, with a powerful pro-Union sentiment among many of the Virginians. Lee then wrote to his cousin: "I wish for no other flag than the 'Star-spangled Banner,' and no other air than 'Hail Columbia.' "

Shortly after Lee returned from Texas, Lincoln signed Lee's appointment making him the commander of a cavalry regiment. This was short lived, for immediately after Fort Sumter was fired upon, Lee was summoned to Washington by Winfield Scott, commander in chief of the armies of the North. Scott was too old to take command of the armies in the field, but he knew of the talent and genius of Lee. Lee had had a distinguished career. In the Mexican war, General Scott was the commander of all U.S. forces. He declared that "the fall of Veracruz must be credited largely to Lee's skill, valor and undaunted energy."[1] It is easy to understand why Lincoln and his advisers wanted Lee to command Union forces invading the South.

On 18 April 1861, Scott offered Lee the command of all Union armies. Lee took time to reflect, ponder, and prayerfully contemplate the momentous decision before him. He retired to his room in Arlington, Virginia. As a deeply religious man, he sought guidance in making that decision. At midnight he emerged with his resignation in hand. He could not lead an army of aggression against his fellow countrymen in the South, who had foolishly (he thought) decided to withdraw from the Union and go it on their own. Any question about who was the aggressor in the Civil War was answered by Lee's decision to turn down the offer to be supreme commander. He had been fully briefed by General Scott of what was expected of him—what his military duties would entail. It was to be, in his mind, an immoral act that he could have no part of.

Lee wrote to his sister of his decision: "With all my devotion to the Union, and the feeling of loyalty and duty of an American citizen, I have not been able to make up my mind to raise my hand against my relatives, my children, and my home. I have therefore resigned my commission in the army."[2] So Lee just didn't turn down the offer to be supreme commander, which he must have wanted very much. He went much further and resigned from his lifetime service in the military because he would be ordered to invade the South.

The very next day, on 19 April 1861, while in Alexandria, Virginia, Lee learned of Virginia's secession following Lincoln's call for 75,000 volunteers. He commented, upon hearing the news, that he could not "see the good of secession." Then, on April 20, he turned in his resignation to the federal army, declaring, "save in the defense of my native State, I never desire again to draw my sword."[3]

Lee returned to his home in Virginia and accepted an appointment as commander of Virginia's forces. He would not be ordered to invade the North but only to defend and repel a foreign invader. With that he had no moral difficulty. He worked hard with great energy and used his extraordinary talents to prepare Virginia to defend itself against the coming assault from the North. It is important to understand Lee's mind and his response to the war. His course of action, his love of the Union, his aversion to secession and to slavery, and yet his final decision based on loyalty to his state were all too common in the Confederacy. His decision to follow his native state, against his other personal views, was a course of action repeated by thousands of like-minded Southerners. We may not understand this today because loyalty to one's state has given way to national patriotism. But in 1861, it was otherwise, at least throughout the South.

A strongly pro-Northern newspaper, the *North Carolina Standard,* reacted as Lee did. The editor wrote on 9 March 1861: "We cannot become parties to the subjugation of our Southern brethren."[4] A cavalryman who rode with the famous Jeb Stuart (Lee's missing support at Gettysburg) expressed this terrible dilemma that faced so many, in these words: "I was opposed to secession. . . . I thought that Lincoln, though a sectional candidate, was constitutionally elected and that we ought to wait to see what he would do. But when he called for troops from Virginia and we had to take one side or the other, then of course I was for going with the South in her mad scheme, right or wrong."[5]

It may seem amazing that the rank and file, those who did the fighting and dying, were more aware of the outcome of the formidable odds the South faced than the leaders were. The father of one Confederate private told his son, "William, it is a foolish undertaking, as there is no earthly show for Southern success," but agreed that his son had no other choice than to "defend your country," which in that case meant Texas.

On the other side, a young lieutenant in faraway San Francisco wrote to a West Point classmate in Georgia: "This war is not going to be a ninety day affair that papers and politicians are predicting. Both sides are deadly earnest, and it is going to be fought out to the bitter end. . . . For your cause there can be but one result. *It must be lost.*"

"Your cause is foredoomed," wrote the lieutenant. The reason was obvious, as time would show. The North had four times the population and manpower that the South had, but, more important, it had a hundred times more of the resources needed for war: a solid money system and a strong economy; the ability to manufacture war materials and develop new weapons; and the ability to build ships and maintain a navy, everything a modern armed force needs for victory. The South hardly had the ability to manufacture a frying pan.[6]

The South put up a good fight, leading some scholars to believe that pro-Confederate Britain stayed out of the conflict because Robert E. Lee would certainly defeat the armies of the North and would not need Britain's help.[7] But Lee, for all his genius and inspiration as a commander to his troops, made one gigantic mistake, which a Southern commander could not afford to do. A Northern commander, with his almost unlimited resources, could make mistake after mistake, but a Confederate general had no such luxury.

Gettysburg was Lee's most significant mistake, and after his defeat there it was only a matter of time before the North would win the war. A Southern private who watched the battle criticized Lee for what he saw happen to George Pickett's division: "Why were we fighting an impregnable position—was it ignorance? It was a very unfortunate condition for . . . an army with true and tried men being shot down like dogs."[8]

What was the cream of the Confederacy doing at Gettysburg, Pennsylvania? They were supposed to be a defensive army, and their many victories over the past two years had been won in the defense of their country. The decision to take the war into Northern territory, from Maryland to Gettysburg, developed from Lee's awareness that time was running out for the Confederacy. His army was badly in need of all kinds of provisions—shoes, food, horses, military equipment, and more fighting men. He saw this in the faces of his soldiers, who loved him like a father.

He also saw the carnage in the Virginia countryside, the destroyed farms, towns, houses—civilized life itself. Demands were being made in Richmond that he share some of his troops with the hard-pressed forces in the West. He must have sensed that the only remaining chance for the South was for him to move his forces into Pennsylvania and strike a knockout blow and defeat the main Union armies. It was a strategy of desperation—the ultimate defense strategy—and it is no surprise that it failed.

The primary objective of the Army of Northern Virginia was to defend Virginia. There was, according to Confederate General Johnston, a higher cause than the North had. They were being invaded by a foreign army. They were tenacious fighters because they were defending their homes, their farms, their cities, their families. From the Confederate generals to the lowest soldier, said one French observer, this was their reason for war:

"everyone held the same language with wonderful unanimity."[9] They were fighting to repel a foreign invader.

Lee's story usually ends in the history books with his surrender at Appomattox, Virginia, on 9 April 1865. A badly defeated army had done all they could against impossible odds. Two weeks later, the London *Times* wrote of Lee:

> Such is the end of the great army which, organized by the extraordinary genius of one man, aided by several other commanders of eminent ability, has done such wonders in this war. Not even the Grand Army of Napoleon himself could count a series of more brilliant victories than the force which, raised chiefly from the high-spirited population of Virginia, has defeated so many invasions of the State, and crushed the hopes of so many Northern generals. Chief and soldiers have now failed for the first and last time. They were victorious until victory was no longer to be achieved by human valour, and then they fell with honour.

As Lee returned from surrendering to tell his men the bad news, they gathered around and cheered this great man. He then said to them, "Men, we have fought through this war together. I have done the best I could for you. My heart is too full to say more." With those final words, Lee disappears from history with comments from Northern historians, like, "No word of recrimination came from his lips; by his example he asked that the country's wounds be allowed to heal."

But the wounds did not heal. The South was overrun by a military occupation and generals with autocratic powers. Then followed Northern bureaucrats and opportunists who laid the groundwork for a bitter peace and an unwise emancipation policy. Again the historians' saying that the root of the "next war" comes from the military occupation of the previous war comes to the fore. There never was another hot war between the states, of course, but a cold war of bitterness emanating from the occupation of the South by Northern armies under Reconstruction lingers to this day. Lee's final acts and words, not noted by Northern historians, tell the rest of the story.

In December 1866, Lee wrote a letter to Lord Acton (the great libertarian historian who said "power tends to corrupt, and absolute power corrupts absolutely"). He expressed the basic Southern position that the limitation of federal power was necessary to "the continuation of a free government." It is only today that the people of the United States are finally realizing the truth of that. He then emphasized that an overblown, powerful national government would engage in aggression abroad and despotism at home.

Figure 14.1. Robert E. Lee: "A Union that can only be maintained by swords and bayonets, and in which strife and civil war are to take the place of brotherly love and kindness, has no charm for me" (1861).

The correspondence between Lee and Lord Acton includes a letter to Lee from Acton lamenting the loss of the Confederacy—a historian consoling a defeated general for having fought for a worthy cause. Acton saw the war as a battle against despotism, pure and simple, a battle that has been going on from time to time over the centuries. "Secession [of the South] filled me with hope, not as the destruction but as the redemption of Democracy. I deemed that you were fighting the battles of our liberty, our progress, and our civilization; and I mourn the stake which was lost at Richmond more deeply than I rejoiced over that which was saved at Waterloo."[10]

Who is to blame? Recently, a respected journalist, Doug Bandow, wrote in a compelling article in the *Washington Times,* "Blame Lincoln for war he could have averted."[11] Debate over the blame question has raged for over a century. But it seems to this writer that Robert E. Lee answered that question about as well as anyone. He was summoned to Washington to testify before Congress. The radicals then in control wanted to tie him to Southern POW camps and to make out a case of treason against him and Jefferson Davis. When he was questioned about taking up arms against the invading armies from the North, he answered by referring to the Act of Secession of Virginia: "In withdrawing herself from the United States, she carried me along as a citizen of Virginia, and that her laws and her acts were binding upon me." With that response, he had set forth the whole principle on which the people of the South stood.

His inquisitors then tried to pin him down again, that maybe he had been "wheedled or cheated" (deceived) by Southern politicians. His answer, which put the blame for the war where it belonged (then and now), was, "I did believe at the time that it [the war] was an unnecessary condition of affairs and might have been avoided if forbearance and wisdom had been practiced on both sides."[12]

Lee's final words of wisdom came shortly before his death in 1870. Under the yoke of Reconstruction and its military dictatorship, Lee was invited by the commanding Union general to arrange a meeting with a number of leading ex-Confederates. The general asked Lee to make a statement, supposedly to indicate how happy he was to be back in the Union with the stars and stripes. Lee said no. He had seen what defeat had brought and the ugliness of Northern occupation. He did, however, set up a meeting for many ex-Confederates to have a say. The last to leave the meeting was the former Confederate governor of Texas, Fletcher Stockdale. Lee took him aside and said, "Governor, if I had foreseen the use those people [Yankees] designed to make of their victory, there would have been no surrender at Appomattox Courthouse; no sir, not by me. Had I foreseen these

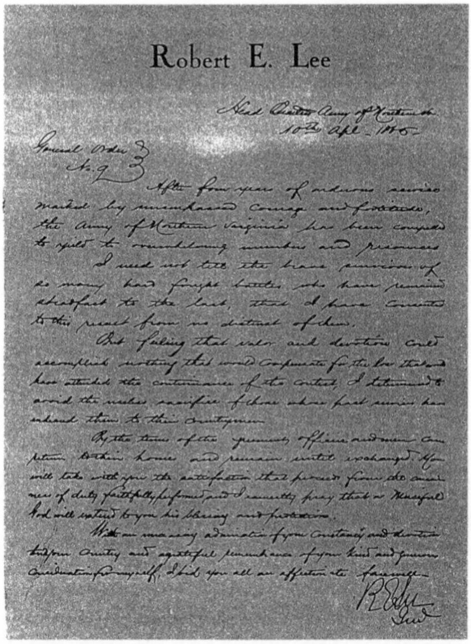

Robert E. Lee

Head Quarters Army of Northern Va.
10th Apl. 1865

General Order
No. 9

R E Lee
Genl

Figure 14.2. "After four years of arduous service, marked by unsurpassed courage and fortitude, the Army of Northern Virginia has been compelled to yield to overwhelming numbers and resources. I need not tell the brave survivors of so many hard fought battles, who have remained steadfast to the last, that I have consented to this result from no distrust of them. But feeling that valor and devotion could accomplish nothing that would compensate for the loss that would have attended the continuance of the contest, I determined to avoid the useless sacrifice of those whose past services have endeared them to their countrymen. By the terms of the agreement officers and men can return to their homes and remain until exchanged. You will take with you the satisfaction that proceeds from the consciousness of duty faithfully performed, and I earnestly pray that a Merciful God will extend to you His blessing and Protection. With an increasing admiration of your constancy and devotion to your country, and a grateful remembrance of your kind and generous consideration for myself, I bid you all an affectionate farewell."

Robert E. Lee's farewell to his troops in the Army of Northern Virginia. It reveals a noble character that has long been the admiration of the South. In the capitol building in Washington each state is entitled to have a statue of two of its most notable citizens. Virginia chose Lee and George Washington.

results of subjugation, I would have preferred to die at Appomattox with my brave men, my sword in my right hand."[13]

A month later Lee suffered a stroke and died on 12 October 1870. He represented, more than any other man, what most of the South was fighting for. In his final words, he pointed out the disaster that Reconstruction had brought to the South—and to the whole country. A disaster that still lingers. The ugly peace forced on the South was only a victory for Republican and Northern control over the nation. The emancipation proved to be the worst in Western civilization in an era in which slavery was abolished everywhere. The corruption and abuse by the occupying armies and bureaucrats of the North produced a hatred that lingers to this day. Southern whites got a raw deal from the Republicans, and they took their wrath out on the newly emancipated blacks, who got the rawest deal of all for over a hundred years.

Lee has not been a controversial figure like Lincoln, Sherman, or even Grant. Like all great men, he made mistakes. But his character and military genius are admired by all. Winston Churchill said he was "one of the greatest captains known in the annals of war." No one ever said that about any of the Northern generals.

War is sometimes called the final arbiter of disputes among nations, even though it creates uncivilized chaos and butchery unrestrained by law. No one has ever suggested that applying the principles of military might—slaughter and devastation—actually means that justice has prevailed. What does prevail is the better army or navy, justice often by the bully. Lawful ideals and principles quickly fade from view as armies take to the field and clash. At that point the combatants start to manufacture reasons for the conflict. And when no good reason can be found, a bad one will do. Facts become distorted, history perverted, and the main reasons for almost all wars—territory, resources, and power—are usually masked over with some sort of moral or social objective.

America's Civil War or, more appropriately, the War for Southern Independence, was decided by military power even though a basic constitutional question was in issue. To this day, that constitutional question has not been resolved in any legal fashion. Neither party in the Civil War wanted it that way, and no effort was made to have the Supreme Court take up the issue. Both sides felt they could win a war and did not choose to risk a judicial determination. It seems to this observer of this most tragic of all events in American history that the zeal for war—the love of the arts of war, in both the North and the South—was the unseen culprit behind the war. There were few peacemakers of any standing. It was not so much a "blundering generation" as a generation enamored with war.

15

Reflections: Healing the Breach

One aspect of the war between the states that did not die with the passing years is a strong sense of Southern nationalism. The numerous articles and books on the theme of the "lost cause" have been wrong. Years ago, as a college student in the West, I had a girlfriend who attended a well-known women's college in Missouri, where there were a number of girls from the South in attendance. My girlfriend recalled that when "Dixie" was played, to her surprise the Southern girls all stood up in reverent attention. At the time, not knowing any better, we thought it was silly. But today I realize the significance of their behavior.

Over six generations have passed since the Confederacy, yet parents and grandparents continue to remind their children that "the South will rise again." In the North no such zeal for the cause of preserving the Union by war can be found, and it is doubtful if many young men today would be willing to give their lives to prevent a state or group of states from withdrawing from the federal system. Most people would go along with Jefferson's view on secession—to let them depart in peace, as brothers. The traitor/conspirator charge of the Republican administration in the 1860s would find few followers today, and certainly very few who would take these criminal charges seriously.

Northern scholars shy away from finding much virtue in dying to prevent the withdrawal of the Southern states in 1861, and most of the civilized world today would look with horror upon an American president who would institute civil war to prevent a state from withdrawing from the federal compact. It is all Northern apologists can do today to avoid having the North end up the "bad guys" in this great national tragedy. Freeing the slaves was undoubtedly a worthwhile pursuit, but it was not even an issue until the war was almost two years old. Lincoln did not go to war to free the slaves—he had no such purpose and he said so time and time again.

To understand the strength of Southern patriotism, the following account of a woman's devotion to the cause of Southern independence may

be helpful: A Southern woman had lost three sons in battle but was willing
to have her fourth and last son serve in the cause. After hearing this story,
Confederate Lt. Gen. Leonidas Polk commented, "How can you subdue a
nation as this?"[1] In one sense, the spirit of Southern nationalism has not
been subdued, and reverence for its cause and its fallen men has not died.
Just as Polish nationalism lived for centuries, and Ukrainian nationalism
has lived even longer, so Southern patriotism may never die either, as these
words from an unknown author suggest:

> You can fight and beat revolutions as you can fight and beat nations.
> You can kill a man, but you can't kill a rebel. For the proper rebel has
> an ideal of living, while your ideal is to kill him so that you may pre-
> serve yourself. And the reason why no revolution has ever been beaten
> is that rebels die for something worth dying for, the future, but their
> enemies only die to preserve the past, and the makers of history are al-
> ways stronger than the makers of empires.[2]

The serious reader or student who reviews the many books written on
the Civil War over the past 130 years is bound to discover the dramatically
changing views about that national blood bath by each generation of Americans. By contrast, foreign accounts haven't changed much. It seems that
each generation of Americans has to write anew about that tragedy, trying
from the Northern persuasion to find a better and more reasonable justification for the carnage. Honest scholarship has destroyed the idea that the
freeing of the slaves was an initial purpose for Lincoln's assault on the
South. And from a legal and moral analysis, "saving the Union" doesn't
hold much water either. The reason the North went to war to coerce the
South back into the federation becomes increasingly indefensible—except
for economic reasons. Even the term "national tragedy" is a dated concept.
In the accounts by Northerners after the war, it was not a tragedy at all, but
a triumph of good over evil, of justice over injustice, of the good guys over
the bad guys. Consider a very impressive history of the war by Charles
Coffin, a former Union soldier, who in 1881 published *The Boys of '61*.
The book is quite long with nice etchings and an account of the war, from
Sumter to the final defeat of the Confederacy. It ends with lofty and noble
sentiments about the Northern cause—a holy war of the forces for God
against the devil. That would certainly justify the slaughter of over 360,000
men in blue uniforms in a gigantic struggle of the forces of righteousness
against the powers of evil.

This view was common among the soldiers who fought in the Union
armies and witnessed the slaughter of so many of their comrades. Hatred
for the enemy and devotion to a noble, often divine cause is what young

men are indoctrinated with during war times, and these powerful emotions and ideas live with them for life. This was brought home to me by an elderly friend who fought in Europe in the infantry in World War II—a man I had known for many years. He shocked a group of us younger men after a golf game when we were discussing the great cars the Germans had designed and built, especially the Porsche and BMW. He suddenly bristled and said, with anger in his eyes, "The only good German is a dead German." He meant it and we changed the subject. Union men, as well as those from the South, were similarly indoctrinated and carried the same kind of hatred, which is inevitably reflected in accounts and studies of the war.

The generation of Union men in the GAR (Grand Army of the Republic) built the memorial to Lincoln in Washington and deified him in history and folklore. If the war was such a great and glorious cause for the North, then Lincoln, as the president who led and even pushed the nation into this war, is easily made into an icon. His secretary and early biographer, John Hay, said Lincoln was "the greatest character since Christ," a view I was taught in my childhood. But this comparison is absurd, since Christ was the "prince of peace" and Lincoln, a prince of war. John Hay's Civil War generation has long since passed away, and the love of money and dominion that provided the dominant motives for the war need no longer be swept under the rug.

Deification of leaders, any leaders—religious or political—creates difficult problems as their words become Holy Scripture; Lincoln, canonized with his death, even became a martyr. The Lincoln Memorial confirms his divinity, just as Roman and Greek temples confirmed the divinity of their rulers. Lincoln, in the form of a god-king, seated on his throne in a huge Greek Parthenon, can only be idolized by the faithful; criticism becomes bad taste, if not blasphemy. And our best and most respected scholars come to the defense of the revered god, as the faithful in our politics defend their chosen leaders. Historians, even the best of them, rewrite history, and then rewrite it again, and when they have been critical, they may even repent of their ways, as one of our leading Northern Civil War scholars, Kenneth Stampp, repudiated his critical views of Lincoln in his later years.[3]

Rethinking the Civil War is nothing new. We have done so with respect to Native Americans as well. In the nineteenth century, as they fought for their homelands, Native Americans were considered evil, blood thirsty savages interfering with the great destiny of the white race to rule over North America. Their status as human vermin was the view of most Americans and few thought of them as anything other than savage and subhuman.

Today we have come full circle and have developed a large sense of collective guilt for our ancestors' ethnic cleansing. We now look upon their

Figure 15.1. The Lincoln Memorial in Washington, D.C., built by those who fought in the Grand Army of the Republic and dedicated fifty years after the war. This Greco-Roman temple, with a huge statue of Lincoln sitting on a throne like a deified caesar, suits a Roman god more than a republican leader. Whether you love Lincoln or hate him, this monstrosity hardly befits the man or his era.

culture, their beliefs, and their love and respect for nature with awe and even reverence, and we are horrified at the way they were treated, as well as the way nature was treated by our forebears. We like to find some excuse for Lincoln when he signed the order approving the hanging of thirty-nine Sioux, the only mass hanging in American history. The leaders of the Sioux were put to death for revolting against the white man's breach of faith, broken treaties, and stealing Indian lands. We've gone from *How the West Was Won* (a popular movie made in 1962) to *How the West Was Lost*. It wasn't Native Americans who were barbarians—exterminating animals and great birds, polluting rivers and streams, and destroying forests and wildlife. We did it, not because we were wise or righteous but because we were the big bullies on the block. It is painful to admit, but we were the bad guys.

But how do these thoughts relate to the Civil War? It was that same generation that engaged in both evils. Where was the moral justification for the Civil War, for sending a million-man army into the Southern states to destroy their civilization? Why the hatred? Why the resort to uncivilized means to settle a legal secession issue that belonged in a court of law or, better still, in the court of public opinion and the democratic process? Perhaps, in the final analysis, the generation of Americans who started the Civil War were not so much a "blundering generation" but a generation of barbarians. The hopes that American democracy offered to the world were damaged beyond repair, as well as the cause of civilized behavior. In the twentieth century, when over a hundred new nations came into being, most often from Europe's colonial empires, it was not American democratic forms that were adopted—it was British parliamentary government that swept over the globe.

These new nations were all seceding from larger imperial orders, and at no time has there been an outcry of "traitors and conspirators" for their secession, even when secession was resisted. Today, the Quebecois in Canada—millions of them, all wanting to secede from the Canadian union—are not looked upon as felons and traitors even though the Canadian Constitution is silent on the issue of secession, just as the U.S. Constitution was silent on that issue. Time has proven the folly and absurdity of the claim of the Republican administration under Lincoln, that secessionists were criminals guilty of treason. Even believing that a state had the right to secede was considered harboring treasonable sentiments, just as being a Communist sympathizer during the McCarthy era was considered. Judge George Comstock, ardent Unionist and founder of Syracuse University, reasoned that if the states were sovereign, they had a right to secede and warring against them was a monstrous crime. He unwittingly condemned the Northern onslaught on the South more than any Southerner ever has.

The Japanese finally apologized for the attack on Pearl Harbor. Would our federal government today apologize for the invasion against the South and the destruction of the Southern civilization—her people, her representative government, her cities, towns, farms, and homes? Not likely. Because then it might have to apologize to Spain for the conquest of Spain's overseas empire in 1898 or for the onslaught on Mexico in 1848 or for stealing almost all of northern Mexico—California, Arizona, Utah, and New Mexico. So far no American government, not even her chief ministers, have ever apologized for their crimes, nor is it likely. In fact, they don't even resign for malfeasance, except to save their pensions, as Richard Nixon did.

Britain and France chose not to recognize or aid the Confederacy to a large extent because of the European hatred for slavery and the Western world's determination to get rid of it. If the South had not been so attached to slavery, Britain and France might have come to her aid early in the war, perhaps bringing Lincoln to settle the secession crisis by peaceful means.

The South's biggest mistake of all was not allowing slaves to serve in the military. Too late in the war, the Confederate government did offer emancipation to slaves who would serve in combat as soldiers; General Lee had made this proposal earlier but to no avail. When the North finally got around to enlisting black troops, they turned out to be able fighting men. If the South could have offered emancipation as an inducement for slaves to join the ranks, it would have been a fight for their freedom as well as to repel a foreign invader. If done early in the war, it just might have turned the tide of battle dramatically, won the hearts of the slaves, and won the war for the Confederacy. The moral flaw in the case for conquering the South would have stood out for all the world to see. Southerners would have been the good guys.

As it was, slavery was the South's Achilles heel, and it was only a matter of time, as John Stuart Mill predicted, before the Republican administration, and Lincoln in particular, would exploit that weakness with the Emancipation Proclamation and later the constitutional amendment abolishing slavery throughout the country.

Today, the South's slave system has done much to tarnish the Confederate battle flag, even though in the 1860s the flag no more stood for slavery than did the Stars and Stripes in 1861 or our revered Constitution. The Confederate battle flag stood for the cause of states' rights and Southern independence, and the desire of the Southern people to control their own destiny. Unfortunately, even tragically for Southerners, the Confederate battle flag—the Cross of St. Andrew, the patron saint of Scotland—has been increasingly used by hate groups, white supremacy fanatics, even neo-Nazis, to support their evil causes. How this can be stopped, I do not know, but this misuse of the Confederate battle flag is as much of an offence to true Southerners as to African Americans and others. If the South had won its independence and, as was inevitable, emancipated its slaves and brought them into Southern society as free men, it is inconceivable that that emancipation could have been as bad as was the emancipation enforced on the South by the bayonet, corrupt carpetbaggers, and Northern do-gooders.

The Civil War was a great national tragedy in every conceivable way: a botched emancipation; the extermination of a whole generation of young men, including hundreds of thousands of teenage boys; the destruction of the constitutional scheme of limited federal power; the end of state sovereignty; the destruction of civilian property in the South in violation of international law; the failure of democracy as a force for peaceful settlement of political disputes; the end of any brotherhood between the states in the North and the South, and its replacement with undying hatred that has lived for generations; the loss of the admiration of the world for America's experiment with democracy as a form of government to bring peace, commerce, and brotherhood among men. Perhaps the most dangerous legacy of the war was the Northern claim that it could use force and go to war to prevent any state from withdrawing from the Union. This has haunted us in the past decade and will continue to do so, as the Soviet Union's Mikhail Gorbachev claimed the right to use force to hold his union together and cited Abraham Lincoln as good authority for doing so. In 1999, the Chinese premier reminded President Clinton that he had the right to use force to hold China together, to go to war to reclaim Taiwan, and he too cited Abraham Lincoln as good authority.

In short, the Civil war was not just a great national American tragedy, but even more so, a tragedy for civilization unmatched in history. In 1861 the world's first great democracy, which was going to show the world what great benefits and virtue this new form of government could bring, failed miserably, tragically, and horribly.

Healing the wounds and the breach between the North and the South can only begin by recognizing what Charles Dickens observed in December of 1861, that "the love of money" was at the root of the North's war objective of preserving the Union.

Notes

INTRODUCTION

1. T. Harry Williams, *Lincoln and the Radicals* (Madison, 1960), 215–216, 240–241.

2. B. H. Liddell Hart, *The Revolution in Warfare* (London, 1946), 8; see also 31, 68, 72–79.

3. *North American Review,* October 1862, 525.

4. Found in Charles Dickens, "The Morrill Tariff," *All the Year Round,* 29 December 1861, 329.

CHAPTER 1

1. Dio Cassius *Roman History* 62.3; compare Tacitus *Annals of Rome* 14.34–38.

2. Michael Hill, "Scots Nationalism, Yesterday, and Today," *Chronicles,* November 1995, 18.

3. Ibid., 19.

4. "British Feelings on the American Civil War," *Chambers's Journal,* January–June 1862, 172.

5. Ibid.

6. Charles Dickens, "Princely Travel in America," *All the Year Round,* 1 November 1862, 177.

7. "American Crisis," *Quarterly Review,* July–October 1861, 257.

8. J. K. C. Wheare, *Abraham Lincoln and the United States* (London, 1961), 174–175.

9. Charles Dickens, "The American Disunion," *All the Year Round,* 21 December 1861, 296; Kenneth Stampp, "The United States and National Self-determination" (30th annual Robert Fortenbaugh Lecture, Gettysburg College, 1991), 10.

10. Edwin P. White, ed. *Great Speeches and Ovations of Daniel Webster* (1894; reprint, Birmingham, 1989), 598.

11. Edgar Lee Masters, *Lincoln the Man* (New York, 1931), 138.

12. John Chodes, "Of Southern Saints and Scalawags," *Southern Events,* Spring 1998, 13.

CHAPTER 2

1. See Richard N. Current, *Lincoln and the First Shot* (Philadelphia, 1963), 69.

2. Howard Perkins et al., eds., *Northern Editorials on Secession* (New York, 1942), 2:826.

3. Current, *Lincoln and the First Shot*, 145–147; John Shipley Tilley, *Lincoln Takes Command* (Nashville, 1991), 180–182, 297–307; see also Charles W. Ramsdell, "Lincoln and Fort Sumter," in *Journal of Southern History*, 3:263.

4. An address to the citizens of Alabama on the Constitution and law of the Confederate States of America . . . at Temperance Hall on the 30th of March 1861 by Robert H. Smith, found in *Southern Pamphlets on Secession, November 1860–April 1861*, ed. Jon L. Wakelyn (Chapel Hill, 1996).

5. *Northern Editorials,* 1:219–220.

6. Ibid., 2:573.

7. Ibid., 2:567.

8. Ibid.

9. Ibid., 1:123.

10. Ibid., 1:219–220.

11. Ibid., 2:298–299.

12. Ibid., 2:600–601.

13. "Of What Use Is the South to Us?" in *Northern Editorials,* 2:563.

14. Jabez L.M. Curry, "The Perils and Duty of the South, November 26, 1860," in *Southern Pamphlets on Secession,* 35–54; compare with an unsubstantiated Northern view that the South "contributed so little to the national treasury," in Joseph Rapes, "Financial Aspects of the Rebellion," *New Englander* 22 (January 1863): 56ff.

15. Robert L. Dabny, "Memoir of a Narrative Received of Colonel John B. Baldwin," in *Secular* (1897; reprint, Harrisburg, Va.: Sprinkle, 1994), 94, 100.

16. J. Barton and J. Hendricks, *Statesmen of the Lost Cause* (New York, 1939), 106.

17. *Southern Pamphlets on Secession,* 332.

18. *Harpers' Pictorial History of the Civil War* (New York, 1977), 88.

19. "Secession Flag Raising in Virginia," in *Leisure Hour* (London, 1861), 741–743.

CHAPTER 3

1. Cicero, *On Duties* 2.8; quoted in *On the Good Life,* trans. Michael Grant (New York, 1977), 162.

2. *Harper's Pictorial History of the Civil War* (New York, 1866), 68.

3. Cited in Edgar Lee Masters, *Lincoln the Man* (New York, 1931), 422.

4. Howard Perkins et al., eds., *Northern Editorials on Secession* (New York, 1942), 2:674.

5. Ibid.

6. Quoted in Alexander Stephens, *A Constitutional View of the Late War between the States* (Philadelphia, 1870), 2:404.

7. "Confederate Struggle," *Quarterly Review* 112 (1862): 558.

8. Harold M. Hyman, *A More Perfect Union: The Impact of the Civil War and Reconstruction on the Constitution* (New York, 1973), 86 n. 15 for sources.

9. Ibid.

10. Ibid., 84 n. 8, for the Lieber papers, which are at the Huntington Library. See also Jeffrey Hummel, *Emancipating Slaves* (Chicago, 1996), 142.

11. William Blackstone, *Commentaries on the Laws of England* (London, 1768), 3:129–138.

12. Found in Joseph Story, *Commentaries on the Constitution of the United States* (Boston, 1891), 2:212–215, sec. 1338–1342.

13. Ibid., 214 n. 2.

14. Ibid.

15. Charles Warren, *The Supreme Court in U.S. History* (Boston, 1928), 1:303–304.

16. Mark E. Neely Jr., *The Fate of Liberty* (Oxford, 1991), 188n.

17. *Ex Parte Merryman,* 17F cas 144 (CCI) MD.186 (N.9481); see *The Tree of Liberty* (Boston, 1986), 180–182, with Lincoln's explanation to Congress on 4 July 1861.

18. *Ex Parte Milligan,* 71US (Wall) 2. 1866.

19. Editorial in *Cleveland Herald,* quoted in Warren, *Supreme Court in U.S. History,* 2:430–431.

20. Warren, *Supreme Court in U.S. History,* 2:433.

21. The leading advocates for exterminating the Southern people tragically occupied the Christian Protestant pulpit. Chester Dunham's remarkable study, *The Attitude of the Northern Clergy toward the South, 1860–1865* (Philadelphia, 1974), helps contemporary readers understand the origins of hatred and venom toward the South.

22. *New York Daily Tribune,* 11 September 1862, 4.

23. *Congressional Globe,* 37th Cong., 1st sess., 45, 75, 91, pt. 3:1338.

24. *Macmillan Magazine,* December 1863, 767–768.

25. *Northern Editorials,* 2:825.

26. Ibid., 2:839.

27. Ludwell Johnson, "PBS's 'The Civil War': The Myth Management of History 1990," in *So Good a Cause,* ed. Oran Smith (Columbia, 1993), 189.

28. For other newspapers condemning the Merryman case, see Warren, *Supreme Court in U.S. History,* 2:368–374.

29. John Clampitt in the prestigious *Encyclopedia of Political Science* (1881) excused the military tribunals of the Civil War but had to admit that the trial of Mary Surratt was illegal—a farce that was organized to convict, not act as an impartial tribunal for a fair trial.

30. Mercy Otis Warren, *History of the Rise, Progress, and Termination of the American Revolution* (1805; reprint, Indianapolis, 1988), 2:660.

31. Ephraim Douglass Adams, *Great Britain and the American Civil War* (New York, 1924), 2:301.

32. *Quarterly Review,* November 1862.

33. London *Times,* 4 November 1862.

CHAPTER 4

1. Doug Bandow, "Blame Lincoln for War He Could Have Averted," *Washington Times,* 17 February 1996, E3. See also Frank van der Linden, *Lincoln: The Road to War* (Golden, Colorado, 1998), epilogue.

2. Philip S. Foner, *The New York Merchants and the Irrepressible Conflict* (Chapel Hill, 1941), 297–298.

3. Kenneth Stampp, *The Cause of the Civil War* (Inglewood, N.J., 1959), 80.

4. Foner, *New York Merchants,* 299.

5. Ibid., 301.

6. Ibid., 303; letter to Gideon Welles, April 11, 1861.

7. Ibid., 304.

8. Ibid., 307–308.

9. Ibid., 308.

CHAPTER 5

1. "Democracy on Trial," *Quarterly Review* 110 (July–October 1861): 247.

2. Ibid., 249.

3. Found in Jeff Hummel, *Emancipating Slaves, Enslaving Free Men* (Chicago, 1996), 352.

4. "The Dissolution of the Union," *Cornhill Magazine* 4 (July–October 1861): 153.

5. *Northern British Review,* February 1862, 36, 234. *Nisi prius* is a legal term for pleading a case, used here in a derogatory sense.

6. Charles Dickens, "New Phase of the American Strife," *Once a Week* (London), 30 November 1861, 638–639.

7. "The Outlook of the War," *Macmillan Magazine* 6 (May–October 1862): 409.

8. "American Crisis," *Quarterly Review,* January–April 1962, 250.

9. "Democracy on Trial," 273.

10. Charles Dickens, "American Disunion," *All the Year Round,* 21 December 1861, 299.

11. "Democracy on Trial," 271.

12. "The Outlook of the War," *Macmillan Magazine* 6 (July–October 1862): 410.

13. "American Crisis," 275.

14. Serge Gavronsky, *The French Liberal Opposition and the American Civil War* (New York, 1968), 89.

15. *Athenaeum,* 6 May 1865, 615.

16. Kenneth Clark, *Civilisation* (London, 1969), 300.

17. "Dissolution of the Union," 166.

18. "American Crisis," 272.

19. "The Danger of War with America," *Macmillan Magazine* 11 (November 1864–April 1865): 419.

20. Gavronsky, *French Liberal Opposition,* 183.

21. "American Crisis," 274.

22. Karl Marx and Friedrich Engels, *The Civil War in the United States* (1861; reprint, New York, 1961), 58.

23. John Ford Rhodes, *Lecture on the American Civil War* (New York, 1913), 2–16.

24. "The American Quarrel," *Fraser's Magazine,* April 1861, 411.

25. "Speech on the Slave Question," in *American Issues,* ed. Willard Thorpe et al. (New York, 1941), 513.

26. *Encyclopedia Americana* (New York, 1971), 27:568.

27. *Pamphlets on Secession,* November 1860–April 1861 (Chapel Hill, 1996), 150.

28. David M. Potter, *The Impending Crisis* (New York, 1976), 424.

29. *Northern British Review,* February 1862, 240.

30. *Athenaeum,* 21 December 1861, 847.

31. "The Confederate Struggle," *Quarterly Review* 112 (1862): 537.

32. Charles Beard and Mary Beard, *The Rise of American Civilization* (New York, 1927), 2:39–40.

33. *Blackwood's Magazine,* January 1862, 130.

34. *Northern British Review* 36 (February 1862): 235.

CHAPTER 6

1. Charles Dickens, "American Disunion," *All the Year Round,* 21 December 1861, 299.

2. Ibid., 296.

3. Ibid., 267.

4. Peter Ackroyd, *Dickens* (London, 1990), 271.

5. Dickens, "American Disunion," 299.

6. Dickens, "The Morrill Tariff," *All the Year Round,* 28 December 1861, 328–329.

7. "The American Tariff Bill," *Saturday Review,* 9 March 1861, 234–235; Dickens, "American Disunion," 411.

8. Dickens, "Morrill Tariff," 330.

9. Ibid.

10. J. S. Mill, "The Contest in America," *Fraser's Magazine,* February 1862, 262.

11. Ibid., 261.

12. Robert Johannsen, *Lincoln, the South, and Slavery* (Baton Rouge, 1991), 60 n. 28.

13. Mill, "Contest in America," 258.

14. Ibid., 361.

15. *Harper's New Monthly Magazine* 14 (December 1861–May 1862): 677.

16. Marshall L. De Rosa, *The Confederate Constitution of 1861* (Columbia, Mo., 1991), 141.

17. *Charleston Mercury,* 3 November 1860, in *Southern Editorials on Secession,* ed. Dwight Dumond (Gloucester, Mass., 1964), 292.

18. *New Orleans Daily Crescent,* 21 January 1861, 408.

CHAPTER 8

1. "A French View of the Stars and Stripes," *All the Year Round,* 6 (September 1862): 615.

2. Ibid.

3. *Records of the Debates on the Federal Convention of 1787,* ed. Charles Tausill (Washington, D.C., 1927), 131.

4. Ibid., 256.

5. Hugo Grotius, *The Law of Peace and War,* trans. Francis Kelsey (Oxford, 1925), 171.

6. The Lieber Code is discussed in Mark Grimsley, *The Hard Hand of War* (New York, 1995), 150–151.

7. Letter to J. B. Fry, 3 September 1884, in *Hard Hand of War,* 193.

8. Stephen Oates, "The Man at the Whitehouse Window," *Civil War Times,* December 1995, 52.

9. James McPherson, "Tried by War," *Civil War Times,* December 1995, 66.

10. See a more recent issue of *Civil War Times* (October 1998) for an article on this issue: "The Wrath of Sherman."

11. *Civil War Quotations,* ed. Darryl Lyman (Pennsylvania, 1995), 205.

12. Ibid., 52.

13. *Wilson Quarterly,* Winter 1999, 6.

14. Charles Carlton Coffin, *The Boys of '61* (Boston, 1881), 396–397; also found in *Civil War Quotations,* 215.

15. Grimsley, *Hard Hand of War,* 182–183.

16. Geoffrey Parker, "Early Modern Europe," in *The Laws of War* (Yale, 1994), 58.

17. *Henry V,* 4.7.1–4.

18. Adam Roberts, "Land Warfare from Hague to Nuremberg," in *Laws of War,* 135.

19. Harold E. Selesky, "Colonial America," in *Laws of War,* 81.

20. "War," in *Encyclopedia of Religion and Ethics,* ed. James Hastings (New York, 1951), 12:685.

21. *Civil War Quotations,* no. 36, p. 15.

22. "The Danger of War with America," *Macmillan Magazine,* November 1864–April 1865, 419.

CHAPTER 9

1. Montesquieu, *The Spirit of Laws* (1751), bk. 15, chap. 11.

2. Nicholas V. Riasanovsky, *A History of Russia,* 2d ed. (Oxford, 1969), 413.

3. "New Phase of the American Strife," *Once a Week,* 30 November 1861, 635–636.

4. Robert Heinl and Nancy Heinl, *Written in Blood: The Story of the Haitian People, 1492–1971* (Boston, 1978), 125–130.

5. Eugene H. Berwanger, *The Frontier against Slavery: Western Anti-Negro Prejudice*

and the Slavery Extension Controversy (Urbana, 1967), 49. Although Lincoln had long been active in state politics, he never questioned this black law. It had nothing to do with abolition; it was against free blacks living in white Illinois society.

6. James Spence, "The American Republic: Resurrection through Dissolution," *Northern British Review,* February 1862, 240.

7. *Macmillan Magazine* 6 (1862): 412.

8. Merrill Peterson, comp., "The Autobiography," in *Thomas Jefferson: Writings* (New York, 1984), 44.

9. James Theodore Holly and J. Dennis Harris, *Black Separatism and the Caribbean, 1860* (Ann Arbor, 1970), 10.

10. "The Slave Difficulty in America," *Once a Week,* 145–148.

11. T. Harry William, *Lincoln and the Radicals* (Madison, 1960), 216; 240–244.

12. "The Character of the Rebellion," *Northern British Review,* October 1862, 529.

13. David Herbert Donald, *Lincoln* (New York, 1995), 315.

14. Abraham Lincoln, letter to Kentucky legislator A. G. Hodges, 4 April 1864, in Philip Stern, ed., *The Life and Writings of Abraham Lincoln* (New York, 1940), 806–811.

15. Robert Walter Johannsen, *Lincoln, the South, and Slavery* (Baton Rouge, 1991), 55.

16. H. Arthur Scott Trask, "Christianity and Slavery in the Old South," *Chronicles,* July 1999, 31–33; Eugene D. Genovese, *A Consuming Fire: The Fall of the Confederacy in the Mind of the White Christian South* (Athens, 1998).

17. "The Crisis in the American War," *Blackwood's Magazine,* 1 November 1862, 641.

18. Ibid.

19. Chester Forrester Dunham, *The Attitude of the Northern Clergy toward the South, 1860–1865* (Philadelphia, 1974), passim.

20. "Crisis in the American War," 640; see also *Civil War Quotations* (Pennsylvania, 1995), no. 913, 149.

21. "Crisis in the American War," 640, 642.

22. Spence, "American Republic," 240n.

23. Ibid.

24. Alexander Stephens, *Constitutional View of the Late War between the States* (Pennsylvania, 1870), 2:617.

25. See *Pamphlets on Secession, November 1860–April 1861,* ed. Jon L. Wakelyn (Chapel Hill, 1996), 146–149.

26. Found in "Crisis in the American War," 644.

27. "The Characters of the Rebellion," *North American Review,* October 1862, 532–533.

28. Charles Carleton Coffin, *Boys of '61* (Boston, 1881), 559.

29. Quoted by Ludwell H. Johnson, "The Plundering Generation," in *So Good a Cause* (Columbia, S.C., 1993), 150.

30. Paul M. Angle, ed., *The Lincoln Reader* (Rutgers, 1947), 407.

31. Stephens, *Constitutional View of the Late War between the States,* 2:615n.

32. E. Ramsay Richardson, *Little Aleck: The Life of Alexander Stephens* (New York, 1932), 280.

33. Thomas Nelson Page, *Robert E. Lee: Man and Soldier* (New York, 1911), 38.

CHAPTER 10

1. Joseph T. Glaithaar, *Forged in Battle* (New York, 1990), 252–253.
2. Fawn Brodie, *Thaddeus Stevens* (New York, 1959), 20–21.
3. Claude C. Bowers, *The Tragic Era: The Revolution after Lincoln* (Cambridge, 1929), 200.
4. Roberta F. Cason, "The Union League in Georgia," *Georgia Historical Quarterly* 20 (1936): 137.
5. *Congressional Globe,* 1871, 6. Thomas Boyard, *Ku Klux Klan Organization* (a pamphlet containing his speech published by the Congressional Globe Printing Office, 1871), 5.
6. Stanley Horn, *The Invisible Empire: The Story of the Ku Klux Klan, 1866–1871* (1939; reprint, Boston, 1969), 17.
7. Leon F. Litwack, *Been in the Storm So Long: The Aftermath of Slavery* (New York, 1979), 268–269.
8. Ibid.
9. Bowers, *Tragic Era,* 200.
10. Congressman Fernando Wood, *Alleged Ku Klux Outrages* (a pamphlet containing his speech published by the Congressional Globe Printing office, 1871), p. 5.
11. Margaretta Barton Colt, *Defend the Valley* (New York, 1994), 377.
12. See George M. Frederickson, "A Man but Not a Brother," *Journal of Southern History* (February 1975), 39–58; R. W. Johannsen, ed., *The Lincoln-Douglas Debate of 1858* (Oxford, 1965), 1:458.
13. John Henry Hopkins, *Scriptural, Ecclesiastical, and Historical View of Slavery from the Days of the Patriarch Abraham to the Nineteenth Century* (New York, 1864). A treatise written by the Episcopal bishop of Pennsylvania, John Henry Hopkins, to the Episcopal bishop of Vermont, Alonzo Potter.
14. See Book of Moses 7:8, 22 in *Pearl of Great Price* (Salt Lake City, 1981), 21–22.
15. 1.15.5.
16. Alexis de Tocqueville, *Democracy in America* (1838), 338.
17. Wood Gray, *The Hidden Civil War* (New York, 1942), 133.
18. Litwack, *Been in the Storm So Long,* 102.
19. Ibid., 263.
20. Darryl Lyman, ed., *Civil War Quotations* (Pennsylvania, 1995), 101.

CHAPTER 11

1. Fred Balhut, "Copperheads and the War between the States," *Barnes Review,* 1977, 9; Wood Gray, *The Hidden Civil War: The Story of the Copperheads* (New York, 1942), 65, 105, 109, passim.
2. Balhut, "Copperheads," 10.
3. Ibid., 11.
4. Ibid.
5. Mark E. Neely Jr., *Fate of Liberty* (New York, 1991), epilogue.

CHAPTER 12

1. Edward K. Eckert, *Fact Distorting Fiction* (Georgia, 1984), xiv.

2. Ibid.

3. William C. Davis, *Jefferson Davis* (New York, 1991), 663.

4. Eckert, *Fact Distorting Fiction*, xl.

5. John Marshall, *The American Bastille Found in Civil War Books* (Baton Rouge, 1967), 197.

6. John Quincy Adams, *The Jubilee of the Constitution* (New York, 1839), 66–69; also in Stephens, *Constitutional View of the Late War between the States* (Pennsylvania, 1871), 2:418; also found in Masters, *Lincoln the Man* (New York, 1942), 336.

7. *Northern Editorials on Secession,* 1:187.

8. Ibid., 225.

9. Ibid., 189.

10. Wood Gray, *Hidden War* (New York, 1942), 66–67.

11. Frank Feidel, ed., *Union Pamphlets on the Civil War,* 1861–1865 (Mass., 1967), p. 893, no. 893.

12. "American Crisis," *Quarterly Review,* 256–257.

13. James Bryce, *The American Commonwealth* (London, 1888), 1:315–316; see note, p. 316.

14. Edwin Whipple, ed., *The Great Speeches and Orations of Daniel Webster* (Boston, 1894), 225–306.

15. Albert Bledsoe, *Is Davis a Traitor?* (Baltimore, 1866), 11, 17.

16. Roy F. Nichols, "United States v. Jefferson Davis," *American Historical Review* 30 (1926): 276.

17. Bledsoe, *Is Davis a Traitor?* 1.

18. Nichols, "United States v. Jefferson Davis," 274.

19. Bledsoe, *Is Davis a Traitor?* 5.

20. Nichols, "United States v. Jefferson Davis," 281.

21. Bledsoe, *Is Davis a Traitor?* 143–145. See also Raphael Semmes, *Memoirs of Service Afloat* (1868; reprint, Baton Rouge, 1996), chaps. 2–3. For a modern analysis of the secession issue, see David Gordon, ed., *Secession, State, and Liberty* (Rutgers, 1998).

22. Found in its entirety in George Tickner Curtis, *Life of James Buchanan* (New York, 1883), 2:337–350, esp. p. 347. See also Philip Shriver Klein, *President James Buchanan: A Biography* (University Park, 1962), 362.

23. Samuel Francis, "Nations within Nations," in *Chronicles,* January 1999, 21. Speech by Richard Alatorre.

24. Ibid. Words of Jose Angel Gutierrez.

CHAPTER 13

1. Jeffrey Hummel, *Emancipating Slaves, Enslaving Free Men* (Chicago, 1997), 352.

2. *Times* editorial, 13 September 1862, 8, cited in *Emancipating Slaves,* 352.

3. Edgar Lee Masters, *Lincoln the Man* (New York, 1931), 431.

4. The full text of this letter is found in Goldwin Smith, "President Lincoln," *Macmillan Magazine,* November 1864–April 1865, 303–304.

5. Masters, *Lincoln the Man,* 429.

6. Cicero, *On Duties* 1.11.35–36.

7. Masters, *Lincoln the Man,* 428.

CHAPTER 14

1. Thomas Nelson Page, *Robert E. Lee: Man and Soldier* (New York, 1911), 25–26.

2. Thomas Nelson Page, *Robert E. Lee* (New York, 1908), chap. 3.

3. Ibid.

4. Dwight Lowell Dumond, ed., *Southern Editorials on Secession* (Gloucester, Mass., 1964), 476.

5. Michael Davis, *The Image of Lincoln in the South* (Knoxville, 1971), 61.

6. Page, *Robert E. Lee,* 73.

7. Sheldon Vanaukan, *The Glittering Illusion* (Washington, D.C., 1989).

8. William A. Fletcher, *Rebel Private: Front and Rear* (New York, 1995), 54.

9. Cited by Charles Dickens in "Princely Stand in America," *All the Year Round,* 1 November 1862, 177.

10. J. Rufus Fears, ed., *Essays in the History of Liberty* (Indianapolis, 1985), 303.

11. *Washington Times,* 17 February 1996, E3.

12. Page, *Robert E. Lee,* 656.

13. Thomas C. Johnson, *The Life and Letters of Robert Lewis Dalney* (Edinburgh, Scotland, 1977), 497–500; also found in James Kennedy and Walter Kennedy, *The South Was Right* (Gretna, 1994), 42–43.

CHAPTER 15

1. Darryl Lyman, ed., *Civil War Quotations* (Pennsylvania, 1995), 187.

2. Charles M. Andrews, "The American Revolution: An Interpretation," *American Historical Review* 31 (January 1926): 219, 232.

3. Kenneth M. Stampp, "My Life with Lincoln" (Bernard Moses Memorial Lecture, University of California–Berkeley, March 1, 1983).

Bibliographical Thoughts

With an estimated 50,000 to 70,000 books and articles on the Civil War, where does one start reading? Rather than list a number of books on the subject, I suggest browsing in the Civil War section of almost any large public or academic library. You will find a smorgasbord of books, from biographies to military action to analyses of the war, that consider its causes and consequences.

Jeffrey Hummel's *Emancipating Slaves, Enslaving Free Men* (1996) is a fine study. Each of his thirteen chapters ends with a bibliographical essay in which he reviews the various books dealing with the subject under discussion. These essays direct the reader to matters that may be of particular interest.

Another book with bibliographical analyses is Gabor S. Boritt, *Why the War Came* (1996). However, it lacks the depth and insight that characterize Hummel's study.

My own recommendation on books about the Civil War—volumes that explain this tragic era and give a broad spectrum of views and insights—includes, first, a two-volume collection of newspaper editorials for this period: Howard Cecil Perkins, ed., *Northern Editorials on Secession* (New York, 1942). These editorials are categorized into various subjects that were of critical importance during the early period of the struggle. The 1860–1861 period is well covered and is of special interest because that was when freedom of the press still existed in the North. Second is a one-volume collection of Southern editorials. In 1964 Dwight Lowell Dumond published *Southern Editorials on Secession* (Gloucester, Mass., 1964). These two collections of editorials represent a good place to start to understand the Civil War.

Similar to the editorials are the pamphlets, which have more of a propaganda flavor than the editorials. Yet they tell much of what Americans were exposed to during the war. See Frank Freidel, ed., *Union Pamphlets on the Civil War*, 2 vols. (Cambridge, 1967). For the South there is the recent *Southern Pamphlets on Secession, November 1860-April 1861,* ed. Jon L. Wakelyn (Chapel Hill, 1996).

There are so many books on Lincoln that reading them would take years.

H. L. Mencken's 1931 comment that "Lincoln has become one of our national deities, and a realistic examination of him is thus no longer possible" seems self-evident, even seventy years later with current biographies
like David Herbert Donald's *Lincoln* (1995). All the tough questions concerning Lincoln's life and presidency seem to be avoided, excused, or
given a light touch.

To counteract this Lincoln adoration, the 1961 English Universities
Press study, *Abraham Lincoln and the United States,* by K. C. Wheare, is
refreshing. A 1997 reprinting of *Lincoln the Man* (1931) by the well-
known poet and writer Edgar Lee Masters is a must read. And another
reprint, *Lincoln Takes Command* (1940; reprint, 1991), by John Shipley
Tilley, should be examined. Gabor S. Boritt's *Why the Civil War Came*
calls Tilley's book "absurd," yet when I approached Boritt for an explanation, my inquiry was ignored. Boritt ignores the economic factors, especially the money interests—what Charles Dickens saw as the cause of the
war. Even in 1860 the business of America was business. Most recent, and
worthy of study, is Frank van der Linden's *Lincoln: The Road to War*
(1998), but it too ignores the tax, tariff, and money interests that were behind those who pushed Lincoln into war. Like so many Civil War writers,
when their research unearths revenue and tax issues, they push this information aside, as if it had no real value in understanding this most tragic
event. Yet it is as important in understanding our Civil War as in understanding our 1776 Revolution. The one standout in Civil War history that
gives the tax and money issue its critical importance, and a must read, is
Kenneth Stampp's *And the War Came: The North and the Secession
Crises, 1860–1861* (Baton Rouge, 1950).

Another important book that goes to the core of the fiscal aspect of the
war—a book that is little known (or acknowledged) among Civil War
writers—is Philip S. Foner, *The New York Merchants and the Irrepressible Conflict* (Chapel Hill, 1941). If money makes the world go around
(private sector) and is the heart of war and the blood of governments (public sector), then the Foner book explains more about the Civil War than
any other study. Two other books missing from the prominent bibliogra-
phies are: Hodding Carter, *The Ugly Scar* (New York, 1959), which tells
the story of Reconstruction as it should be told; and *The American Heresy*
(London and New York, 1930), a no-nonsense look at the Northern dog-
mas on secession.

As a primary source on Lincoln, read carefully his first and second inaugural addresses. They are worth more than volumes of slanted biography.

Finally, I found that the most fascinating and honest accounts of the war
were written by Europeans, especially the British. Every periodical in

Britain ran continuing accounts of the Civil War, focusing on just about every phase of the conflict. British editors wrote in an atmosphere of pure freedom of expression, something totally lacking in America, then and even perhaps now. Periodicals worthy of study are

All the Year Round (Dickens)
Athenaeum
Blackwood's Magazine
Chambers's Journal
Cornhill Magazine
Fraser's Magazine
Leisure Hour
Macmillan's Magazine
Northern British Review
Once a Week
Quarterly Review
Saturday Review

These journals are a gold mine of information and insights into the war.

As for British newspapers, *The Times* is all-important, but there were newspapers in every town and village, let alone cities, in Britain, and they all were obsessed with the war in America. Although they didn't have the touch of the scholarly periodicals, they saw the war in much the same light as the more popular journals.

Index

About the Author

Charles Adams, the world's leading scholar on the history of taxation, is the author of the best-selling books *For Good and Evil, Those Dirty Rotten Taxes,* and *Fight, Flight, and Fraud.* Known as the "tax writer," Charles Adams entered the field of international taxation after ten years in private legal practice and became a certified specialist in taxation law. His writings have been published in magazines, newspapers, and periodicals with lead stories featured in the *New York Times, Washington Post,* and *Wall Street Journal.* Mr. Adams is also an adjunct scholar at both the Ludwig von Mises Institute at Auburn University and the Cato Institute and a visiting lecturer on U.S. tax history at the National Archives, George Mason University, University of Rochester, University of Toronto, and New York University. He is the author of *For Good and Evil: The Impact of Taxes on the Course of Civilization,* Second Edition (Madison Books, 1999).